THE FEARED

Praise for *The Feared*

'Foregrounding the stories of these activists will contribute to creating an enlightened public awareness of their plight. As this movement gains momentum, it can help create a social climate that will oppose the suppression of democratic dissent and the targeting of human rights activists that take up the cause of such dissenters.'

—Rudolf C. Heredia,
Author of *Reconciling Difference: Collective Violence in India*

'As a seasoned journalist with decades of experience, Kolhatkar brings unparalleled insight to this crucial and sensitive subject matter.... I recommend "The Feared" as essential reading for its timely exploration of the erosion of democratic freedoms in India.'

—Monideepa Mukerjee,
Director General (Retd) Press Information Bureau, West Zone

THE BEARD

Praise for The Beard

THE FEARED

Conversations with 11 Political Prisoners

NEETA KOLHATKAR

YODAPRESS

London · New York · Sydney · Toronto · New Delhi

First published in India by Simon & Schuster India and Yoda Press LLP 2024

1 3 5 7 9 10 8 6 4 2

Simon & Schuster India
818, Indraprakash Building
21, Barakhamba Road
New Delhi 110001
www.simonandschuster.co.in

Yoda Press LLP
C-28 Basement
Mayfair Gardens
New Delhi 110016
www.yodapress.co.in

Simon & Schuster: Celebrating 100 Years of Publishing in 2024

Paperback ISBN: 9788198128522
eBook ISBN: 9788198200396

Typeset in India by SÜRYA, New Delhi
Printed and bound in India by Replika Press Pvt. Ltd.

To

the spirit of dissent and resistance, which is integral to our democracy

CONTENTS

Acknowledgements ix
Foreword by Julio Ribeiro xiii
Foreword by Justice (Retd) B. N. Srikrishna xvii
Preface xix

1 SUDHA BHARADWAJ 3
'Starting over at sweet 60, on a road never travelled...'

2 NILOFER MALIK AND SAMEER KHAN 23
'*Mein kranti launga.*'

3 KOEL SEN 41
'Bonkers has helped me from going bonkers.'

4 PRASHANT RAHI AND SHIKHA RAHI 51
'From age 24 to 40, I was fighting for my father's freedom.'

5 SANJAY RAUT 73
'Irony dies a hundred deaths.'

6 KISHORECHANDRA WANGKHEM 87
'They write and wrath is wrought upon them.'

7 ANAND TELTUMBDE AND RAMA AMBEDKAR 99
'Prison is the centre of sadism.'

8 BINAYAK SEN 127
'I will not come out alive if I am jailed again.'

9 KOBAD GANDHY 155
'I was wondering whether I would ever come out alive.'

10 MURALIDHARAN. K 171
'There seems to be some sort of a central directive being given to all the prison authorities to act tough with the Maoist prisoners.'

11 P. HEMALATHA 195
'His bail is jail for me.'

Notes 224

About the Author 241

Acknowledgements

This book has been realised after constant conversations with various friends, peers and academicians. I am deeply indebted to my friends and classmates from St. Xavier's College: Naazneen Humza asked me to reach out to Maya Pinto, to request Mr Julio Ribeiro to write the Foreword. It was Maya who led me to Arpita Das, founder of Yoda Press. I am eternally grateful to Maya, Arpita and Ishita Gupta, the commissioning editor. In today's times when there is an underlying diffidence, Yoda Press and Simon & Schuster India have shown courage to publish this book.

I am also immensely grateful and honoured that Justice (Retd) B. N. Srikrishna, who promised to read all the 11 chapters, has written another powerful Foreword for my book. His endorsement means the world to me. Both Mr. Ribeiro and Justice Srikrishna's endorsements will certainly motivate the reader to understand the importance of these conversations and the reason to document the experiences of political prisoners.

Every interview has impacted me, as I was drawn deep into the lives of every person, their life experiences and how they and their families were deeply affected by the experience. I remain indebted to Sudha Bharadwaj, Nilofer Malik and Sameer Khan, Dr Binayak Sen, Pranhita and Aparajita, K. Muralidharan, Kishorechandra Wangkhem, Anand Teltumbde and Rama Ambedkar, Shikha

Rahi, Prashant Rahi, Kobad Ghandy, Koel Sen, Sanjay Raut, (Rajya Sabha MP and Executive Editor of *Saamana* newspaper) P. Hemalatha and Venugopal. I value the time and energy they all invested in speaking to me over long durations. Thank you for allowing me into your lives, your homes/offices, and sharing your deepest emotions. Thank you for permitting me to publish your interviews in this book.

While they are fighting to have the charges against them dropped, their spirit remains intact and spurs them on to not give up.

I am immensely grateful to Rediff.com for allowing me to publish this book, a compilation of interviews I had conducted under its aegis. My sincere thanks to: Mr. Ajit Balakrishnan (the Founder, current Chairman, and Chief Executive Officer of Rediff.com) for reposing his trust in me and giving me blanket permission to publish the book. Sincere thanks are also due to Mr Nikhil Lakshman (Editor-in-Chief), for featuring some of these interviews on their wonderful platform. I feel lucky to have been given the editorial freedom to go out and explore new subjects.

I truly appreciate the various conversations I had with my dear friend Ramya Sarma, who keeps a constant, watchful eye on me. No amount of appreciation and thanks would suffice to encompass the handholding and guidance she has extended. Ramya has been the first to goad me into writing this book and in introducing me to leading publishers and editors to try to get this book out there. Thanks also to Nataraja Sarma, for his support and his sense of humour which helped me tide over some dull moments.

Thank you, Carol Andrade for guiding me and helping me shape this book into one good effort. I am grateful to Father Rudi Heredia for his guidance and help as well.

A special thank you to Sanober Keshwar, for all her guidance and for helping me connect with many of the interviewees. She and Freny Manekshaw have helped me immensely. Thanks are also due to advocate Susan Abraham for sharing her contacts and giving critical feedback. The help and guidance of all my friends has been instrumental in conducting quality interviews and shaping this book. Thank you also to Advocate Nilima Dutta and Rupa Panalal for their support.

Thank you to Ujwala Mhatre, for her warm hospitality and support. Thank you, Pravin Kajrolkar and Samar Khadas, for often putting in a word for me when I have sought your help.

I am also deeply indebted to my friend Geeta Bhagat, whom I can call at any time of the day or night, to vent my feelings and frustrations. Thanks for reading, scrutinising every word, and believing in my effort. She has the knack for spotting errors and most of all I admire her finesse in language, having cut her teeth in journalism under the late and distinguished Mr. Behram Contractor. She has contributed to this book in many ways. Thank You, Nichola Pais for being a kind and encouraging friend.

Immense thanks to Ms Monidipa Mukherjee and Advocate Sunip Sen for reading the book, encouraging me, and giving their feedback. I am also immensely thankful to Sabrina Qazi Modak for being supportive in this entire process. My immense thanks to my close friend, Shernaz Tyebjee for her faith in my work and giving her critical feedback.

I thank all my colleagues and journalist friends who have supported me, few who shared contacts and their experiences which helped get the book published. Also, there are few who can't be named, you know who you are, thank you for reposing your faith in me.

I am immensely thankful to my rock support in life, dear friend, Anne Margaret George. My gratitude to Altaf Shaikh for being the friend who will tell me what I need to hear, always.

My immense thanks to Roshni and Amaan for their love and immense support. A special thanks to my family, sister Smita and my brother Madhav, who are appreciative of me and my work. Most of all, I am indebted to my Aai, Baba and Aaji, who loved me and believed in me throughout their lives.

Foreword

Julio Ribeiro

Neeta Kolhatkar is a journalist who has worked in both print and electronic media. In this first attempt at writing a non-fiction book, she interviewed 11 political prisoners, mainly about their experiences of being an undertrial or a convict in an Indian jail. Of necessity, the reason for their being jailed would also enter the dialogue, as would the social, cultural, and educational backgrounds of the prisoners.

The very first interview is with Sudha Bharadwaj, arrested by the NIA on the charge of consorting with the banned CPI (Maoist) organisation,[1] along with 15 others of similar persuasion in the notorious Bhima-Koregaon Conspiracy case, from Pune in Maharashtra. Sudha was an American green card holder as she was born in the US, but moved back to India as her life's ambition was to work for the poor and dispossessed in her native land.

Anti-national charges were pinned on her and she spent three years in Yerawada Jail in Pune and Byculla Jail in Mumbai before she was released on bail. Sudha was imprisoned for a year and three months at Pune's Yerawada jail, and another year at Mumbai's Byculla jail. On August 28, 2018, Sudha Bharadwaj, along with 15 others, including lawyers, civil society activists, professors and others, was charged with UAPA (Unlawful Activities (Prevention) Act, 1967. A special NIA court granted bail to Sudha on December 8, 2021, on a surety of Rs 50,000 after three years of incarceration. She is facing a trial which will last a decade or more, robbing the poor, for whom she worked in Chhattisgarh, of her dedicated services. At the end of the chapter, Sudha herself sums up her philosophy: 'My love for them (Dalits and Adivasis) should not be construed as being anti-national or that I do not love my country.'

In the three years she spent in Maharashtra's two jails, she describes her life there and those of the other inmates in graphic detail. Our jails are a disgrace, as anyone who has been condemned to spend time there knows. My college friend, Rajamani Iyer, had a son Shyam who was confined in the Arthur Road prison for a white-collar crime he swears he did not commit. The evidence against him revolved around a signature which he denied was his. The matter could have been resolved if the police had got the signature verified by a handwriting expert. Since that one crucial process was inexplicably delayed, he languished in Arthur Road prison as an undertrial. On being released on bail after eight months, he recounted to me his experiences. He had to pay for a mattress which he just about managed to spread out in the overcrowded jail. Those who could not afford to pay, slept on the bare floor in close proximity to other prisoners. There were many more undertrial prisoners charged with minor offences like ticketless travel on the railways. They had no means to pay for bail or get a surety for bailing them out. Shyam, incidentally, paid for one such undertrial whom he had befriended.

Listening to his account of life in Arthur Road prison, I understood why the big offenders that the Indian government wants repatriated from London or other western cities to India, always plead that the conditions in our jails in India are inhuman and this plea resonates with judges in those countries. All boasts about India becoming the third largest economy in the world by 2030 fade when such facts are publicised.

Sudha Bharadwaj was lucky. She was treated with some semblance of respect and was even 'privileged' enough to have the company of another activist, Shoma Sen, in Yerawada Jail.

Neeta Kolhatkar is, first and foremost, a journalist and her style reflects this, making it one of the strengths of this remarkable book. Easy to read, her interview with Bharadwaj moved me to agree to write this. It also helped that the author was in college with my niece.

Another interview that struck me was the one with Kishorechandra Wangkhem, a journalist from Manipur, whose writings have displeased the BJP government in the state time and again. From his name I presume that Kishorechandra is a Meitei. Yet he was very critical of the Meitei-dominated government in his state. He said that he has spoken truth to power as all good journalists should do even if that does not go down well with the authorities. For his principles he was repeatedly arrested under the draconian National Security Act which makes getting out on bail very difficult.

When the Manipur government of Biren Singh decided to publicise the role of Rani of Jhansi in our Freedom Struggle, Kishorechandra wrote that she had no relevance in Manipur. He pointed out that Manipur was not even a part of British India during that time and was, in fact, ruled by an independent prince! For his views, he was put away under the NSA for 140 days before he was given bail. Kishorechandra was, in fact, jailed four times under the NSA. The last time was when the state BJP president died of COVID and the journalist (along with a colleague) pointed out that the deceased had persistently advocated cow-dung and cow-urine as a cure for COVID, going to the extent of falsely claiming that the dung and urine of our Indian cows were being exported to the US as cures!

If the chapter on Kishorechandra reads more like a criticism of the ruling potentates then a commentary of conditions in jail, the third chapter I read was about the Telugu poet and leftist intellectual, Varavara Rao, jailed like Sudha Bharadawaj in the Bhima Koregaon Case. The prisoner was old and sick, yet no consideration for his age or ailments was shown. He was kept along with other inmates in the overcrowded Yerawada Jail in Pune. His health deteriorated till the Supreme Court let him out on bail after nearly four years in detention. Rao was still fortunate. On the other hand, Fr. Stanislaus Swamy, a Jesuit priest and tribal activist detained in the same Bhima Koregaon case, was not so lucky. He died in a hospital on 5 July 2021 of the COVID he contracted in jail. He was 84 at the time.

The chapter on Varavara Rao talks mainly of the poet's background and his journey to the far left, as well as his life with his family. It evokes a lot of human sympathy for the man. For the discerning reader, eager to know about the conditions in our jails, the chapter enlightens you about the difficulty posed by the State in communicating with one's family, despite rules inscribed in Jail Manuals. Much depends on individual Jail Superintendents and even the Jailors on duty and their personalities.

Neeta Kolhatkar's book opens a door to a different world where human beings, born to be free, are incarcerated for their views which are not in tune with the lexicon of the prevalent political regimes. It is certainly worth a read, especially by students of political science.

Foreword

Justice (Retd) B. N. Srikrishna

I read with interest the book *The Feared* which describes in detail the stories of eleven political prisoners garnered by interviews with them and their kin.

That the system of prisons in our country badly requires improvement cannot be gainsaid. The convicted prisoners are treated as less than humans and subjected to treatment which probably enhances their brutality quotient instead of engendering a sense of contrition in them. The story of the eleven political prisoners is all the more pathetic, because they are not convicted of any criminal charges but languish in prison pending formal criminal proceedings against them. Regardless of merit in the allegations against them, holding them in gaols to silence their voicing of political thoughts is wholly unacceptable. Even if a person is convicted, he does not cease to be human, even though some of his Constitutional Rights may be restricted. As long as this country believes in Constitutionalism, Rule of Law, and the Presumption of Innocence of the accused, until proven guilty beyond reasonable doubt, it would be travesty of justice and derogation of human rights to subject persons detained for political activity to long periods of incarceration along with hardened criminals. However anathematic the political views held and propagated, it would be unjust and even illegal to treat the persons holding and propagating such beliefs like ordinary convicts, while they are detained pending arraignment and trial. Even assuming there is good reason to detain such persons, there is no reason to treat them as less than human beings. Human dignity is their fundamental right and that is non-derogable, whatever the allegations against them.

If details narrated in the interviews contain even a modicum of truth, it would be a matter of great shame for our criminal justice system. It is time that these issues are openly debated and pointedly brought to the notice of those in power.

Neeta Kolhatkar is to be commended for boldly undertaking the task of interviewing eleven political prisoners and their kins and for highlighting the pathetic conditions in which they find themselves. I hope the plaintive cries of the prisoners and their families reach the ears of the authorities and impel them to take prompt remedial action.

Mumbai
19 February 2024

Preface

> *Collective fear stimulates herd instinct and tends to produce ferocity towards those who are not regarded as members of the herd… Fear generates impulses of cruelty and therefore promotes such superstitious beliefs as seen to justify cruelty. Neither a man nor a crowd nor a nation can be trusted to act humanely or even think sanely under the influence of a great fear.*
>
> —Bertrand Russell

> *Justice will not be served until those who are unaffected are as outraged as those who are.*
>
> —Benjamin Franklin

It may seem unlikely that a pediatrician, politician, editor, publisher, journalist, professor, housewife, businessman, and activist could be remotely connected. Furthermore, it is impossible to think that all of them could have been incarcerated. This is true, however, and through these deeply emotional conversations, we discover how these eleven have shared the terrifying experiences they, or in some cases, their family members, have undergone after serving lengthy periods of time—months or even years—in prison.

These are political opponents, also known as 'prisoners of conscience'. Peter Beneson coined the term 'prisoner of conscience' to describe two Portuguese students who had been sentenced to seven-year prison terms for their alleged 'crime' for making a simple toast to freedom in the time of the dictatorial government of António de Oliveira Salazar. The situation in Portugal from 1932 to 1968 has been no different in India. While we got freedom in 1947 and we claim to be a democracy, every government in our country has responded in the same manner as Salazar, by incarcerating their political opponents. It has to be said, however, that since 2014, there has been an increasing number of political opponents and journalists who have been imprisoned under severe criminal charges. Some among those arrested and their family members have shared their experiences in this book. Each of these individuals was denied bail for a few years thereby being forced to remain in incarceration. Among these cases, some are yet to come up for trial. Their crime was to speak up against the Government of India and the Prime Minister.

Through these interviews, we learn about Indian prisoners of conscience or political prisoners, as we shall be referring to them, who are out on conditional bail, and continue to live restricted lives because they were taken against their will from their homes, communities, and people. They have paid a high price for freedom, as it has come with them needing to remain silent. I first interviewed the trade union activist and well-known advocate Sudha Bharadwaj, in January 2022. She was one of the 16 well-known individuals detained in the Elgar Parishad and Bhima-Koregaon cases of 2018. After three years Sudha was granted conditional bail and released.[2]

Varavara Rao, an octogenarian, is similarly prohibited from returning to Hyderabad after being released on bail, as Sudha was. He and his wife are compelled to live in a new city where they are surrounded by strangers, and in order to survive, they have had to pick up a new language. Aside from being cut off from their own family and locality, they are restricted in their travels because they are unable to utilise public transportation, which raises their costs. In certain instances, they are required to make an overnight journey to appear in court. Even though their cases are still pending, they are required to travel to the police station once a month or once every three months, depending on their bail requirements. Some members of the 16 Elgar Parishad and Bhima-Koregaon are still behind bars—Mahesh Raut, Hany Babu, Sudhir Dhawale, Rona Wilson, Surendra Gadling, Sagar Gorkhe, Ramesh Gaichor and Jyoti Jagtap—despite the efforts of their relatives to secure their release on bond.

The great majority of people in society are unaware that not everyone who is incarcerated is guilty. In our daily life, if we ask around, most citizens would say if anyone has been imprisoned it is because they are guilty of a crime; in few rare cases, people might agree that the accused have been falsely implicated. Most are not aware, however, that every prisoner is not a criminal. Moreover, what these interviews make evident, is that the police treat all people equally, without making a distinction between criminals and undertrials. There is an inherent contradiction in such an attitude because many hardened criminals and other prominent accused people are first granted bail and are allowed to live their lives as they please. Keeping this in mind, the conditions inside prisons are highlighted in each of these interviews. Criminals are feared by society, but political prisoners are kept in separate cells, by their own admission in these interviews, because the authorities are aware of their influence in society and in the communities in which they have been working. Many political prisoners like Kobad Gandhy have also written articles and letters from inside jail describing the terrible conditions. These political prisoners are known to the prison authorities due to the intense media focus through television channels and newspapers.

As I started speaking with political prisoners, a startling observation became apparent: writers, intellectuals, civil society leaders, politicians, lawyers, and even poets appear to have been feared by the ruling political party, whether the Congress, Communist Party of India (CPI), or Bharatiya Janata Party (BJP); whether it was the Union or state government. All the same, it has to be said that since 2014, the situation has only become worse because of the current dispensation's zero-tolerance policy, which has resulted in lengthy jail terms for many political prisoners. Initially, the zero-tolerance policy was against corruption. However, it soon turned into zero-tolerance against any criticism of the Union government, their policies, and mainly against the Prime Minister. This has resulted in lengthy jail terms for many political prisoners.[3] These political dissenters have been increasingly subject to harsh legal penalties under (repetitive) statutes such as the Sedition Act and the Unlawful Activities (Prevention) Act, (UAPA). Furthermore, they have been denied the ability to post bail, with the exact phrase 'bail is the exception and jail is the rule' applied.[4]

In this book, the reader will find in-depth descriptions of the appalling conditions in our prisons, particularly in Maharashtra. The worst scenario one can imagine is when a prisoner falls ill while being incarcerated. This is borne out by what many of my interviewees have to say about extreme indifference displayed by the jail authorities when they fell ill. Prompt medical care is often purposely withheld in Indian jails. Regretfully, in these kinds of cases, even the judiciary has been unable to discern between political prisoners and professional or hardened criminals. Perhaps the most egregious example in this case was that of Father Stan Swamy, who was even refused a sipper in jail.[5] He eventually succumbed to the COVID-19 virus on July 5, 2021, in custody.

These political prisoners have time and again drawn attention to the violations of their fundamental rights that occur within prisons, such as the denial of mulaqats, or one-on-one meetings with attorneys and family members. The COVID-19 pandemic made matters worse by preventing the families of these and numerous other prisoners from being able to meet with their loved ones for several months. The families wondered if their loved ones were still alive while being incarcerated and struggled to obtain basic information about their well-being. They were sometimes forced to sprint from one signpost to another in an effort to pressure the jail administration into offering medical attention to their incarcerated family member. In the case of Maharashtra, which is where most of the political prisoners interviewed were incarcerated, these conditions are also a consequence of the political opposition to prison reforms in a state that is otherwise viewed as liberal and progressive. Member of Parliament, Sanjay Raut, has earlier expounded on the irony of this political resistance to implementing prison reforms. He did so from personal experience. He had been to the Arthur Road jail's anda cell (a high-security prison) as a member of the Committee on Home Affairs (2004-2010), in his first tenure as a member of Parliament for improving jails. He went back to the same cell a few years later while being incarcerated for political reasons. In this matter, Maharashtra can learn from the neighbouring states of Gujarat, Andhra Pradesh, Telangana, and West Bengal, which have reformed their prison systems as a result of vocal social movements and media pressure.[6] The first night in jail is reputed to be the hardest. After that, you learn how to survive, though many prisoners carry lifelong scars. Even though these prisoners of conscience are free on bond, their cases are still pending. We also learn from these interviews how damaged the family members are, in the process, and how difficult it is for them to function on their own on a number of levels. It is fascinating to observe how political prisoners adjust to their situation though, and through their stories, we get to know the bonds they create, the friendships they develop, and the relationships they form while being incarcerated. These individuals have shared how they are trying to help the less fortunate inmates with legal aid, because those who are still inside the jails don't have any clue about the courts and the way they function. They don't even have lawyers since they can't afford legal services. As a result, thousands of undertrial defendants continue to languish in our jails.

In this regard, we can draw parallels with various points in history when similar patterns unfolded across the world. The one that stands out distinctly and is rather similar to what India has been witnessing for the last decade is how events unfolded in pre-war Nazi Germany. In their article, for instance, scholars Timothy Ryback, Wendy Lower, Jonathan Petropoulos, Michael Berenbaum, and Peter Hayes write:

> While the Nazis were focusing on putting Germans back to work in the midst of the Great Depression, they also unleashed attacks on their political opposition as soon as Hitler became chancellor. On the evening of February 27, 1933, alarms suddenly rang out in the Reichstag as fire destroyed the building's main chamber. Within 20 minutes, Hitler was on the scene to declare: 'This is a God-given signal! If this fire, as I believe, turns out to be the handiwork of Communists, then there is nothing that shall stop us now from crushing out this murderous pest with an iron fist.'[7]

Ryback et al. point out that by the end of March 1933, the Nazis had arrested 20,000 Communists, Social Democrats, union officials and other radicals.

In this book, I have spoken to Communist leaders, Union leaders, activists and even a Saffron party leader (Shiv Sena—Uddhav). The idea of this book evolved after I began speaking with the political prisoners. With every interview my point of view too began to change. While some of the political prisoners are out on severe conditional bail, a few like Sanjay Raut have been luckier, but many others like Professor Shoma Sen and Prashant Rahi, languished in jail for over five years.

Whatever their ideology, they all appear to be feared by the authorities, be it the state government, central government, or the police. There is a concerted modus operandi to keep many of them away from their core work of reaching out to people, because they wield a lot of influence.

It must be clarified at this point that the first government to start taking severe action against political activists was the United Progressive Alliance (UPA) between 2004–14 when they proposed action against the Naxals, also referred to as Maoists by government agencies. On April 13, 2006, then Prime Minister, Dr Manmohan Singh, stated in his speech at a meeting of Chief Ministers, 'I came here with the primary purpose of listening to your views and the strategies you are adopting to face the challenge of Naxalism. It would not be an exaggeration to say that the problem of Naxalism is the single biggest internal security challenge ever faced by our country.' He also talked about the police response recommended by the CMs at this time. 'We may need specialized force on the pattern of Andhra Pradesh's Greyhounds. This investment is essential if we need to turn the tide in favour of the Government.'[8] Further to this, in 2010, when P. Chidambaram was the central Home Minister, he said their government, in response to 76 jawans being allegedly massacred by 'Maoists', would also consider using the Air Force against the perpetrators of the crime.[9]

Every Indian government thereafter has targeted the Naxals. Among the first intellectuals to be arrested in this connection was Dr Binayak Sen, whom the authorities alleged to be a Naxal ideologue.[10] Dr Sen who is a reputed medical professional was first arrested on May 14, 2007, from Bilaspur, Chhattisgarh. He was accused of acting as a courier between jailed Naxalite leader Narayan Sanyal and businessman Piyush Guha and charged for sedition. He was held for seven months and the courts refused him bail till May 2009. On December 24, 2010, he was sentenced to life imprisonment after being convicted of sedition and conspiracy, leading many international health professionals and Amnesty International to term it 'an unfair trial'. There was international appeal to release Dr Sen. On April 15, 2011 he was granted bail by the Supreme Court, which gave no reason for the order. He continues to face the charges despite failing health.

However, as already mentioned, after the Modi government came to power, there has been a zero-tolerance attitude towards any protest or opposition. In fact, between 2018 to 2021, India witnessed many protests due to controversial bills that were passed by the BJP-led government on December 12: the Citizenship Amendment Act (Bill) and the National Register of Citizens (NRC). CAA is an amendment to the Citizenship Act of 1955. Under the Act, fast-track Indian citizenship is extended to Hindus, Sikhs, Buddhists, Jains, Parsis, and Christians who had migrated to India before the end of December 2014 from the Muslim-majority nations of Afghanistan, Bangladesh, and Pakistan. Muslims have been excluded from this provision. The amendment introduced religion as a qualifier for citizenship for the first time in the history of modern India, a secular state.

These protests first begun in Assam and then spread to nearby states, and later to Delhi and Mumbai. One of the most important protests was the one in Shaheen Bagh in Delhi. The Shaheen Bagh protests were led and organised by Muslim women from December 15, 2019, and continued till March 24, 2020.[11]

However, as soon as the national lockdown was imposed with the outbreak of the COVID-19 pandemic, the protestors were arrested and moved forcibly from the site. While the protest was ongoing, the protestors faced criticism for blocking a public space; petitions were filed in the Delhi High Court to stop the blockade and the protestors faced severe police action. Interestingly, the peaceful protests received immense support from across the globe, even though they were criticised by the mainstream media in the country. However, the anti-CAA protests were not the only peaceful protests which earned the ire of the central government.[12]

In November 2020, 200 unions of farmers called for a strike against three agricultural bills passed by the Indian Parliament. The farmers demanded the creation of a Minimum Support Price bill to ensure corporates don't control farm prices. They launched a protest march in Delhi moving with their belongings and families, but were stopped by the security forces who used anti-riot measures like water cannons and fired teargas shells at them. They even put iron spikes on the roads to prevent the farmers from marching ahead.

Over a dozen rounds of talks between the central government and farm unions took place between October 14, 2020 and January, 22 2021, but did not yield positive results. Eventually in late 2021, the Modi government repealed all three farm bills. These striking farmers were mostly from the Sikh community. Many of the BJP leaders including the Prime Minister had termed these year-long protests as anti-national. The striking farmers were called Maoists and termed 'Khalistanis' by various leaders of the BJP.[13]

The farmers once again began protests from February 13, 2024 and were yet again met with anti-riot security forces. Among the demands made by the farmers this time, was that the government was yet to enact a law that ensured a minimum guaranteed price for all crops.[14] Yet again the farm leaders faced stiff resistance and inquiries from the law enforcing agencies. On

August 30, 2024, the NIA even raided a woman farmer leader's residence in Bathinda.[15]

The government action against civil society isn't restricted to the political sphere. In fact, the current Union Government has put together a list of farmers, lawyers, journalists, comedians, activists, students who are labelled as anti-national. In one such case, even a climate change activist faced three FIRs.[16]

This intolerance has also been extended to journalists covering serious issues in India. A report titled 'Behind Bars: Arrests and Detentions of Journalists in India' states the following in this regard:

> In the last decade, at least 154 journalists were either arrested, detained, interrogated or served show cause notices for their professional work and notably more than 40 percent of these instances were in 2020. At least three journalists were killed due to their work in 2020. Out of three, two belonged to Uttar Pradesh and the third killing took place in Tamil Nadu.[17]

According to a website analysis, the annual number of sedition cases filed increased by 28 per cent between 2014 and 2020.[18] According to a different report, there were almost 985 UAPA cases filed between 2014 and 2020, and the number of pending cases has grown annually by 14.38 per cent.[19] Furthermore, since 2014, the Enforcement Directorate (ED) has booked 95 per cent of politicians who are members of opposition parties.[20] In most cases, the politicians have been accused of corruption and many have got a reprieve after joining the BJP government.[21] It is interesting to note here that every political party demands the repeal of these harsh laws like Sedition and UAPA when they are in the opposition. However, after they come to power, they employ the same laws to subjugate their rivals.[22] All the same, the truth is that a strong opposition is essential for both the electoral process and for our democracy to genuinely function as one.

It is without doubt a fact that only when Indian citizens are better informed will they be able to overcome their 'fear' of the authorities, and make our democracy more enduring. 'Because a better-informed society is a freer society,' as Rosa González, the Regional Communication and Information Advisor for Latin America and the Caribbean at UNESCO, stated on World Press Freedom Day in June 2021.

While a journalist's job is to act as a 'watchdog' and question the government, bureaucracy, and judiciary based on the fact that a free press is the fourth pillar of democracy, it is undeniable that this role has been steadily eroding, and we have witnessed mainstream media outlets being taken over in India. As a result, India's 'free press' seems severely hobbled. It is not surprising, therefore, that India was recently ranked 150 in 2022 and 159 in 2024 on the World Press Freedom Index. As a matter of fact, 16 journalists have faced charges under the harsh UAPA law between 2010 and 2023. Till now, only one has been acquitted while yet another case is being discharged. In yet another report by The Committee to Protect Journalists published on December 1, 2022, seven Indian reporters remain behind bars. Six of these seven journalists who were subsequently imprisoned had UAPA charges against them.[23] According to another report, by the Free Speech Collective Behind Bars, 154 Indian journalists were either arrested, detained, questioned or given show-cause notices for their work between 2010 and 2020. Of these, almost 40 per cent were processed in 2020 alone. Furthermore, nine foreign journalists were detained, arrested, questioned, or refused permission to enter India in the same years. It is evident that the government does not want to see any negative publicity in the press, and they condemn those who ask questions and demand accountability.

To return to the prisoners themselves, one of the most damaging effects of these long periods of incarcerations is the severe impact on the mental health of the prisoner and even their immediate family members. This brings us to the dire need of mental health experts and relevant medication being made available in Indian prisons, something that emerges strongly from many of the conversations in this book. After all, prison life is tailored to break a person's mental strength and determination. Even in prisons where there are facilities for counselling and medication, not all prisoners are allowed to access these facilities.[24]

Given all these circumstances, I was determined to compile these conversations in a form of a book in order to reach out to more readers. These stories are important on their own but especially in terms of the fact that they bear witness to an era.

THE FEARED

flourish
and
prosper
Happy Birthday

1

'Starting over at sweet 60, on a road never travelled…'

Sudha Bharadwaj

I first interviewed Sudha Bharadwaj in January 2022. I wanted people to know the person she is—an advocate, educator, activist, a woman, and most of all, a mother. Through my various interactions with common friends, I got a lot of information, especially of her experiences in prison, and that was something I wanted to ask her about, particularly about the various experiences with her fellow inmates in Yerawada which included some cute interactions with cats. I had researched her work as well, and since I had been covering the Bhima-Koregaan and Elgar Parishad cases, I was aware of the conditions placed on her by the court, and I was determined not to compromise her safety in any way. I had all of this on my mind as I prepared to meet her.

After three years in jail, on December 9, 2021, Sudha Bharadwaj was released on conditional bail by the Special Court, after the Bombay High Court granted her bail. The conditions imposed on her were that she could not speak about her case to the media and that she would have to live in Mumbai and go to court and jail whenever asked to register her presence. At the advanced age of 60, Sudha, an advocate, was forced to start life all over again, and at a steep price. She had to live at quite a distance from her daughter for a few years. Later, Sudha had to move house three times and began living in the distant suburbs, travelling long distances in Mumbai's local trains to reach court.

Many readers might be aware that Sudha has been a member of the trade union movement in Chhattisgarh for more than 30 years. She has consistently fought for the rights of marginalised communities: protecting their right to land, exposing atrocities against them, and preventing tribals from being displaced. Just before her arrest, Sudha had moved to New Delhi, to be close to her daughter. She had begun teaching at the prestigious National Law University, Delhi, where she worked as a visiting faculty and taught tribal rights and land acquisitions, law, and poverty.[25]

I had butterflies in my stomach while sitting face-to-face with Sudha, but once we began to chat, she too warmed up to the questions I was keen to ask and the issues I was interested in. She sat on the floor surrounded by a pile of letters and cards gifted to her by fellow inmates at the time of her farewell. She spoke to me flashing her megawatt smile, her best ammunition, and remained optimistic about this new phase in her life throughout our conversation. We ended up speaking for more than three hours.

I must add here that in the meantime, she has also begun working as a lawyer and travels like lakhs of other Mumbai commuters. She is now part of the local train routine of this city and recently, when I bumped into her near Churchgate station with a common friend at night, she was rushing to catch a train to Borivli by herself. Suddenly she met another friend and turned around to bid us goodbye as she said, 'Now I have company till Kandivli.' She has adapted to Mumbai's grind, which is such a far cry from the remote villages in Bilaspur. It is deeply inspiring to witness her steely resolve.

Neeta Kolhatkar: You are starting all over again, that too at 60, and you still must go to court and visit the nearest police station.

Sudha Bharadwaj: Yes, every fortnight I go to the police station and attend all court dates, which means the entire day is spent there.

NK: Not only must you start all over again at this age but do so in a new city. How do you find my city?

SB: Well, yes... I like Mumbai city. It is efficient and gives work. My first impression of Mumbai is, 'Yeh kaamkaji logon ka sheher hai (It is a city of working people)', which has given me the confidence to find work here. Even though the rents are expensive, it is an efficient city, as work gets done rather fast. In smaller towns, you have to chase people to get simple work done.

NK: It must have been tough for you to move houses at least three times and start anew every single time—from Thane to Andheri and now, Borivli. You've travelled across Mumbai and its suburbs. How are you finding your way around?

SB: It is quiet here, though I have to travel a long distance. Thankfully, Borivli station is a major junction, so it is easier to get direct trains and there is no further travel. It has not been easy for friends or contacts to share their homes because we know these cooperative housing societies have their own rules. There are police verifications and other questions asked. My friends are brave and have tackled it all for me. With my qualifications, skills, and practice, I would like to extend help to the indigent undertrials, as I received many requests when I was in jail. I am writing, doing background work for labour cases for trade unions, and I also do drafting for a senior advocate.

NK: This being conditional bail, you are not completely free. How free do you feel, Sudha?

SB: Well, I don't feel completely free. I am in a new city, while till now work has always been in Chhattisgarh. My union is there, I used to practise in the High Court over there, and most importantly, my daughter was studying in a college there. This was the most painful part of being in Mumbai, being away from her.

NK: This restriction also means you cannot live with your daughter when she needs you the most. How has that affected you both?

SB: This has been the hardest period of my life. I could never have imagined living my life and not meeting her. All the years I spent working in Chhattisgarh from 1986. She was born in 1996. Throughout, I was a trade union activist and later, a practising lawyer. Even though we were together, I had to share her time with thousands of people. She was denied dedicated attention and time. I have missed out on precious moments with her and that has affected her deeply. I wish I had understood this all better. I took up work at the National Law University in Delhi. In 2017–18, I taught and even got an extension for the next term. It was just as she was entering college and needed me to be around. When I thought I could give time to my child, as her board exams approached, they put me in jail. I have been deprived of time with my daughter. This anger I do have against the State. The State snatched it away from both of us. In the period when a parent needs to be around, she has been forced to do everything on her own. I can only hope she forgives me because a mother's love is unconditional.

NK: You have been a practising lawyer and have experience dealing with law and prisons. Despite this, how was it when you were taken to jail for the first time? Do the authorities leave you with any shred of dignity?

SB: My 15 years of providing legal aid and practising law did not prepare me for the initial shock and indignity of it all. I still remember the first day I was taken to Yerawada Jail. I was taken there at night and the prison was too dark. The first taste of humiliation was when I was asked to strip. It was a harsh reminder that I was a 'criminal' and I would be treated like one. The procedures they follow are aimed at breaking the person, like they rummage through your bag and empty it. They refuse to allow you to take things like t-shirts or track pants. You are not given options and must carry your things in your hands and under your arms—patti, ghungri, and chaddar (bedsheet). You are given an aluminium plate and bowl, which resembles a begging bowl. As I was ushered into the barracks, it was a sight. I saw no space for any new person and they were reluctant to allow a new inmate. The first night was tough, as I barely slept and before I knew it, it was morning. Yerawada is cold during winters and worse, they would wake us up in the wee hours. We were made to sit in line as we were counted. Every prisoner is called by another name in jail. When it was my turn, they announced, 'Yeh naya Maowadi aaya hai' (Here comes the new Maoist). (Laughs)…they count you by your crime. Then they sent me to a separate cell in Yerawada. Slowly, you get used to your new environment and the jail. I was treated with respect though I couldn't say the same for those around me. Moreover, I learned that the jail staff used crass Marathi words. I remember how in Byculla, they would not say, 'Turn around' respectfully; instead, they would say, 'Tumcha thhobad, line mei jao (Show your black face, get in line)'. Maybe I was spared due to my age and they even knew who I was because jails have televisions and they are watching the news all the time. Another favourite of theirs was to refer to us as 'Bahut chapter hai'.

NK: Did they mean prisoners were acting smart?

SB: They would address us prisoners as 'chapters'—every chapter of the CrPC (Code of Criminal Procedure).

NK: Oh, interesting. Can you elaborate?

SB: Like the chapter on maintaining peace. So those who had been slapped with cases of 107, 110 or 116 were all 'chapter' cases, which also meant they were habitual offenders. Another bigger shock was being addressed as 'Tu' ('You' without respect in Devanagari). One has gained enough age and experience to be treated with a little more respect and one would expect that they would use 'Aap' when addressing women over 55 years. This was a rude shock, like someone had thrown a bucket of ice water at you. (*Smiles*)… of course, once the jail staff became friendly with us prisoners, I realised, we were all in the same boat.

NK: Where were you kept the first time you were imprisoned?

SB: Every prison has its own rules, even though there is a prison manual. We were not allowed to interact much with other inmates in Yerawada. Moreover, I was put in the 'phansi yard'—where two prisoners who were served death sentences were kept. It so happened that Professor Shoma Sen was there too.[26] The prisoners who had been served the death sentence were the famous Gavit sisters [sisters Seema Mohan Gavit and Renuka Kiran Shinde, who were serial killers convicted of kidnapping 13 children and killing five of them, between 1990 and 1996]. Along with their mother Anjanabai, they were active in western Maharashtra cities like Thane, Kalyan, Nashik, Pune and Kolhapur. [As per the Wikipedia entry on them, the modus operandi they used for kidnapping was to take children to crowded places, where one out of the trio would try to steal people's belongings. If the thief was caught, they would try to evoke sympathy through the child or create a distraction by hurting the child. Later they would take the child to a remote place and would kill them].

NK: When you were in Yerawada, were there many cats roaming freely in the open? Jailed humans seeing free cats, isn't it philosophical?

SB: Hahaha, that's a nice question. There were many cats in Yerawada when I was there but none in Byculla and those two (Gavit) sisters would interact a lot with those cats. I was told that in the 25 years the siblings lived in that yard, they had brought up many generations of cats. Watching them was fascinating. Till I was jailed, I had never liked cats and would not interact with them. When I was working, I barely had enough time to look after myself and my daughter. Now, it was beautiful watching those cats lazing in the sun and running around. They had become the universal pets in jail, as most inmates seemed to have taken a liking to them as though they were one of us. There was a Bhil lady; she was old and had been there for many years. She would sing in Bhilala and speak in a sing-song manner. She too loved those cats. She would share her quota of milk with a kitten. Maybe they reminded her of her village days.

NK: Prison is tough and sometimes, it is tougher to keep oneself emotionally and mentally fit. How did you manage?

SB: Well in Yerawada, I had Professor Shoma Sen in the adjacent cell. So yes, we were close. She was my life support. I don't think either of us could have done without the other, living in those separate cells. We could at least eat together. She and I subscribed to one newspaper each and after reading it in detail from the first page to the last, we would exchange papers. We read the *Indian Express* and *The Hindu*. We would solve crosswords and Sudokus and would laugh at the witty columns. It gave us something to talk about, at least. A lot of the time I was writing and reading. It felt like being caged. We could only look through the bars and watch children playing outside. The Yerawada campus is a very old jail, built in 1926, and has a lot of tree cover. In summer, we would watch some women throwing stones to steal mangoes. It was therapeutic to watch the coping mechanisms of other inmates.

Sometimes, Shoma and I would come out to walk in the sun and we sang songs from *The Sound of Music*, by the Beatles, Simon and Garfunkel, and some women's movement songs. Here, I learned to take care of myself. Earlier, in Yerawada, I would take walks inside my cell because we were allowed to get out of our cells for only half an hour daily. Even in Byculla Jail, I would take time out for a half-hour to do some exercise, because there was no place to walk around.

NK: What was the situation in Byculla Jail? Are there women who have been languishing for many years? How was your experience?

SB: The Byculla jail was different from Yerawada. There, I was kept in the barracks. Here, I saw that many more women had been languishing for years. One thing I also noticed was that a lot of them had been abandoned by their families. Especially in cases where the woman had been served punishment under the Immoral Traffic Prevention Act or if they had murdered their husbands; then they would be disowned mostly by both sides of their families—paternal and maternal. These women usually are the ones who cannot afford to pay a lawyer or their bail sureties, and are still in jail. I am rather fortunate compared to most. (*Smiles*).

NK: How different is your case, considering you too were forced to spend a few years in jail as you were arrested under UAPA, a draconian law? Even you were denied bail initially.

SB: I have the backing of the Chhattisgarh Mukti Morcha and also the union I work for and I am lucky to have my daughter and friends who supported me. I have a team of good lawyers and they are fighting my case in court even today. Yes, I was denied bail and it took some time, yet I have these people fighting for me.

Moreover, being a lawyer, I was following the developments. It is not the same with these women. They have no clue—they are not aware of their next date; they don't know the latest developments regarding their case, they are clueless. It was much worse during the pandemic, as there was a complete pause in their cases. All mulaqats (the current mulaqat system is the standard protocol of allowing family members and lawyers to visit inmates at prisons) had stopped during the pandemic lockdown and the inmates were not being taken to court. We didn't know what was happening and naturally, these women were frustrated.

NK: Speaking of the COVID-19 pandemic, it must have been extremely scary. What was worse—the virus or the lack of hygiene and social distancing inside the prison?

SB: First, everyone needs to understand one basic thing about our Indian jails, it is impossible to maintain social distancing. We were sleeping on 3'x6' (feet) laadi (tiles). We would be stuck to each other. In Byculla jail, there were 56 other women in the first barracks where I was put, while the actual capacity is 36. You can imagine how few the number of prisoners would be, had we observed social distancing—barely two-thirds, only 35 could have been housed there. This was the admission filed by jail authorities, in response to my medical bail application. We slept close to one another; the bathrooms were common and there was no body space anywhere as we stood in queues. We were spared in the first deadly wave when I was in Byculla. However, it was serious in the second wave as 56 inmates tested positive.

Honestly speaking, many inmates tasted some freedom when they were shifted to the Brihan Mumbai Municipal Corporation COVID centres. At least they could sleep on mattresses, instead of the normal laadis. They had not seen beds in a few years! Some charity organisations served vegetarian food, and even though these prisoners were not vegetarian, it was good quality and tasty food. Initially, when these women inmates were being shifted to these centres, they were petrified. They were not sure whether they would survive and cried, fearing for their lives. When they returned, they looked happy. They shared their experiences with us.

Many others including me escaped the virus because of the rapid antigen testing. I had mild fever and diarrhoea, and now doctors say I may have had the virus. Otherwise, every second inmate had caught the virus. We faced the problem of being stuck in quarantine barracks. It was depressing as everyone around had fallen sick. Most of the toilets in these barracks were choked as the sweepers refused to come inside to clean them, fearing infection. On the other hand, the women inside the barracks were too sick to clean them. We ate food thrown through the bars. It was like living in a horror for over a month. Till then, I had been managing barrack duties of sweeping, swabbing, and washing my clothes. After I fell ill, I just couldn't do them; I had become extremely weak.

NK: There is a class system even in our prisons, it is said. Is it true you can get things if you have the money?

SB: Yes, a different class exists inside the jail. Of course, the currency is the canteen. Someone can send you money if you have a PPC (Prisoners' Personal Cash) account. You can then purchase toiletries, biscuits, snacks, and such things. Then one can also eat special food on Sundays, like chicken. Now this is also beneficial because you can buy things for those who are poor and have them do your work, like washing, swabbing and other barrack duties.

NK: Were you allowed mulaqats with your daughter, friends, and lawyers?

SB: Now, mulaqats under UAPA are extremely strict even though on paper they are allowed, as per the rules. Only blood relatives and lawyers were allowed to meet me and no friends were allowed. Even lawyers are allowed to meet you only twice a week. I eagerly looked forward to all my mulaqats. During COVID, these were stopped; after a gap, they allowed phone calls. This was a huge relief. Since my daughter was far away and she could not come more than once in three months to see me, we eventually came to depend on these phone calls. Sometimes if the police were kind, we were even allowed video calls. At other times, they would be overzealous and refuse to allow us to take the food inside our cells. They have even prevented me from hugging my daughter.

In the three years I was inside, I only had four to five mulaqats with her. She wanted to visit me on my birthday in 2021, despite the long distance she had to travel to meet me. The jail officials made her run around for an entire day to get permission from the NIA. She was sent from one authority to another and finally, she was not allowed to meet me. We could only meet two days later and both of us were miserable. Now see, she was allowed to meet me in Yerawada but was refused permission to meet me in Byculla. Why must things have to change, when we are the same? It all depends on the prison staff who are present on duty. They tend to be nice on rare occasions and will allow you to speak for more than 15 minutes and since she visited only once in three months, they were kind. They were particular about phone calls, which could not exceed 10 minutes and they would cut the call abruptly, mid-sentence. They would not permit video calls and each time, we were subject to a lot of police verification for this. Even during the verification of phone numbers, they would unnecessarily complicate matters. You don't have the freedom in jail to speak to your blood relative on any new or unverified number. Every time, one wrote out a new application and all these were sent to the original police stations, where the police took their own sweet time. Phone calls were a huge relief to many, as they could at least keep track of family matters.

Often, the investigating officer prevented my union people, who had come all the way from Chhattisgarh, from meeting me, because they were poor. They were dismissive about these visitors and once, I complained to the court about it. Just because these are poor people, don't be classist and harass them. They acknowledged it and at least stopped doing so.

NK: What coping mechanism did you all develop, to help each other? Was it like an extended family?

SB: Humans can develop amazing ways to cope with any situation. While many rely on prayers or religion, a lot of women express themselves in their creative ways. See these letters and cards they have given me as farewell gifts. They would make special birthday cards for each other. Also, though things were rationed and we only had limited ingredients in the canteen, inmates would make delicious cakes from whatever was available. So each one of us had these extended friendships to cope inside. There was conflict due to limited space. But we learnt to share, though sometimes people got in the way of the other, because we were forced to do so. But along with fights, strong bonds were formed. See, these were 24x7 friendships. Further, there are no barriers between you and the other person and most of all, there is no time for any formalities. You automatically responded to anyone crying. I must say one thing. You couldn't have imagined the kind of people you make friends with in jail.

NK: Many learn different skills in jail. Did you pick up a new language or any new skills?

SB: Before being jailed, I did not know Marathi. When I went to Yerawada, I had to pick up Marathi. Initially, we struggled to get books from outside and our only source for reading was the jail library. In a very typically patriarchal system, the women's jail was always subordinate to the main prison for men. Now, the main library was in the prison for men and only 25 books from there could be brought to the women's jail (*laughs*). We had fun reading the English books, but finally, I ended up reading a lot of Marathi books. I actually read many interesting Marathi books like *Shyamchi Aai*, and *Dr Babasaheb Ambedkar*. Yes, I also read Veer Savarkar's *Jeevan Thep*, of which there are several copies. In the end, I learned to read Marathi and I read Anne Frank's diary in Marathi. I don't understand the nuances of this language, but I got the general drift of it. Another problem in Yerawada was that the women constables would speak to us only in Marathi, so one was forced to learn the language. In Byculla, it was more cosmopolitan, as everybody spoke Hindi.

NK: How was it in Byculla? What were your other experiences?

SB: In Chhattisgarh, I have been practising labour law, land issues and conflict, human rights cases, and so on. In Byculla, I learned about other legal issues. I had never been a criminal lawyer and that is what I learnt a lot about in this jail. I also learned what was entailed in giving them legal aid. This is a very important and serious issue and I will try to file a Public Interest Litigation regarding this—providing legal aid to undertrials is a constitutional mandate and we should not rely on ad hoc methods; effective legal aid is essential.

NK: While you inmates shared space and life, did you share your knowledge and skills with one another?

SB: Just watching women cope was such a relief. Women would make rangolis, draw mehendi, do needlework; some would cut their maxis and convert them into beautiful tops. You simply have to see their creativity to believe that they could make beautiful things with such limited items and without any support from the jail authorities. Can you expect women to not find a needle and thread to survive? We find a way to get around. Wait, I will show you the little potli (pouch) that was made by a Finnish lady for me. She was jailed and later, her plea bargain was accepted and she left for Finland after she completed her sentence. She was an interesting lady, a pianist. She had been jailed for two years and she gifted this to me. (*Sudha went inside the house to bring out a tiny, green handmade pouch*).

NK: Your mother has been your inspiration. How was it living on the JNU campus? Why did you choose to live in India and not go to the US, as you had a green card?

SB: My mother Krishna Bharadwaj was a socialist, Marxist, and an economist. She belonged to Karwar (in Karnataka, barely 79 kilometres from Goa), an area influenced both by Socialism and the Goan liberation movement. She was a good singer when she was a child. In the beginning, we lived in Karwar. As a child, I remember the entire area being influenced by the Goan liberation movement and Socialism. She was a brave girl and yes, it runs in the family. At that time, youngsters would sing these povadas (ballads) as they set off on prabhat pheris (dawn marches, a subtle form of protest against the British). Her parents always kept an eye on her because, if she saw anyone singing during the prabhat pheris, she would join them and would have to be brought back from another village. My mother went to Cambridge and came back to India. After spending a year or so at the Delhi School of Economics in 1972, she founded the Centre for Economic Studies and Planning at the Jawaharlal Nehru University (JNU). She was a renowned economist. In that sense, we both came back home. I was born in the United States and I returned to my home country. After 21, I had to decide whether to stay here or go back to the US and I chose to live and work here. Later, we moved to the JNU campus. I had a nice childhood there. The JNU campus is a beautiful place to live in and an exciting place for politics, far removed from all the violence seen on other campuses. On that campus, I saw students studying not for a career but wanting to do something with their lives. They wanted to change society and were idealists, and not aspirational.

NK: Do you think the popular notion of nationalism is more accepted than yours, which is inclusive and fighting for the rights of the poor?

SB: I love working for the people of this country and I cannot help it if others don't love all the people in this country. (*Laughs*). It is that simple: I love workers, but we have seen they are not loved by their employers and end up losing their jobs. I can't help it if people don't love the Dalits and Adivasis, they are as important to this country as anyone else. My love for them should not be construed as me being anti-national or that I don't love my country. It is ironic and funny that they have put such severe anti-national charges on me. It means you would have much preferred that like typical IIT students, I should have gone to the US after my degree and lived there forever. There is a beautiful poem that speaks of diverse paths and taking the one less travelled, which made all the difference. I have enjoyed my journey and if I were given a choice, I would go down this same path.

NK: How tough has it been for you to adjust to Mumbai and being forced to live here since your release? Starting to practise anew in a metropolis and not in Bastar?

SB: Of course (it is hard) being away from a place where you have spent half your life, from the age of 25; for nearly 30 years, all my conscious working life has been spent in Chhattisgarh. In that sense to be exiled from there, from the Comrades there, from my union colleagues, my lawyer colleagues, as I had a group of lawyers and of course the people I worked with, I'm away from them, also, an area I was familiar with—it has been very difficult. It is a feeling of exile. I do video conferencing with the people and my colleagues, sometimes I appear by video conferencing in the Chhattisgarh High Court also. But the civil society in Mumbai has been extremely supportive; trade unions are supporting me and I am working with a senior advocate here. I am doing a similar mix of cases (as I did before), matters related to slums and forest rights, these are things close to my heart. In that sense wherever you go you find issues close to you. In that sense I am busy, I am working and like every other Mumbaikar there is a long commute each day. I travel nearly four hours to and fro: that is part of life in Mumbai. In a way that is also nice, being a part of the flow of normal life. It is at times tiring at my age, now I am a senior citizen, that's what life is like now. When I have my daughter with me, it is very nice. She will be leaving again soon to pursue her Master's. She is going to Kolkata, so she will be away again for another two years. She will be coming and going, plus we have the great luxury of phone calls, so that is wonderful. One of the heartiest developments for me is that my neighbour (in prison) and partner, I can say, in a way the invisible presence in my book,[27] Shoma Sen has been released from jail yesterday (April 17, 2024). It is great news and a source of happiness for me, because she, in an unsaid way has been part of every page of that book. It is unfortunate that my bail conditions don't permit me to communicate with her. There is nothing more I would love than to go and give her a big hug.

NK: When we spoke the first time, you had said Mumbai is a city of the working class. Does this city live up to this emotion and expectation?

SB: It still does, surprisingly. Mumbai city is a great equaliser in many ways. The other day, we were having a chat on the local train about how we were all very annoyed with the air-conditioned trains. We all agreed that rather than the 27 AC trains, just increase 27 ordinary local trains, since people can also travel by first class in the same trains. The minute you have a hierarchy in the local trains then the AC trains will be given priority over other trains. If there is any kind of hindrance in the local trains system then this city will collapse. These local trains are the arteries and veins of Mumbai city. In other ways also, you get down at any station in Mumbai and you walk around. On either side of you there are trains, lines, and you see people selling all sorts of things, from cut vegetables to fruits, everything under the sun. Obviously, a large number of people are eking out their livelihoods from all these cracks and crevices. I once asked someone what happened to the mill workers because this was a city of mills and there were lakhs and lakhs of mill workers (here).[28] They said at least half of them are still here. So these are the people giving you the vada paavs, gajras, nashta (snacks), and cut vegetables, and selling wares on the trains, driving your taxis and autos. It still is a working-class city.

NK: There are reports stating long periods of incarceration can lead to depression and other mental health issues. How did prison impact you mentally and psychologically? Even if you are a strong person, it can have an impact, right?

SB: Of course, no doubt about it (prison impacts one's mental health), even if you are strong, it makes a difference. Personally, I was lucky. I had an issue of depression even before I went to jail and I was on medication (for it). After that I continued to be on medication and maybe that helped me. I am a person who associates easily with others and in Byculla jail, I didn't have even a minute to myself because I was busy writing applications for others. When one was locked in for the time, that night till the next morning is tough. There would be many sleepless nights. Of course it takes a toll. In the jail there would be a lot of women who are really suffering from mental stress. You can't imagine, there are many women who have been incarcerated because of crimes within the family. Now many of them are totally abandoned. Just imagine a woman who has in self-defence murdered her abusive husband, she will be left alone by both her families—na maika na sasrual (Neither her maternal nor marital side of families) is going to visit her. She probably doesn't have a lawyer and she is probably ragged by guilt. They are thinking of their children who they are separated from. I mean almost every second woman is affected. We saw many women crying or not eating and, in such cases, the tragedy is that there is no regular counselling. Of course there is a regular psychiatrist who visited every week, but she would examine and treat only those who were referred to her. It is not our choice to go to her. Those who are referred are those who are seen to be making a nuisance of themselves—those who throw things around, those who are violent or attack another inmate. These are the sorts who the jail authorities cannot manage (on their own). If you are the kind who sits in a corner crying to oneself for one's daughter, then at the most, your neighbour will come and persuade you to eat and console you. But a vast majority are troubled who need help. Will their families accept them, how will they go back, would they be able to adjust? Will they get jobs once they are out of jail, what will their children think about them. There are so many issues going on in their minds. Imagine the foreigners, the Bangladeshis who come here, they have nobody.

NK: Speaking of your case, did the uncertainty of your case adversely impact your daughter?

SB: Yes, very much. It was ironical, after working a large part of my life in Chhattisgarh, working with the union, as a pro-bono lawyer, I hardly had any time for my daughter. Later I made a conscious decision to give her my time and be with her and that is why I had shifted to Delhi to be with her. This period of separation from me, when I was in prison and she was in Delhi, was extremely difficult for her. It was tough for her and I was extremely aware that it was difficult for her. When she wrote letters to me, I used to be almost afraid to read them. It took me a lot of courage to open those letters. I would think innumerable times before opening them. It was really painful to see her pouring out her anger, her loneliness and her sorrow. She felt let down and by the time I would write back to her, I knew it would take time for her to receive my response. They would take a week to censor her letter, then I would write a reply, again the jail authorities would take a week to censor it, by which time her next letter would be on its way. The time gap between her writing a letter and receiving my reply was long and my response would have been meaningless. I couldn't comfort her and then again, I would be afraid, what if I said something sharp, or suppose I had scolded her. Then she would have held onto it until the next letter arrived. It would have been terrible; I was extremely careful and would re-read my letters repeatedly. I did not want to hurt her. She suffered a lot and she was extremely brave. I must also share, she suffered through COVID-19 and she was all alone, without me, that was tough. The only good thing that happened were the phone calls. It was our lifeline. This is the only number I remember by heart and the only one I shall remember in my life. Her number, which was the only one on which phone calls were allowed. All of a sudden, the constable would call, madam ab aapki baari ayi hai (Madam now it is your turn), so it made no sense to write it down on a chit and then go looking for it. It was better to memorise it.

NK: Did your daughter take help?

SB: Yes, she did, though it was tough. It did help her.

2

'Mein kranti launga.'

Nilofer Malik and Sameer Khan*

(I will bring revolution) said Nawab Malik to his daughter, Nilofer.

On January 9, 2021, the Narcotics Control Bureau (NCB) arrested Sameer Khan, a businessman and the son-in-law of the then cabinet minister and Nationalist Congress party leader, Nawab Malik. This was just the beginning of Malik's troubles with Central agencies. In March 2022, he was arrested in connection with money laundering by the Enforcement Directorate. After repeated applications for bail were rejected, finally on August 11, 2023, the Supreme Court granted Malik two months' interim bail.[29]

After a few requests, I finally convinced Malik's daughter Nilofer to speak to me, as people needed to know the harrowing times their family had endured. It has been a tough journey for the family, doing the court rounds to get bail, first for Sameer and then for Malik. Their rock has been Malik's wife, who ensures that he maintains his diet even in jail, given his health issues.

Sameer Khan was arrested on January 9, 2021, in connection with a drug case and was released on September 27, 2021, by a special NDPS (Narcotics Drugs and Psychotropic Substances) Act court after eight months in prison.[30]

In the period between Sameer and Malik's arrests, the latter had taken on the NCB authorities for falsely charging innocents like Aryan Khan, the son of Bollywood superstar Shahrukh Khan, who was arrested on October 3, 2021. From day one, Malik had maintained that the entire case against Aryan was fabricated and had exposed the then NCB Mumbai chief, Sameer Wankhede in the matter. He had even accused Wankhede of extortion at that time. Malik was arrested on February 23, 2022 by the Enforcement Directorate, which alleged that he was connected to another property in Mumbai's Kurla.[31]

I went to Nilofer and Sameer's office in the suburbs to meet them on March 15, 2022. Initially, Nilofer spoke to me as Sameer went about his work, occasionally dropping in to listen to us. When he finally spoke, he sounded shaken. One could imagine how the incarceration must have left him emotionally scarred. Together, they spoke of their ordeal and how their family was still being hounded by the central investigative agencies.

Neeta Kolhatkar: Were you all prepared the day your father, Nawab Malik, was arrested?

Nilofer Malik Khan: The previous night I had gone to meet him and shared my misgivings, but Daddy had assured me nothing would happen to him. Our lawyers too went through the entire process with us and (advised us on) how to handle any situation. As I was leaving, he said, 'See you tomorrow, beta.' The next morning, everything had changed. My aunt called me to say some people had come to my parents' home and I needed to talk to my mother. When I spoke to her, she said Daddy had been taken by an officer for questioning and she was expecting him to return soon. After quite a few calls to Daddy, because the officers may not have allowed him to answer, he spoke with me. I insisted on knowing where he was and he said he was being taken to the Enforcement Directorate's office at Ballard Pier. I immediately knew something wasn't right, but again he insisted all would be fine and I was panicking unnecessarily. I knew he wouldn't return home because that is the way these agencies function. In the last two to three months, many things had occurred, which had put me on alert. ED officers had been calling a few people close to our family for questioning on some pretext or the other. Their matters had nothing to do with Daddy, but those people were close to him. There were other indicators of something brewing. The most shocking thing was how they had barged into his house at 6 am, causing alarm.

NK: How has your mother coped with these developments?

NMK: She has been through a lot. First, my husband, and now Daddy was jailed. Initially, she had believed the officer when he said Daddy would return home after questioning. I could understand her predicament because that is exactly how naïve I was when Sameer was served the summons. I had been confident he would come home because he had done nothing illegal. After Sameer was taken for questioning, I had not even told any of my family members (about it). Once he left, he did not return for over eight-and-a-half months. I could see the same pattern unfolding in this case. The officers try to finish you by making you run from pillar to post. You are left trying to persuade your lawyers to get one hearing and then comes the fight for bail. Now imagine, if this is the sort of harassment people like us, with all the connections and resources, are put through, what is the plight of those who don't have the money, power, or experience to fight for their rights? So far, my father has fought for the rights of such people who lacked the resources to stand up to the tactics of NCB officers. These poor people were being harassed and falsely charged. There are still some matters pending, some who have been falsely charged and my father was waiting to expose those cases. As a result, some are languishing in jail for want of justice.

NK: First, they came for your husband, then for your father. How have simple processes like mulaqats been for you? Has it been tough?

NMK: The first time, with Sameer, it was sad because the jails had shut down completely since a national lockdown was declared to combat the COVID-19 pandemic. At that time, all mulaqats were stopped and they allowed only one call per week. Also, as per protocol, we had been informed that we could speak only for five minutes, but they would cut the call before the five minutes were up. After they lifted the lockdown and we were allowed to visit him in jail, I was excited because finally I thought I would be able to see him, touch him. I think it is very important in a married relationship to have these feelings and touch is important. Just imagine, when I finally got to see him, it was from a distance. There was a glass partition between us; we were nearly five feet apart and could only speak over a telephone. I couldn't feel or touch him when we first met face-to-face. Forget speaking to him, seeing his plight, I burst out crying. Today, I understand the whole process and how the jail system functions. We were better prepared this time for Daddy than before. Everyone in my family, my mom and sister had gone to meet Sameer at Arthur Road Jail, so now they knew what was in store. My first mulaqat with Sameer had completely shattered me but it wasn't so bad when I went to meet Daddy for the first time.

NK: Though your mother had met Sameer back then, how tough was it for her to go again to meet her husband in jail?

NMK: Yes, like I said, the process is emotionally draining. The fact that you have to leave your house early, go and stand there in a queue, then wait to register your name, and then stand there till your name is called out. It is not easy for women. This is all rather time-consuming. To reach the jail by 8 am, we had to leave home an hour before. It takes more than an hour and a half to complete all the formalities. They take your Aadhaar card, it is sent inwards to all the desks there and they call out the name of the visitor and the one jailed. Then, a policeman goes in to bring the person from his cell and you continue to wait. I would accompany my mom because none of this was easy for her at this age. It also got crowded after a while and there was just no scope for social distancing and sanitising the area. After all this chaos, we would meet the person. Of course, we were all happy to see each other. His spirit is just amazing, he kept us going and told me, it was a long battle and we had to fight; 'Hum kranti layenge (We shall bring revolution),' he told me, with all of us smiling hard.

NK: Visiting a jail must have been a huge culture shock for you. How did you cope?

NMK: It is sad and a huge culture shock. It gets extremely crowded for the relatives who line up to meet their loved ones. People would be surprised to know that it is not only hardened criminals or the poor who are in jail. There are many privileged people serving jail sentences. Each one of us waits with utmost anticipation to catch a glimpse of their relative. All are like one extended family, the minute a person's name is called there is a sigh of relief, as each person is optimistic that their name too will be called out. The one who gets to visit the relative turns around and reassures the others, everything will be fine. Each one comforts the others. Till now, we have met Daddy twice. Sadly, the authorities don't distinguish between the undertrials and others. Not all are guilty. The system functions rather cruelly.

NK: Is a strong message being sent out to society through your father's arrest? For him to remain silent

since he was raising questions on the functioning of the narcotics bureau? Asking to remain silent?

NMK: Evidently, the message is asking people to remain silent. If anyone asks questions, they will be put behind bars. My father told me clearly, 'Main kranti launga (I will bring about a revolution),' and I have immense faith in him. At one of our mulaqats, he raised his fist in the air, assuring me, 'Beta, hum kranti layenge (Child, we will bring revolution).' This will hopefully give courage to at least one person to speak up. My father had been exposing the wrongdoings of an investigative agency that had put many in jail under false charges. These are all simple people, scared to speak against any officer and the agency. My father is a brave man and has only spoken the truth. When he took it upon himself to expose the NCB corruption, he had alerted us about the repercussions, that the authorities would hound him. Our parents have instilled strong values in us—even if you have few clothes to wear or little to eat, don't ever do things that will tarnish the reputation of your family.

(*Sameer has walked in and out of room where Nilofer and I sit and chat a few times. Finally, he joins us. He is soft-spoken and weighs his words carefully before speaking.*)

NK: Sameer, how severe was the initial trauma for you? How big a shock was it for you, being arrested and serving a term in prison?

Sameer Khan: Prison is uncharacteristic and I felt lost in there. It was uncomfortable and I felt rather uneasy. You don't know what to do—whether to stand or sit? One is constantly restless. One second, you want to stand and the next, you want to sit. Then again, in the next second, you want to do just the opposite. I can only say one thing, jail is not for anyone. You can never be at ease. To begin with, you are reeling under the shock and trauma of the severe sections the authorities have slapped on you. It has been extremely tough for the people around me who have languished in jail for years. The whole experience of getting out on bail was painful, lengthy, and stressful.

NK: What helped you survive in prison?

SK: I read a few books, including a book on Jyotirmoy Dey's murder.[32] Since I was kept in a general cell, there were many inmates and we could only speak with each other. It is no place for a human being. Sadly, in our country, the minute you are in prison, you are termed guilty and the onus is on you to prove your innocence. No one should be treated so ruthlessly. It is one of the most painful experiences to go through.

NK: What did you do to drive away your negative thoughts? How did you battle your emotions?

SK: Jail is fodder for all kinds of negative thoughts, and I too had to battle them. You start doubting yourself and the system because jail simply erodes any positive rationale. You are constantly battling, on multiple levels—first, fighting your negative thoughts, then the adjournments in court; and the constant battle to get a date for your bail hearing. You are taken to the courts (which is a whole process) and then you just keep getting dates; it is like that scene from the Hindi film *Damini*;[33] tareekh pe tareekh, one date after another. To add to all this, you are cut off from the outside world and you don't know who to consult about your case. There is nobody with whom you can discuss this and that is when you begin to have doubts—you doubt your very existence. When they have snatched your liberty from you forcibly, you even have doubts about being Indian. They arrested me under the severe sections of the NPDS Act.[34] The authorities ensure your lawyers are left with no grounds to fight for your bail. Well, as per these laws, you can't fight for your bail till the chargesheet is filed, by which time you end up spending more than six months in prison.

NK: Imagine, despite all your connections and resources you were treated in this manner; how bad was it for others around you?

SK: Most of those languishing in jails cannot afford to hire lawyers. Their condition is pathetic, as they have no clue about the status of their cases, whether they have even got bail or not. I used to write down their case numbers and would send them to my wife, to see if she could get some help for them. It is bad not to have money because these people cannot pay the surety amounts for their bail, which means they continue to remain in prison for long. Many of them have been disowned by their families for the stigma they face.

NMK: There is huge stigma faced by many of these families, especially if the main bread-earner has been jailed, it is truly sad. People stop purchasing goods from these families, they are ostracised from society, which eventually depletes their resources. Ultimately, in such cases, the fall is taken by the wife and children, who have to face taunts from their community. Many families struggle with loans and fees. They struggle to survive since they have no one to fall back on. On top of all this, these women have to fight against all odds trying to get their spouses out of jail. They don't even understand legal and judicial nuances and they face the pressure to arrange the lawyer's fees. Most of these families are left to fend for themselves.

NK: Do you feel you were being targeted because you are the son-in-law of Nawab Malik? Do you fear for your life?

SK: The officers hinted at this to me on many occasions during their questioning. The day I was brought to the NCB office, the

Investigative Officer in my case announced my arrival as 'Cabinet minister Nawab Malik's son-in-law, Sameer Khan has come'. It gave away their plot. Thereafter they were not ready to listen to the truth. I stood my ground that I was being falsely accused, but of course, they would not listen to me. Then later, they said they wanted to break Nawab Malik's chair, indicating he would be ousted as cabinet minister. There was a vendetta against me. They want to make a person feel so helpless and paralysed; I am still living with this trauma. They ensure you can't live a normal life. The false charges they levelled against me have affected my children and my work. Many have distanced themselves from our family. People fear if they are seen interacting with us, the authorities may target them, so they prefer not to remain close to us.

NK: How severely were your children affected after you were jailed and released?

SK: They have been severely affected. When I came home and I'd go to the toilet in the middle of the night, the younger one would wake up crying and ask his mother where I had gone?

NMK: They were traumatised when he was jailed. The younger one would not stop crying. He would keep asking my mom when his father would return and she would tell him to stop crying; that his father would be back soon. I would tell her not to give the kids any false hopes. One time, when I had taken them to a toy shop, my younger one saw some superhero toys and told me, 'Don't worry mamma, this Batman will release my Dadda and all those in jail.'

NK: How has jail scarred you, Sameer?

SK: Prison scars you no doubt, but you also know the worst is behind you and that actually makes you feel fearless. But this is not how I felt when I first came home from prison. I would tremble in the middle of the night, talk in my sleep and it worried my wife a lot. She would wake me up and speak to me. My children can't sleep alone anymore. A lot has changed in our lives. Just as we were beginning to get on with our lives, they arrested my father-in-law. He was our great support. The trauma was back, all the bad memories and fears returned to haunt me.

NK: Sameer, were you able to speak with other prisoners? Could you interact with people within your jail?

SK: I did meet many people; I even met Father Stan Swamy. He was truly a lovely person. Initially, I was taken to Taloja Jail and that is where he was kept. He was unwell and he couldn't move. It was sad to see him in such a condition. Yet, he was enthusiastic, extremely nice, and welcoming. Even though he couldn't move, he was energetic. We spoke a lot and he explained a lot about life and philosophy. The first two days, I faced immense dilemmas and struggled to understand all that was going on. I didn't know who he was, to begin with, and I had no idea about the legal battle he was facing and the struggle he was undergoing (physical). After I was released, I read the news of his death and how he had been denied treatment. He was so humble; he did not even let me know who he was and the extraordinary work he had done in tribal areas. There was a young man taking care of him; he too had been arrested in the same case. (*I asked whether he meant Arun Ferreira*). Yes, Arun Ferreira was the first man who had spoken to me when I entered Taloja jail. He gave me a rundown of the rules and procedures and explained the drill. I was put in the cell next to Arun's. After the initial introductions, we began speaking. Both Father Stan and Arun conducted deep conversations, as compared to most people in Taloja. The first two nights I was put in the jail's hospital and then suddenly, I was just taken to a cell. After I entered my cell, I got the shock of being in prison. Their handholding was reassuring to me.

NK: Jail can break a person mentally; how did you cope? How were the other inmates?

SK: Apart from Father Stan and Arun, there were some other kind people too, who helped me a lot. At first, when I did not have my canteen money, the inmates around me did not hesitate to share their quota of water, snacks, and the food that I wanted from the canteen. I will never forget their hospitality. This help is crucial because it is difficult to deal with the rude shock of being in jail. I grew up drinking mineral and filtered water and then suddenly… (*pauses*). Once I was released, I began reading up on Father Stan and Arun. I learned about the immense work he (Stan Swamy) had done; it was such a pity he was denied medical intervention and the conditions in which he died were heartbreaking.

NK: Can you describe the condition in Taloja jail to us?

SK: The conditions in Taloja are pathetic. There is a huge problem with drinking water in that jail. On many days, you don't get water and as you may be aware, there are timings for every activity in jail. First, to deal with the schedule, and on top of that, the water crisis would mean more crowds at bathing time. There are a few storage tanks, yet there is permanent water shortage. Of course, there are fights and the cause is not water. We have seen some worse times, like during the COVID-19 pandemic when we were kept indoors. The staff would open the bars only to slip our food inside. For the rest of those 15 days, we were locked up around the clock. I did not see the sun and worst of all, did not speak to any other human for that entire period. Only after the quarantine period was over were we allowed to interact with others. They finally allowed us to speak with our family on the telephone three days after this quarantine period was relaxed. They gave us specific timings as per the cell numbers and we were allowed to queue up to make calls only after our names were called.

NK: Do you remember the day you saw the sun after a fortnight of being in quarantine? How did you react?

SK: I took my first step out in the open after over a fortnight. Initially, I felt giddy when I looked at the sun and thereafter, I couldn't bear to see the sun. It felt rather strange. I had not even seen myself in that entire period and I had forgotten how I looked. At that time, when I was allowed the first video call to my wife, I was horrified to see myself. I did not recognise myself. (*Gets misty-eyed and looks pensive*).

NK: Have you spoken of your experience in prison before? Have you shared this with anyone?

SK: No (*whispers*), this is the first time I am speaking (*Chokes… recomposes himself*). That day, when I saw myself on the video call, I was shocked to see my long beard. When I was first arrested, the NCB had kept me in their custody for 12 days, then two days in the hospital and a fortnight of quarantine in Taloja Jail. There was no access to a mirror. So that day, when I saw myself, I just couldn't believe it. That shock was… (*pauses awhile*). I did not want her to see me like that, I was worried and she wanted to see me because she hadn't heard from me or even seen me on video. I didn't need three minutes of conversation because all I wanted was to hear her voice. When she saw me, she couldn't control herself and began crying. (*Sameer and Nilofer weep for a few minutes. The room is silent*).

NK: Did your incarceration change you as a person once you were out on bail? What are the small ways in which you feel change from within?

SK: Small things in our everyday life that we take for granted are denied to us in jail. As I mentioned before, I didn't know what life looked like outside my cell. I hadn't even seen the sun for a fortnight. Later, all I saw were mountains, metaphorically speaking. I felt as if I was stuck in a hole, with only tall mountains surrounding me and blocking the sunlight. One fine day, I was uprooted from Bandra and was taken to some remote place. We take our lives for granted. Simple things like people walking on the streets I couldn't see. In that sense, coming to Arthur Road Jail was a relief. The conditions there were much better than at Taloja. There is no problem with water and food in Arthur Road Jail. The food at Taloja was inedible—everything was diluted and tasted like boiled water. They would serve rice with a lot of water and the same with curries, again watery. We were not given any cups, bowls or cutlery. You learn to survive in jail with several hacks to make life easy. The bottled water came in handy, as we would cut up the bottle and make a cup to drink curry/beverages. That is how I learned to have tea in Taloja Jail. At Arthur Road, we were given plates, bowls, and cutlery. It was a relief. Even the kinds of inmates in both prisons were different. I could only speak with a few in Taloja Jail. In Arthur Road prison, there were more people with whom I could interact. Fellow prisoners become your family and friends inside the jail. I am keen on fitness but sadly, I just couldn't exercise in Taloja. So we would buy water bottles and salt from the canteen. After we had finished consuming the water, we would fill them with salt and turn them into dumbbells. We used to work out with that. (*Smiles at the memory*). I could even walk in Arthur Road Jail but only for a short while because every time my court date got close, I would get stressed. Once my mind got restless, I couldn't do anything. I couldn't lift a dumbbell or even go for a walk. I would get bogged down with thoughts of whether I would get bail or not. I would worry about what my lawyers would say. Other times, I would be left wondering whether I would get an opportunity to talk to my wife. I would wait for my wife's letters and would go looking for them. She would write to me every night.

NMK: It was my nightly ritual and all my family members would say: don't go near her, she is writing a letter to Sameer. Every night after I would write him a letter, I would burst into tears. I would assure him in every letter that everything would be okay. Then I would send him a message saying I was not going to write a letter anymore because I did not want this to be a part of my life. I did not want to spend the rest of my life writing letters; instead, let me start manifesting your being next to me.

NK: How did you cope with this huge change in your life? You were away from your wife and sons for over six months.

SK: Once you are thrown in a situation, you have no choice but to accept everything that comes your way. Even if it means accepting you are thrown in prison. You have no choice but to accept it and you realise you are in no position to lay down any condition. This experience has been a huge learning experience for me and I know I can survive anything in life after living in prison. Anything apart from that is good and you know then life can't get worse than this. I can tell you this, freedom is extremely important… just be free…. I value my life and all my relationships. I have started valuing people around me a lot more than before. (*Nilofer adds he has become humbler*). I saw people die in front of my eyes in jail and you can do nothing. A person who would eat with me in my cell just dropped dead in my presence and I couldn't do anything. Life is brutal in jail and you have to learn to survive. The other disturbing situation was when a man in the cell next to mine in Taloja killed himself. I was scared to death. I recall the first night I was brought to Taloja, when I saw a huge rodent running around in my cell. It was as long as my hand. Later, when I went to Arthur Road Jail and was taken for a medical check-up, I requested the doctor to give me sleeping tablets. I didn't want to stay awake because I didn't want to relieve those experiences. I did not want those memories to haunt me every night.

NK: Has your perception of jail and people who are imprisoned changed since your incarceration?

SK: We are judgemental about those sent to jail because we are not aware of the truth. After what I have been through, though I am out, I still face stigma because our society is trained to perceive people who have been jailed as offenders. I can speak for myself. I saw the kind of people who have been jailed and these are not from our strata of society. How many of us can say we have friends among people we know who have been imprisoned? How will we be judged if we say we do know? I now keep wondering how others will judge me because I was imprisoned. All my perceptions about life, in fact, everything I believed in, have changed. I have lived this entire experience I saw around me, so many innocent people being in jail for years, without any hope. They are clueless about their sentences; they don't have any information about their cases, their punishment, bail, etc. Since the time I have been released, I have been talking about these cases with my family.

NK: Sameer, was the media particularly harsh on you?

SK: Journalists are used by the investigating agencies to spread false news and lies about some of us who have been sent to prison. This is the main reason for the media conducting trials on their news channels. The media does not distinguish between leaked false information and tips on actual investigations being carried out. I remember the day I was taken for investigations to the NCB office, I saw my face on their notice board. That news clipping claimed that I had helped the NCB bust a cocaine racket but none of it was mentioned in their chargesheet, because there was no racket nor had I busted anything. The agencies merely use the media to serve their ends.

NK: Nilofer, this is a tricky situation. Nawab Malik is a Muslim and he has also been exposing the modus operandi of the central agencies. Is that why he is being made to suffer?

NMK: I wouldn't say that he has gone inside because he is a Muslim. Yes, he is extremely vocal and he has been exposing this particular conspiracy and the wrongdoings of any agency or people. My father has not targeted any one person or officer; he is just exposing the injustice done to not one, but numerous people. These are simple people who are scared to speak up against any officer or agency because they fear they will be charged under severe sections or get arrested. So, they came forward and shared information with my dad. He is not the sort to get scared; he will expose wrongdoing and speak up against injustice. At that time, he had told us that he was likely to get hounded. The values my father and mother taught us were, 'Do kapde kam pehno, do roti kam khao, lekin kabhi ghalat kaam mat karo. (Even if you get fewer clothes to wear or little food to eat, don't ever do any wrong in your life). Don't do anything that brings a bad name to your family.'

NK: What support have you received from political circles?

NMK: Leaders of all the parties in the Maha Vikas Aghadi alliance—the NCP, Shiv Sena and Congress, have extended support to us. I have no complaints. They have called on us to assess the situation and speak to us, which is important. We are glad that they are here as a family. Until now, they were close to Daddy and now they have bonded with our family too. We are all one now. They have come home and met us and call us from time to time. I think these are very important things and it makes you feel good that they are here for us. Even my mother feels reassured. The most important thing that they have done is they have not accepted his resignation and they are not giving in to the demand made by the opposition. Yes, they stood up against the morcha, 'Nawab Malik hatao Maharashtra Bachao' (Remove Nawab Malik and rescue Maharashtra). Every party in the MVA government has said from day one that he will not resign. (*This was in March 2022, over a year prior to Malik being granted medical bail*).

**Publisher's note:* Sameer Khan passed away during the production of this volume, on 3 November 2024.

3

'Bonkers has helped me from going bonkers.'

Koel Sen

At the time of her arrest. Professor Shoma Sen was the Head of the Department of English at the Rashtrasant Tukadoji Maharaj Nagpur University. After completing her Master's from Elphinstone College in Mumbai, she went on to pursue her MPhil and PhD in Nagpur. Dr Sen was among the five people to be arrested in the early hours on June 6, 2018, from different parts of India. The other four who were arrested with her were Surendra Gadling, Rona Wilson, Sudhir Dhawale and Mahesh Raut. All were charged under the Unlawful Activities (Prevention) Act, for distributing pamphlets which the authorities said were controversial. They were also accused of making hate speeches in connection with the Bhima Koregaon violence that broke out in January 2018.[35] *Her arrest came a few days prior to her retirement in the following month. However, she was suspended immediately after her arrest. On February 14, 2021, Sen's case was transferred from Pune and Mumbai to the National Investigation Agency (NIA) court in Mumbai. On September 21, 2021, Sen's application for interim bail for medical reasons was rejected by a court.*[36]

After six years of incarceration, Sen was granted bail on April 5, 2024, by an Apex Court bench of Justices Aniruddha Bose and Augustine George Masih. In the bail order the judges stated that the restriction for grant of bail as per Section 43D(5) of the UAPA would not apply in case of Sen.[37] *In fact, the National Investigative Agency after nearly six years declared in the Supreme Court that 'they no longer needed to keep her in custody'. Sen, like others arrested in the case, has also been released on conditional bail.*[38] *She has been ordered to keep her mobile phone switched on round the clock; she has to inform the investigating officer (IO) of her place of stay and she has to submit her passport, address proof and mobile number to the IO; furthermore, she is not permitted to leave the state of Maharashtra without leave of special court.*[39]

I met with her daughter Koel Sen, who is a film director while her mother was still in jail. Koel talked of the time when things went 'bonkers' in her life. On March 24, 2020, a national lockdown was announced, on account of the COVID pandemic. As a result, jails were suddenly shut down and the families of those incarcerated suffered immense trauma; suddenly, there was no communication possible, as phone calls were barred and so were visits. The whole process took a toll on Koel, and it was her cat 'Bonkers' who offered a distraction at this time.

Neeta Kolhatkar: You have a cat named Bonkers? How did you get him?

Koel Sen: Just looking at him, you would think he is Bonkers. This name was suggested by my friend. His expression looks like he has gone bonkers. Bonkers has kept me from going bonkers. (*Laughs*). A friend and I found him. Now, he has adopted me. Since then, he has been with me. It has been amazing to have a friend. It is amazing how therapeutic cats can be. He has helped me tremendously in feeling less lonely and is a good companion. Cats are actually giving. (*Smiles*). It really helps to have him around.

NK: Due to the COVID-19 pandemic, mulaqats had stopped completely. How has it been, especially since you met your mother in person after a long time?

KS: It was after more than two years that we met for the first time, in proximity, and spoke face-to-face. The last physical meeting was in February 2020, that too in court which was prior to the national lockdown. We had three meetings because there were no fixed rules regarding mulaqats during this period. I was happy to see her in person but was also sad to see the changes she had undergone. Prison seems to have aged her. Her health too has become frail, and she already had glaucoma and arthritis. She also shared with me how her reading has been impacted and the pain in her knees has worsened, making it difficult for her to get up and sit. She has to do that often while in court. It saddened me to see her condition. In fact, these physical meetings also have their limitations because she is surrounded by constables all the time and even though we get some time to speak in private, they keep a close eye on us.

NK: Is her health a cause for worry? Does she tell you about it?

KS: Yes, I had heard about an episode from Sudha Bharadwaj (*they were in adjoining cells at Yerawada prison*), but Ma doesn't tell me anything. Maybe she doesn't want me to get disturbed. There was an episode of her blood pressure dropping and she experienced a blackout. Or that she felt giddy. She doesn't want to burden me with her ailments. Being a mother, she is concerned about me and the impact it will have on me and I completely understand her predicament.

NK: How alert are jail authorities and do they allow medical intervention immediately? Have they taken her to the hospital regularly?

KS: The jail authorities couldn't be bothered, to be honest. They don't bother about the health of the prisoners. Ma has to ensure she is taken to a government hospital for her treatment and she has to follow up with the court and authorities, telling them of her health problems and that she needs treatment. Then, there are procedures to be followed. Once she is taken to a government hospital, since she is a prisoner, they are always seen by interns, and not doctors. They are treated like second-class citizens. Doctors are scared of prisoners. In such situations, Ma has to explain the details of her ailments. Her eyes need to be checked and she needs better treatment. Before she was arrested, we had taken her to the best ophthalmologist and given her good quality treatment. We have no clue about the government hospital and the services there, and no new tests have been conducted. It is definitely a cause for worry.

NK: First of all, a parent being in jail is sad enough, then to be denied basic rights, like touching, hugging or sharing food with your loved one, just because she is in prison must be heart-breaking. How tough has it been for you?

KS: It is sad. I tried to hug her initially, but the police will simply not let you do that. In fact, on one occasion, my friend had brought some nice food, kebab, biryani and some sweets, which we wanted to share with her. We gave her a small bite and after eating the brownie, she was thrilled. Her eyes lit up and all of us were happy. The constable immediately suspected something was brewing because we looked happy and were smiling. She cautioned us and meekly, we too apologised, to divert her attention. It was quite funny actually. There was nothing wrong in what we had done, yet the officials see everything in the context of laws. It is behaving humanely with my mother but the jail rules prevent her from having home food. Actually, prisoners can be given packaged food like biscuits, wafers, and chips but home-cooked food is not allowed. Previously, Ma was allowed to eat food from home, but later, the rules changed. However, the staff are also rather patriarchal when enforcing rules. When male prisoners are brought from Taloja Jail to the court, they are given permission to eat any food, which is not so in the case of Ma or other female prisoners. It is just that the rules change from one prison to another; there is no single rule for all.

NK: It is now nearly five years since your mother was imprisoned. How tough has it been for you? Also, adjusting to the rules to different prisons must have been rather tough?

KS: It was difficult for me when Ma was in Yerawada. First, I had to get accustomed to the fact my mother was in prison and I had to go all the way to Pune to meet her. Just the thought of going to meet a person in prison impacts you when you are at the gate. These thoughts occur—that you have to go to meet your mother in prison even though you know she is innocent, and there is nothing you can do. Just the structure, look and feel of the prison, the walls, the uniformed staff and the way they examine you, all this deeply impacts you. It is a huge shock initially, and extremely painful. The treatment meted out to a visitor is also rather violent, since you are perceived as the 'family member of a criminal'. They size you up because for the prison staff, there is no distinction between the undertrial prisoners and those termed guilty. For the police, all are guilty. You can feel their fixed glare as they see family members interact with their loved ones in prison.

NK: What has been your experience visiting the Byculla women's jail?

KS: When Ma was first taken to Yerawada, there were several visits because I had to take her some things. I had to get her clothes, medicines, and most of all, it was overcoming our shock at her imprisonment. In the beginning, it felt so sudden; later, when she was shifted to Byculla, we were beginning to get used to it. But then we had to endure the COVID-19 pandemic and the two lockdowns. In the end, I could only see her four times at the most because their rules kept changing with each lockdown. Like when I would visit Ma in Yerawada, I had given them all my identity proof for verification. When she was shifted to Mumbai, imagine, we were the same two individuals, but I was made to go through a whole new process of verification, running around with the paperwork and providing the same proof, even though it existed in their records. They gave me a deadline for the meeting and in that stipulated period, we had to juggle the verification and the eventual meeting. In the end, I could meet her only once a month and come to think of it, she was in this same city. I met her more often when she was in Yerawada. These processes make you feel frustrated.

NK: What about your emotional and mental well-being? How have you managed to keep yourself together?

KS: I have had bouts of anxiety and depression and had to even take medication. All of this has affected my life and work, and it has been tough. It was particularly bad in 2020. At that time, I had a nervous breakdown. It was a wake-up call for me to get away from all this. Initially, my mission was to get Ma out of jail. The same goes for the families of all the 16 people arrested in this case. (*Father Stan Swamy passed away in 2021*). We have all gone through the same phases of anxiety, the extremely stressful and emotional times. When the lockdown was suddenly announced, they shut down the prisons and stopped all communication—letters, and phone calls. There was absolutely no news from within the jails, especially regarding the health conditions of the prisoners and the medical facilities available inside the prisons.

It was also the time I took the decision to stop speaking to the press, because they kept hounding us for minute information. I also learnt that when one is in a vulnerable position, people don't necessarily protect you. They want something out of you. I experienced it with the media and my extended family, who did it despite knowing about my predicament.

NK: You have tried to reach out to people by writing posts on social media. How has your experience been? Did you receive support?

KS: It has been helpful and I have received warm wishes from a lot of people. One also has to build a strong support system, which helps one remain strong, as one has to get on with one's own life. Of course, there have been times I have felt completely lonely. I am an only child and sometimes I feel there is just too much pressure on me. These posts are also important to keep Ma alive in public memory because prisons make a person absent from the lives of others. I share these posts so they learn of her well-being, of the developments in her case, the updates on her health and basically, to inform the people connected with us. I have also seen from my posts people are genuinely concerned because I have just been talking about Ma. Most of those who have responded have expressed their shock and then shown concern and have been extremely supportive.

NK: Most of the families of the 16 arrested know each other. Some of you children have grown up together. Do you all share a close bond and interact regularly to get each other's support?

KS: We are still there for each other. We are all learning from these experiences, as we exchange our thoughts and feelings and continue being with each other through this emotional journey. We do step aside, or sometimes boost each other's morale but it is still difficult. We are being watched and the officials know when we visit prison. Police use their tactics and try to get information on us from the others. They try to get information from us to see if we communicate with each other, since all our cases are similar. Of course, one gets sharper along the way because initially, one isn't aware of these queries as being ways to keep a watch on all of us. They, of course, have ways of snooping on us.

NK: Can you recall the day your mother was arrested?

KS: It was a complete shock. It was unexpected and I would have never imagined she would be picked up by the police. Since I was on a shoot and working till late at night, my cell phone was out of network. I was told later that Ma had tried calling me before she was taken away. Later, my father couldn't call me because both their phones were confiscated. I wasn't even aware of the police raids on their house in Nagpur. A few days later, our maid's daughter called to share the details and that's when I checked all the details online.

NK: Have you and your mother exchanged letters? Does she share her experiences from inside?

KS: Her letters do describe her life in prison—the food she eats, the celebrations too, of the various festivals they have. She has written that she wanted to wear a saree for the Ganesh festival and I took one I liked, but she felt that a silk saree was too nice to wear in prison. They all learn ways to make the most of the little content available in jail. Like, they make cakes from biscuits and using Bournvita. Such amazing things they do, and use various hacks, like using the back of a bottle to crush peanuts. She finds the food in jail problematic. Also, they are woken up early, for tea, biscuits, and a snack. Then they are given a tasteless lunch and the same food is served for dinner in the evening. The canteen is shut at 6pm, so nothing is available, it is not easy.

NK: How have you changed in these last three years?

KS: I have changed a lot and I look at it as a positive thing. I think I've learnt to be more independent. Another thing I have learnt, which is a good thing but also sad: I have been able to keep certain people away from my life, those I know who have not helped us. They are close people, even extended family, who have not come out and supported me. In fact, they completely ignored me when I was looking for emotional help. When your mom is not around and you are in a bad shape, you look out for people like her to help you out. I am thankful to my mother's friends. They have given me a lot of emotional and mental support. They have really looked after me in these times. I am pretty sorted now and things have fallen into place. Now I know what is right and what to do.

NK: Has your mother's arrest affected your ideology and politics?

KS: It is pertinent to have an ideology, especially in today's times. There is nothing wrong in believing in an ideology and politics which is not majoritarian. In fact, this belief system is important for one's own growth, in my art and overall understanding and it eventually reflects in my work. People are being silenced for holding contrarian views and opposing policies, which is a part of public discourse. It is suffocating to not be able to speak and one needs to find a way. My mother has faith in this country and is extremely optimistic. She believes that change is possible in small ways and she may not be around to see it, but there will be a change. We respect each other's views.

4

'From age 24 to 40, I was fighting for my father's freedom.'

Prashant Rahi and Shikha Rahi

Prashant Rahi completed his BTech (electrical engineering) from IIT-BHU, in 1982 and his MTech (systems engineering) from IIT-BHU in 1985. From 1985 to 1988, he was a senior research fellow in what was then a new frontier, Power Electronics at IIT-BHU, under the UGC scheme for doctoral researchers. He later worked at the HINDALCO's captive, thermal power plant at Renusagar, Uttar Pradesh. For a year, he served as a reporter at Himachal Times, Dehradun, then in UP, in 1993.

Afterwards, for nearly seven years he was the staff correspondent based in Dehradun, for The Statesman, between 1994 and 2001, till a year after Uttarakhand was formed. He had an impeccable record as a conscientious supporter of the Uttarakhand statehood movement. He also supported the democratic struggles of the youth, peasantry, and the masses to fulfil their livelihood needs and regional aspirations, right until his first arrest. Uttarakhand Police arrested Rahi in December 2007, for sedition, waging war against the State, conspiracy for being a Maoist and he was charged under the Unlawful Activities (Prevention) Act (UAPA). He was later released on bail in 2011.

In 2013, however, Rahi was re-arrested by the Maharashtra police, again on charges of being a Maoist. He was released 14 years later, on January 7, 2022 when Rahi and his three co-accused were acquitted of all charges by Udham Singh Nagar Sessions Court Judge, Prem Singh Khimal.[40] *It was the same case in which Professor G N Saibaba*, who was teaching at a Delhi University college at the time, and others, were convicted in 2017.*[41]

Rahi's daughter Shikha is a filmmaker. Prashant was in different jails over the last 12 years of his incarceration and Shikha travelled to various prisons across the country to meet her father. She singlehandedly fought his legal battles to get her father his freedom. I first interviewed her in 2010, when she younger, more vulnerable, and just breaking out into the world. Over a decade later, I met her again for the first interview I did for Rediff.com. We met at her place in the city's suburbs. Her mother and she cooked a delicious meal and we sat for a few hours over a heart-to-heart chat. Later, we met again, to update the interview, in a café in the suburbs.

Today, she has transformed into a bolder, more confident woman. Although she is fighting her own battles, she has become a conscious social observer of the world around her and more sensitive to marginalised people. She is not afraid to tell her story. Over the last few years, Shikha moved the Nagpur Bench of the Bombay High Court to get her father medical treatment as he was suffering from Sciatica and was not taken to the hospital for treatment. A harsh truth slowly came to light as it was found that some of his fellow inmates had conspired to give him laxatives.

Finally, on March 5, 2024, the Bombay High Court's Nagpur Bench acquitted GN Saibaba and five others, overturning the 2017 verdict of the Gadchiroli Sessions Court which had sentenced them to life terms. A division bench of Justices Vinay Joshi and Valmiki SA Menezes ordered the acquitted accused to be released after depositing Rs 50,000 each as bail bond. The Court declared the sanction against the accused under the UAPA as 'null and void'.

**Publisher's note:* Professor Saibaba passed away on October 12, 2024, as a result of medical complications, seven months after his release.

The six who had originally been convicted in the case were Professor GN Saibaba, journalist Prashant Rahi, Mahesh Tikri, Hem Keshavdatta Mishra and Vijay Nan Tikri. They were acquitted of all charges. Pandu Narote, the sixth person who was implicated in this case and convicted in 2017 with the others had died in August 2022 after the authorities delayed giving him treatment while he was in jail.

After the acquittal on March 5, 2024, I re-interviewed Shikha, along with Prashant, in order to get a fresh perspective on life inside Amravati prison and what the verdict of acquittal means in these times. This time, Shikha left the centre stage for her father as he responded to my questions. She would only add something when she felt there was an important point to be made. It goes without saying that she is much relieved and happy to see her father acquitted of all charges, and this time, for real.

Neeta Kolhatkar: Congratulations Prashant on your acquittal, this is a big decision.

Prashant Rahi: Thanks for your congratulations, it is freedom for not only me, but it is freedom for a certain cause. So, congratulations for us in this case, and to all those who are still inside in other cases.

NK: Last time when you were acquitted (in 2022), you were not allowed to come out of the prison even for a second. This time as soon as the judgement was pronounced were you finally convinced it was for real? Or did you have any doubts, going by the precedent?

PR: Yes, this question was there in our minds. Due to a lot of confusion, even though I was to be released on March 6, at the eleventh hour, I was put back in prison. I was only released the next day, March 7. On the day before we really got out, there was a big struggle inside the prison. This was the first time I was released and put into jail again. March 7, I was finally released, but on the night of March 6, I was put back inside the cell. On the evening of March 6, I was told that all the procedure and paperwork for my release was completed then there was a phone call from some higher up (official). There was an officer from the Intelligence Bureau who was present inside the prison. He had interviewed me and asked where I'd studied, who was there in my family, where I lived. The prison staff settled my accounts exactly like you check out of a hotel and that is when the jail staff received a phone call. I got to know the Superintendent had called. I could hear her voice. She outright refused to let them release me, said it is not done, it was 7.30pm and no prisoner is released in the dark. Law is something and practice another thing and rules are another thing. It is not as if prisoners haven't been released at night before, but they simply refused.

NK: Is it then that you thought yet again you will not be free?

PR: Yes, when the Superintendent insisted, the lower rung officer had to capitulate. That constable who was completing my formalities came to me with a sullen face and bashfully told me that he wasn't being allowed to release me. When I asked what had stopped him, the policeman said he would lose his job. So, I said, that would be better. He should leave his job for the sake of our country. If he let me go and if he were to lose his job for this, I would raise the issue (outside). I told him I would go straight to North Block from Amravati prison and visit the Home Minister (in his defence). I don't know where the voice came from, somewhere deep within my heart. Then other officers came in and the policeman got scared. I realised I had to change all their minds. Meanwhile, my lawyer had moved to file a contempt petition against the Superintendent. Obviously, this policeman would have to face the consequences. He understood he was doing his job on behalf of the Superintendent. I had to explain the same thing all over again to the other senior officers. I gave them a half-an-hour-long speech. If they didn't let me go now, the government would move the Supreme Court to challenge my acquittal and would have a strong argument against me. If I were not released, then they would claim I am still inside the prison and reluctant to get out. They won't cite the rules. They would claim I did not go out, which will then be seen as fait accompli. It would also have given them the ammunition that since I was inside the prison, I should continue to remain there. This was a real possibility. I then struck a compromise. I reluctantly agreed to remain in jail but asked them to put me in some other cell and not the anda cell: the aadan, a place when prisoners come late at night. I tried convincing them to keep me outside, but it wasn't possible. They took me back to my cell and promised to release me by 8am the next day.

NK: Did you feel reassured they would release you, eventually?

PR: There was no guarantee they would and predictably they didn't take any steps to release me. So I began creating a row in the anda cell and finally at 10.30am, I was released. Later I was told, the authorities wanted to first release G. N. Saibaba, and minutes after his release I was set free. Nagpur is the Headquarters of this division and Saibaba was given priority, as the prison where he was placed, is close to DIG of prisons too. Amravati prison is of the lower category of prisons, so we were not a priority.

NK: What happened when you stepped out? How was it to be free?

PR: You know when I stepped out, I told them I was going to the Home Minister. Two senior police officers were waiting outside the gate. I turned to them and said 'Jai Hind' and they saluted and reciprocated. *(Laughs)*. The lawyer had a cellphone and tried to take a photograph but you are not allowed to click photos outside the prison. That drama happened. I enjoyed it as I enjoy all kinds of drama. I don't like a mundane sort of life. (*Laughs*). Once I was out, I was sure it would be difficult for them to put me back inside. It makes a great difference when you step outside the jail. It is a world of difference.

NK: What is this difference that most won't understand?

PR: Once you are registered as a prisoner, you are helpless, whether you are an undertrial or a convict. Whatever be your intentions or spirit, you are helpless. Whatever be the level of your struggle, you just can't do anything. When you come out, you can boss over anybody. There in prison you have to succumb to everyone's rules, you have to be subordinate to everybody. Officers would tell me while bossing over me, 'We shall be friends once you get out.' These are the power relations of prison. Like what Michel Foucault, the French philosopher, wrote when he spoke of power relations. Foucault's theories addressed relations between power, knowledge and how they are used as a form of social control.

NK: You've been to how many prisons till now? What are the stark differences you noticed and experienced? Also, Maharashtra is considered progressive, how are the prisons in this state and how are the political prisoners treated?

PR: Five jails in Uttarakhand and two in Maharashtra—the first was Nagpur and the last one was Amravati. I have been mulling over this the last few years. I spoke to the staff and other undertrials about this as well. There is the usual subordination, loss of dignity, it is all common. There are differences, like what matters the most to all prisoners are the mulaqats. I was told by a few police officers that in Maharashtra, previously there were some incidents wherein organised criminals misused the mulaqats for other reasons. Like not only passing on illegal information but also used them for intimidating and threatening rival gang members. It is due to the gang warfare and such incidents that severe restrictions were then put in place. These are inhuman restrictions. Now these laws and rules fall under the Home department, they just need an excuse to clamp down on the rights of people. These restrictions are there in other states too. However, in Uttar Pradesh and Uttarakhand, where I have spent a few years, mulaqats are held rather freely. However, the system uses excuses to restrict all democratic facilities. For example, if I say I want my right, one has to fight against the nature of the system and not simply say this is my right and I want to assert it. There is a nuanced difference. Maharashtra has a strong security presence inside the prisons and jails as compared to the north. Like in Uttarakhand, for 1000 prisoners there would be hardly 30–40 staffers. Here, against 1000, there would be not less than 150 police staff. The proportion of police presence inside the prisons is important, and in spite of such high police presence they have also imposed severe restrictions, which amounts to a denial of basic human rights. One would expect better facilities in an advanced and progressive state such as Maharashtra. Then they allow this symbolic gala bhet mulaqat (hugs) to those prisoners who have children below the age of 16 years on November 14 and on two other occasions, as if they are extending favours or giving liberty to inmates. I don't know how we can hope for a change regarding mulaqats, because the situation is rather bleak.

NK: What about the other issues inside prisons, if you compare Maharashtra to other states?

PR: Where other things are concerned, it is better here; food, for example, is much better in Maharashtra prisons. They at least use all kinds of spices and ingredients in their cooking—-turmeric, masala, onions, tomatoes, and generally the taste is like that of home-cooked food. However, since it is cooked in large quantities, the quality ultimately depends on supervision. In some jails, there is minute supervision, while in some others it is not so, and then the taste and quality of the food suffers. The point is, there is provision in the system to provide good food. In comparison, the system itself doesn't have this provision in UP and Uttarakhand prisons.

Another issue is that of the canteen facilities available in prisons. In the north, one gets all kinds of cooked food at different intervals throughout the day. Like one can get pakodas, choley puri, tea, eggs, dal fry, etc., round the clock and every day. Here, in Maharashtra, such cooked food is not available on a regular basis. Only recently, when this particular IPS (Indian Police Service) officer, Amitabh Gupta, took over as Inspector General of Police, he introduced a few new facilities like cooked food periodically. Of course, different jails have different kinds of cooked food. Among the nine central jails in this state where I have been, Amravati is the most backward. Previously, three times a month, we would get chicken on Sundays, also egg curry or Kabuli chana, which of course we had to buy. On the contrary, in Nasik you get cooked nashta (snacks) every day, like medu vada, dosa, omelette and so on. A medu vada plate costs Rs 70, which is the cheapest. Only rich prisoners can afford (cooked food). There is a disparity between different areas and jails. Where there is buying power, they have better facilities. Amravati has the lowest purchasing power so we get pathetic facilities. Nagpur is relatively better. They give them fruits once in two or three months, like apples, oranges, bananas, and guavas.

NK: Are family members allowed to send food to prisoners in Maharashtra?

PR: No, families of prisoners cannot send food to jails in Maharashtra. This makes it different for this state. In Uttarakhand for example, we can get all sorts of things from outside. Family members can send fruits, pickles, desi ghee, cucumber, radish, onions and tomatoes, except for zeera and condiments used for cooking. We are not allowed to cook. In Uttarakhand, we can apply ghee on rotis or add a spoonful to the vegetable or dal. In Maharashtra, none of this is allowed. Even biscuits, Shikha would bring some for me; while in Uttarakhand they would let her bring, here in Maharashtra they would not allow it.

NK: How are the conditions inside the prisons?

PR: Oh, the conditions are different across prisons in India. To begin with, the mattresses are different. In the north, they give us kutta kambals (dark blankets made from rough wool), which are used even by the police. In Maharashtra, these are made of cotton wool; they are called kambal but not made of wool. These are greyish in colour. We have to wash our kambals and these double up as mattresses as well. It is only after the arrival of the new Inspector General that prisons introduced the new kambals and we can now purchase one mattress and one pillow for Rs 800. This was introduced just six months ago. Now, the mattress looks very nice, but once you start using it, it becomes very thin; it kind of shrinks with use. They want us to be in trouble always.

Shikha Rahi: It gets extremely cold in winter. Prisoners shiver in that extreme weather.

PR: They are not concerned and are least bothered with the prisoners suffering in the barracks. We prisoners in the anda cell are better off than those in the other barracks.

NK: Can you explain why you were in a better situation than prisoners in other barracks?

PR: In the anda cell, the numbers are fewer than in the other cells. Another important point is, all of us in the anda cell were not the sort to get cowed down easily. Some of us would have private blankets and our own sheets. For instance, I could keep six blankets. There was a senior jailor who sympathised with me.

He said I was a senior citizen and I could keep any number I required. However, their attitude is one of laxity towards the general prisoners. Most of the latter do not get more than three blankets. Because I could keep six, let me tell you, I didn't feel cold, otherwise it can get severe in the winters. Sometimes they give only one blanket. Every prisoner gets one dari and one blanket. There is a quota for every prisoner of two-three, but there is also a paucity of blankets in our prisons.

SR: Once some institution had donated a number of blankets to the prison.

PR: Yes, an NGO or an institution can donate, not an individual. While a family member can give a blanket to a prisoner.

NK: The first time when you were arrested and brought to Maharashtra, how were you treated? Were you stripped down?

PR: I wasn't stripped down. I went inside the prison as a convict. The minute I stepped inside I was sent immediately to the kapda godaam (clothes godown). I had to drop my luggage there. It is like a cloakroom where they check the belongings, make an entry and a number is put on it and kept safely. Ninety-nine per cent of the time, your luggage is safe. As soon as we complete this procedure, those who are convicts are given a uniform to be worn. In fact, convicts and even some undertrials are given uniforms. Prisoners who are booked under Section 302 (for murder) and Naxal prisoners are given uniforms, for instance. Earlier, when we were imprisoned as alleged Naxals, we didn't have to wear these, but now it is compulsory for Naxal prisoners to wear the uniform. There is a green band at the edge of the sleeve of the shirt the Naxals have to wear. There is a yellow band for life sentence convicts and 302 undertrials.

SR: They are demarcating these types as the most dangerous prisoners within the jails.

PR: Obviously. This band is part of the uniform which is categorised according to the gravity of the offence. I had to wear the green band uniform. All other prisoners wore white uniforms.

SR: Not the undertrials, they could wear their own clothes.

NK: Did they treat you differently because you are a 'Naxal'?

PR: No, they did not. They should have treated me differently and with respect, but they didn't. They treated me like any other prisoner. In the Nagpur central prison things are bit different because there are many Naxalite prisoners. I was first there as an undertrial, and then as a convict, (I was given bail but was re-arrested in jail itself, so I was kept there); both times, I noticed that the Naxal prisoners are treated with some regard by the jail staff. However, here in Amravati prison there is no dignity and regard, whether you are a hard-core criminal or a Naxal. This could also be because Naxal prisoners are rarely kept in other jails, including Amravati prison. You have to fight for your dignity in other prisons, while in Nagpur, Pune and the more prominent ones, the Naxal prisoners are respected. Generally, most prison authorities believe Naxals are those who fight for peoples' rights and there is a positive perception about them. Some jail staff even maintain that they know that Naxals are pro-people who have dedicated their lives for the rights of the uneducated and the poor. That is why they have been jailed. So, there is an element of sympathy towards the Naxals.

In fact, one jailer whom I shall not name, was a constable at the time of this incident. He had to go for an interview for the post of a jailer. In Amravati, he was asked by the then IG, who are the Naxal prisoners and what are they like? He later told me that he had summarily stated at the time, 'Naxals are those who fight for rights of people.' He said the IG was pleased with his reply. The officials don't mind if the subordinate policemen and jailers have this opinion; of course, this is not true of all officers, only of those considered humane.

NK: Let us now go back to March 2022 onwards, when there was a national lockdown for most part of the year, due to the COVID-19 pandemic. How were the conditions in Amravati prison? How was your condition and that of your other fellow prisoners? How bad was it, considering in the city of Mumbai and Pune, the conditions inside the prisons were pathetic and inhuman?

PR: Actually, Amravati prison cannot be considered a representative of what happened in the rest of this state. At that time, we feared a complete lockdown in jail, which did not happen in our prison. We were free of any lockdown, which meant the staff could go back home on a daily basis, which would not have been possible in the case of a complete lockdown. In other big central prisons, the jail staff could not visit their homes for weeks. This may be due to the fact that the overcrowding in our prison was far less. Say the capacity of the prison is 1000 prisoners, and the actual number of prisoners was around 1500, so it was rather comfortable. This is the primary reason for us being better off compared to other prisons. People did fall ill, even the prison staff. In fact, we also had a few deaths. 5–6 prisoners died at the time, but among them two were already in terminal stages of illness. Since I was in the anda cell, we would get the information later, but we were curious because all of us had heard reports of the pandemic and deaths in prisons and we were concerned. So, in a way, in Amravati prison, it was business as usual. We would interact with each other when we came out of our cells. All visitations had been stopped.

SR: We were not allowed visitations or phone calls. The Bombay High Court allowed us to resume voice and video calls in May 2022, after a Public Interest Litigation was filed. They started with the regular audio calls for only five minutes once a week, then they increased it to 10 minutes and then much later did they allow video calls. Only the lawyers had the provision to call any time. Only Amravati had a regular schedule for calls. But there were other issues in Amravati, like the network would be weak, calls might drop and we couldn't complete conversations properly. Or there would be a lot of noise in the background making it difficult to hear anything or even speak.

PR: After the court order the prisons slowly resumed the calls. Shikha had sent me the court order and I had read it thoroughly wherein they had allowed the number of calls per prisoner. I calculated the number of calls per prisoner, the total number of prisoners and the number of smart phones the jail staff would require. I handed a letter to the jail staff informing them of these details. I am a qualified systems engineer, so it was no rocket science for me. When I gave this to the jailer, he responded, 'Iska kya fayda, rakhiye', (Leave it, it is of no use). Then after several months, the staff were forced to purchase those many smart phones which I had calculated (*laughs*). For most of the time, there were too few smart phones. This went on for a few weeks and then soon it got regularised to video calls. But even the lawyers, they were allowed calls only once a week. We had some good sub-inspector rank jailers; they were hardworking and nice. The main issue there was no over-crowding in our prison. The jailer, who was in-charge, had completed his Master's in Agriculture and he wanted to be a teacher. He was a nice man, he was sensible. He would try and do a lot in the prison. I used to feel proud that the PUCL had moved the PIL and got us the right for the audio-video calls The officers don't want to make these facilities available, they want to minimise them. As for the prisoners, the big shots, who have the money and muscle, want to corner whatever little there for themselves. Sharp inequalities are stark inside the prisons.

NK: From the time you went to prison as a convict and an undertrial, did you at any time reconcile with the idea that you may never come out? Since the first time you were acquitted, they re-arrested you.

PR: Since my conviction seven years, 2017 to 2024, and one year as an undertrial, I did consider the possibility that I may never get out. It was neither implausible nor impossible, considering the precedent the State followed. However, at the time when our judgement was reserved by six months before the pronouncement of our order, I thought they would delay it by another six months during which time the political situation may change and the court might relent. As time passed, my anxiety increased. But by March we were out. On the eve of this judgement, for the first time I did not get good sleep. I used to keep well almost every day of my time in prison; however, on the eve of the judgement I just couldn't sleep. I had written a long letter to Shikha, which of course I did not post. I thought if they delay setting me free further, then there were many issues to be raised with our lawyer. I held back the letter because I thought I might have to edit it because I had written it in the middle of the night.

NK: Were you pleasantly surprised with the judgement, pronouncing your acquittal?

PR: (*Laughs*) Yes, of course. I didn't allow my feelings to appear on my face, because we were on video call. My co-accused was also there. Only one of us expressed happiness, Hem Keshav Dutt Mishra.

SR: From the moment he was brought on the video call, he was smiling. He was brought in front of the camera for the first time. Till then only Saibaba would be brought to attend the court proceedings. The minute he saw all the accused, he couldn't contain his happiness.

PR: Meanwhile, our other two co-accused, Mahesh Tikri used to come along with Saibaba, pushing his wheelchair and even Vijay would accompany them.

NK: Wait, you were telling me about being pleasantly surprised. So, did you respond and when?

PR: I respond to emotions rather late and that is why I was late in showing them or expressing myself.

SR: No, I distinctly remember baba being on a stretcher during the earlier Uttarakhand judgement and despite being on a stretcher he had put his arms out and had said 'yes'. Which is why I was very confused when I saw baba's blank face this time, when the judgement of acquittal was delivered. I was wondering what happened? What is he thinking? It didn't look like he hadn't got it. I was wondering why was he not happy or what was he worried about?

PR: I don't know why it happened or why I came across differently. This case has been entirely different. In fact, Uttarakhand was a more serious one for me as I was the main target and we had fought it with all our resources. We had won and I was happy.

SR: He had argued for his own matter and he had worked a lot on it.

PR: This case was entirely different kind and I had worked a lot on this case, after our advocate Surendra Gadling was arrested. I still haven't expressed my happiness over this case. Whether be it conviction and acquittal; everything in this case comes with a lot of responsibility. This case brings with it a certain phenomenon in the polity of this nation. Even now that we are out, it brings with it a lot of responsibility for us. It is my hunch that there were attempts to target the accused from some other case with this one. Never considered disconnecting from the world. I happened to be among the fortunate ones. Generally, the uncertainty of a case does affect the incarcerated badly enough to despair or suffer anxiety symptoms.

I kept resetting my assumptions about how much more time it would take. It varied from weeks and months to years and even a decade or more, depending on the possibilities of the outcome. The greater of the anxieties happened when my sentence suspension (post-conviction bail) applications—four in all—were to be filed. Filed or pending, all to no avail from early 2020 onwards till early 2022, and until the final hearing began, and also when the SC stayed the HC verdict which set aside our conviction. When the final hearings were on—anxieties ebbed.

My anxieties, big or small, tended to cause havoc with Shikha. In the 20 minutes of time we got to meet or talk each fortnight, my anxieties prevented me from being adequately sensitive towards her emotional and other issues. I used to try and reserve five or at least two minutes to address her personal issues, using up all the rest for communications to be made on my behalf for the case hearings.

Had I not had her visiting or available on video call, I might have suffered on account of my anxieties. Prisoners in general tend to go despondent when nothing seems to happen in their cases. When hearings are held, there generally is an element of satisfaction or normalcy.

Excerpts from the previous interview with Shikha

NK: We have seen how medical intervention is deliberately delayed by jail authorities in many cases—Father Stan Swamy, Vernon Gonsalves and Pandu Narote's case. Two of them—Father Stan and Pandu died. How tough is it to get basic rights like medical treatment, in jail?

SR: News of Pandu's death shook me terribly. You know, it is extremely easy to lose someone if they fall sick while in jail, and it is impossible to shake the bureaucracy into getting timely medical treatment. We don't seem to care when something happens to marginalised people. We don't care because it won't make a difference to society. Sadly, these days, stray animals get more attention than humans. It is much worse for the prisoners, as they are considered the scum of society. It was the same with Pandu. His family had not seen him since he was taken into custody—which was after his conviction in 2017. They live in the interiors of Gadchiroli and they don't even have the resources to travel to Nagpur, where he was jailed. They finally saw his body. As it is, we have heard stories of medical negligence in Father Stan's case. Pandu's news hit me harder. Pandu was given a life term based on the identity cards of his family members and the platform tickets that were found on him.

The judge had said there was no industrial development in Gadchiroli due to the Naxals' presence. His hands were tied, and he could give the maximum punishment of a life sentence. That is the reason Pandu spent years in prison and died of medical negligence.[42]

NK: It's been a 15-year struggle for you, from jails in Uttarakhand to jails in Maharashtra. Prisons are a stark reality for you. How has this journey affected you, and is there a difference between the jails?

SR: I have gone from age 24 to 40 fighting for my father's freedom. In this period, I have seen different jails, and I had never imagined I would be visiting courts, fighting legal battles, and visiting jails. There may be minor differences in the jails around the country, but the ordeal the prisoners and their families go through is the same. My memories of seeing relatives waiting to meet those jailed in Uttarakhand or Maharashtra are harrowing.

In most cases, the families are from the marginalised sections, and invariably, the sole breadwinner is jailed for some trivial offence. Also, seeing how these people suffer and the way they struggle with their legal battles, I do feel there seems to be little justice. Earlier, when this case started, I felt extremely burdened by the whole experience. I would feel helpless. It is still very painful to imagine a parent in solitary confinement, knowing this could be a life term for him. There are constant ups and downs with the legal battle. Even in the last year, when he fell ill, I hit rock bottom. There were times I couldn't breathe. It was so painful that I felt only the end of life could rid me of this pain. I now think less of my misery, and what keeps me motivated is an understanding of the systematic repression of all voices of dissent by the State. What gives me strength is knowing that it is not just me and my father; there are many more who are victims and probably in a worse situation than us. So, my hope is to at least get my father out.

NK: How have you evolved, Shikha?

SR: Honestly, I feel like the whole world around me has moved ahead, and I am stuck in time. We have been acquitted in the Uttarakhand and Maharashtra cases, but my father is still in jail. The struggle seems endless. My journey has been such that I have not been able to evolve in my personal life and take things forward at the pace I could have done had this matter not been weighing on me. I am compelled to be more resilient and patient. Right now, though, I haven't been able to travel because of the legal limitations. Yet, I admit, the case doesn't weigh more on me than the thought of my father having to spend his life in an 8x8-foot cell. I have to switch off and not think about this too much to be able to lead a somewhat normal life. In terms of evolving, I have become more resilient, patient, and tolerant. This problem is one of unending pain, and at some point, I have to pull myself together and not break down. I did undergo therapy, which has helped me cope with this crisis to a great extent. Beyond therapy, I had to figure things out for myself to maintain my sanity. There were times when I felt all was lost, only to realise later that the only way to go forward from that point was to rise.

NK: Do you miss the normal father-daughter relationship?

SR: In my childhood, my father was often absent due to his work. I did miss him a lot. At that time, I also wasn't aware of his ways of nurturing me. He emphasised more on knowledge rather than materialistic treats. Back then, other kids had more of these, and I definitely missed that sort of pampering. It is now that I appreciate his unconventional ways of raising me. It is these unique values inculcated by my parents which have enabled me to take on this humongous task singlehandedly. Looking back, I do feel I wasn't sensitive to my father needing more attention and care after his release from prison in 2011. I went back to catching up with my life as fast as I could. We didn't realise that after having spent four years in prison, he was lagging behind in worldly ways and would need some handholding to get back on his feet. I believe that keeping a man like him behind bars is a grave injustice. He has genuinely worked hard to improve the lives of others while never prioritising his own needs. It is difficult to watch him suffer. I cry and get upset every time I see him, but I know I have to get over my feelings and just keep fighting. The most important thing is to fight on and prevail in this battle. When they see me struggling, my friends and family tell me, 'Shikha, you have stretched yourself more than you could have done,' or they will ask why I'm doing all of this and why the lawyers aren't taking care of it. It doesn't matter when someone you care about is incarcerated. It is not about me; you cannot simply watch the person you love go to jail. If the person is dead, you won't even be informed and you won't know what to do. According to some family members, 'Your father hasn't done as much for you as you have for him.' This is not a barter system. It has to do with the fundamental human values that my parents have taught me.

NK: Have your friends or business associates cut you off since they found out about your father's case and your legal battle?

SR: Till a few months ago, my perspective was different, because only one in a hundred may have distanced from me. Apart from that, my friends, co-workers, and other professionals have always shown empathy and a willingness to assist me in any way that they can. 'You know, I want your father to come out as soon as possible,' a friend of mine once said to me, 'You must write him a note congratulating him on his wonderful work. These days, nobody goes that extra mile for someone else. Tell him how wonderful he is and how appreciative you are to have him for a father.' They are usually shocked at how I have been getting by without giving up. I identify myself to everyone I know; I also speak of my father, the work he has done, and the fact that he is incarcerated.

NK: Do you feel weak and want to give up at any time?

SR: Yes, of course. But I can't fall apart and be weak because there is still a lot of work to be done. I speak openly nowadays and I feel proud talking about my Baba. He is the medal I now show off! I don't think I will have anything to show off once he comes out. Like my childhood friend tells me, my life would have been a boring one had it not been for this drama. She tells me, I now have a great purpose in life, which keeps me going.

NK; When was the last time you hugged your father?

SR: I had not done so since he was convicted in 2017, because the prison meetings are conducted through a glass partition and we can converse only over the phone. It was only because of his illness, when he was finally brought to a hospital that I could quickly steal a hug before the police instructed me to keep a distance. We were both happy to get this personal touch even though I could get a small hug of two seconds. It made me feel relieved he is still there.

NK: How did the uncertainty of your father's case affect you. Because even after his bail and acquittal he was re-arrested. How did it all impact you psychologically?

SR: The long, unending and uncertain nature of this case always kept me anxious. It made me unstable and volatile in situations of distress. The constant worry exhausted me. I was not left with any time or energy to pay attention to my life. I kept working mechanically in a creative field.

As a freelancer in films, I avoided films with long shooting schedules for the fear of having to leave midway in case of a sudden legal development. Whenever I was tempted and took up big films, I ended up leaving them midway as something or the other happened which needed me to personally go to another city and meet the lawyers. I had to be there physically at the court for things to move ahead.

I could never commit to any plans much in advance with friends or family for a holiday or any other event because kya pata kab kya ho jaaye (Who knows what will happen).

Since the final hearing was over, I did not take up any job as I was expecting the judgement any time and I knew if my father comes out of the prison after so many years, I'm going to have to be around to help rehabilitate him. What I thought would be a wait of 2–3 months ended up becoming 10 months. That's how long the bench took to come out with the judgement. Thanks to my grandmother I don't have to pay rent or I could not have sustained in a city like Mumbai just with my savings.

I had begun therapy (counselling) in 2018–19 and that helped me in dealing with extremely stressful situations to some extent. Though it is my opinion that psychotherapy is something everyone should undergo to understand themselves and others better.

5

'Irony dies a hundred deaths'

Sanjay Raut

Sanjay Raut had visited the Arthur Road Jail in Mumbai and several other prisons in India as a member of the Committee on Home Affairs (2004-2010), in his first tenure as a member of Parliament. Little did he know that he would come back a few years later as an undertrial.

Sanjay Raut is the executive editor of Saamana, a leading Marathi newspaper that has actually set the agenda for television news channels since the 1990s. He is also a politician and has been a member of Parliament in the Rajya Sabha for over 22 years. When it comes to giving out news, he has never let us journalists down. Every time he gives an interview, he will make some pointed comments that could lead to some new political controversy. Speaking of op-eds, I remember a time when the late S. P. Singh, who was my boss, editor, and founder of Aaj Tak, asked me which newspapers I read on a daily basis. When I gave him the list, he asked whether I read Saamana. I remember telling him, not daily. At that time, he had advised that I read Saamana every day for its '10 percent news', which one would not find anywhere else, and especially the editorials. Since then (in the 1990s), it has become a mandatory read for me.

As the Shiv Sena joined the Maha Vikas Aghadi in 2021, the post-poll tripartite alliance with the Nationalist Congress Party and Indian Congress, Raut became the go-to person for most news channels. We saw a new persona emerge at this time who began tweeting pointed remarks, reciting lines from Urdu poetry on social media. The Bharatiya Janata Party was at the receiving end of his pointed criticism after Eknath Shinde toppled the MVA government and formed a new one on June 30, 2022.[43]

The build-up to Raut's arrest was expected, as the government's message of silencing was clear by then. There were reports that the investigative agencies were linking Raut and his wife to the Patra Chawl redevelopment project.[44] *Soon enough, the Enforcement Directorate accused Raut of being directly involved in the project, which they claimed necessitated his arrest.*[45] *Along with this, Raut was accused of money laundering. The political environment was simmering against the Uddhav Thackeray faction at this time. Yet in these times, Raut is 'Fearless like a tiger', as he says is the symbol of his mentor, Balasaheb Thackeray, the founder of Shiv Sena. Raut says prison hasn't broken his spirit. He knows he is being targeted because he is a political opponent.*

Eventually, on February 19, 2023, the single-judge bench of Justice Nitin R. Borkar termed Raut's arrest as 'illegal and witch-hunting by ED'. On the very first day Raut was out on bail, he promised he would give me an interview. After this, it was a marathon chase trying to track him down and get some time from him. On the day of the Karnataka election results in May 2023, Raut agreed to this interview. That afternoon, I entered the revamped Saamana office at Lower Parel. Raut's cabin still has the decadent charm of old-world wooden furniture and the fragrance of an incense stick. His tall chair has Balasaheb's photo frame above his head and a television screen on the opposite wall (on mute). After initial queries about the purpose of the interview, Raut asked how much time I would require. When I asked for an hour, he willingly kept his cellphone silent and asked me to 'shoot'. Even as we began speaking, there was excitement in the air as news of the Karnataka poll results started coming in.

Neeta Kolhatkar: There was a build-up to your arrest. Do you think the agencies were targeting you when they arrested you? Were you mentally prepared for it?

Sanjay Raut: Many political developments were taking place in Maharashtra at that time. First, the Bharatiya Janata Party leaders were angry with me because they felt I was the person from Shiv Sena who had pushed the party to join the Maha Vikas Aghadi (MVA) government (the tri-party alliance between the Congress, Nationalist Congress Party and Shiv Sena). In June 2022, when our MVA alliance was broken, Eknath Shinde and the other representatives had gone to meet the BJP central leadership. BJP leaders from Maharashtra and Delhi had informed their central leadership that I was the leader at the forefront and had helped form the MVA alliance. I was seen as the main person driving a coalition against their party. It is evident how these agencies function, as we have seen with the way Sameer Wankhede conducted investigations against many people. We stand vindicated now. The government has misused these central agencies. Not one word I had spoken against the Enforcement Directorate, and those I have uttered in my conferences at Sena Bhavan, were mere accusations. They have all come true. They are extorting money from people and threatening the innocent. The ED has only taken revenge against me because I have been exposing their dealings. I would like to reiterate that I never pleaded with any person to give me any protection or urged them to prevent my arrest. It was evident I would face consequences, and I was prepared for every eventuality. I did everything to save my party, and I cannot allow my party to fall apart.[46]

NK: Suddenly they have dug out the Patra Chawl case. What is it (the case) and why are you being dragged in that case?

SR: I had taken a loan of Rs 50 lakh from my brother to purchase a small house for my daughters. My daughters were studying at Podar College. Both had to wake up every morning at 5am to reach Dadar to attend their college. We decided we could either rent a house or purchase one. Even after selling our house in Mulund, we fell short of some money. My brother offered me a loan and asked me to purchase a house for them (with it). In fact, after a few years, I even returned this amount to my brother. Moreover, every time I file my nomination form for the Rajya Sabha seat, I have to file an affidavit and declare my assets and financial information. I had even filed taxes for this. The government then tried to drag (in) my brother's name because he was working at HDIL, then (they) dragged my name into the working at HDIL, then dragged my name into the Patra Chawl redevelopment issue. I had not heard of this chawl in my life, and I don't even know where it is located. The residents of that chawl have never met me. Yet the government dragged my name into this case and filed false papers against me. They conspired to put me behind bars.

NK: Do you recall the events on the day you were arrested?

SR: Of course, I remember them distinctly. My brother had called to tell me something was cooking against me and I should be alert. I told him to let them do anything, I'm not afraid, I told him. Now, our party had collected a hefty amount (donations) for the Ayodhya yatra; Shiv Sena had booked two trains to show strength. I had kept the accounts sheet with the cash in the house, which my brother thought would create a problem. This was to be handed over to the party office, and I am chokh (meticulous) with every paisa. It is our party's money, which I refused to send away, as he had suggested. Later, the ED officials leaked the news that they had found Rs 10 lakh (in my home), which was the donation amount.[47] They are predictable when they want to make false allegations. They came early in the morning, though they eventually showed that I was arrested at midnight.[48] These are ways to harass people. I know they feel they are extremely powerful because they are using the Prevention of Money Laundering Act, 2002 (PMLA) like a weapon. According to this draconian law, you are not innocent[49]—though it is imperative according to the constitution to get bail; and it is tough to get bail.[50] On the day I was arrested, around 7am, Sunil (my brother) knocked on my door. (We live in a joint family.) He informed me that the ED team had come home. Now, these ED officers behave as if it were their father's property. They don't even conduct themselves well in front of women. I insisted they leave the family members alone. At that time, I told them to wait as I had to go about my activities and bathe. I woke up the family. Then they demanded to search the house, and I told them to go ahead if they had a search warrant. They showed me some paper and went about ransacking the premises. Then I insisted they take me away with them at that very moment. They refused and said they didn't have an arrest warrant at that time. I told them I was aware they would be given the order at 4pm. By then, they had taken over our entire house; they went to our terrace, and sent one man into our water tank to check if we had stashed money in there. They even looked under the staircase. *(I asked, wasn't all this rather 'filmi'. Raut said, of course, what else could one expect?)* They barged into my mother's prayer room, searched the drawers, and ransacked the tins where we store flour and foodgrain. They behaved as though I were a criminal or a dacoit. They showed no respect for my having been an MP for 22 years and for my brother having been a legislator for two years from this constituency, and most of all, I am an editor of a leading newspaper. We have some status in society. They were so unkind, behaving as though they were ambassadors of God and we were Satan's. This is solely due to the sections in some laws, like the Prevention of Money Laundering Act, 2002 (PMLA). In fact, the death penalty is better because it completely disregards the prestige a person has earned over many years. Prior to raiding my house and arresting me, these ED officers went to the homes of various professional contractors my daughter had hired for her wedding, like decorators, florists, mehendi (henna) designers, etc. They asked them how much we had paid them. This is not the way investigative agencies function in a democracy. I asked them to take me away immediately, but they arrested me at 5pm and took me to their Ballard Pier office. By then, thousands had congregated outside my house and I began getting calls on my phone. The ED officers got upset and instructed me not to answer any calls. I dismissed their authoritarian attitude. I told them I was still inside my house: 'ani shahanpana karayacha nahi (There was no need to throw your weight around)'. When I asked why they had not shown me the arrest warrant, they became defensive and said they were searching my house. I said, go ahead; who has stopped you? By then, my supporters had gathered and they tried to prevent it, but I happily went with the ED officers.

NK: Was this a huge culture shock for the investigating officers to see you not crack under pressure?

SR: I made one thing clear to them. I am different from the others—the legislators and MPs who had joined Eknath Shinde's faction. I told them I wasn't scared. These officers kept telling me to speak at a 'higher level'. I asked them to name the 'higher level' person and made it clear that I would not ask anyone to help me escape jail. If they have found any evidence against me, then they should record it and arrest me immediately. I am prepared to go to jail, but I will not ask anybody for mercy. I reminded them that they hadn't shown us my arrest warrant and had detained me for quite a few hours. They had detained me seven hours prior to my actual arrest. In fact, at their Ballard Pier office, I told them I was particular about my daily schedule and that I needed to go to sleep by 10.30pm, but they kept me waiting till midnight. They just want to harass you to see if you'll break.

NK: Why did they take you early in the evening if they recorded your arrest at midnight? What did they do for so many hours?

SR: They detain you many hours in advance before actually arresting you. They have their usual tactics of taking you through the usual rounds of questioning and tiring you by repeatedly asking the same questions. Prior to this arrest, both my wife and I had gone to give our replies when they had issued summonses. They didn't even spare my family. They told me I had to stay awake till midnight as a senior officer from Delhi was supposed to sign my arrest warrant.

NK: How are the conditions in the ED office? Is there a lock-up? How were you treated? What about the investigation during your arrest?

SR: They have no lock-up facilities at the ED (office). We were kept in the conference room. We were made to sit there and sleep on the table at night. The place has nothing and is the epitome of an inhuman, 'nirghrun (merciless)' agency that breaches every human right of a citizen. I told the court I was a heart patient with seven stents, and the room I was kept in had no light or ventilation. While questioning me, they showed me some stupid paper, and I told them outright that this had been brought from elsewhere; it was not from my house, and I would just throw it in the dustbin. They would wave silly papers in my face as though these had been found either in my house or office. They didn't stop here. One day they took my younger daughter with them, brought her to our Dadar house, and made her open it. There wasn't even a lady police officer who accompanied her. They asked her to sit while they searched the premises. Afterwards, the court slammed them, and the judge clearly said it was an illegal arrest.[51]

NK: Which prison were you shifted to after your ED custody? Do you remember your first night in jail? How bad was it?

SR: After my ED custody tenure was completed, they shifted me to a jail because they didn't ask the court to extend my custody after the stipulated eight days. I was then sent to Arthur Road Jail. Remember, once you enter a jail, every right of yours as a citizen is breached. Listen, I was a member of this country's Prison Development Committee as a Member of Parliament (Rajya Sabha). I visited prisons across India to see how we could reform them and make changes. As a member of the delegation of five, I had even visited Arthur Road Jail. At that time, I was welcomed with a lot of respect, and the irony of it all is that I went back there as a prisoner. One thing I must say is that the staff treated me with a lot of respect and warmth.

NK: Have the suggestions of this committee for prison development and reforms been implemented by any state? What about Maharashtra?

SR: Other states have implemented the reforms we suggested but not Maharashtra. Our state hasn't accepted them. We will have to work towards that.

NK: Despite your being mentally prepared, how bad was it to actually go through the grind in a jail?

SR: Once you know you are going to be arrested, you have to prepare yourself mentally and emotionally. This is also what I told the fellow inmates to follow: many accomplished professionals who have forcibly been imprisoned for a few years now. I wasn't allowed to meet people often, but whenever I did, I would boost their spirits and tell them: this is a battle, and we have to fight. I was put in the anda cell, where we can only smell our body odour. The only way we would see something different, apart from the cells, would be from behind the bars, when we saw someone patrolling. Also, we would know when it would rain outside because it would begin pouring down from the ceiling, and we had to keep swabbing the floor. There were also rats scurrying about. Worst of all, we were forced to sleep under bright lights all the time. Those bright lights are never turned off. The only small consolation I had was eating home-cooked food due to my medical condition. However, by the time the food was brought to your cell, it was in such a sorry state that you would be put off to eat it. The food package would have been opened and checked by numerous staff members at various points. They would have rummaged through every box and pressed every morsel to see if a blade, pair of scissors, or something pointed had been smuggled in it. There are other security drills that you have to endure. We are not terrorists, goondas, dacoits, or anti-nationals; we are political prisoners who have been framed under false charges by this government and sent to jail to serve their vested political interests. Some may have buckled under pressure and joined their party (the BJP) out of desperation, like some of our party legislators did. I am not like them. The ED has named some of them in different cases, and warrants were served to them.[52] In fact, they were on the verge of arrest. Most of all, Eknath Shinde is a victim of the ED. The only difference between them and us is that they are scared, while we are not. Some of us have faced the agencies fearlessly.

NK: Were you allowed mulaqats? Were your wife or your daughters allowed to meet you?

SR: We were allowed to have these mulaqats once a week. They too were allowed in such a way: there is a glass partition between us, and we are only allowed to speak over the phone, and that too for 10 minutes. It is a long-drawn process until your number is called out. My wife never came to the prison. My brother would come to meet me. Once, my daughter came to see me, and I told her not to come ever again since prison is not a good place for women to visit. They would all come to the court to meet me. We would be given some time to meet and speak.

NK: Did you think you would be released earlier, as compared to other prisoners?

SR: Every hour spent in prison is equivalent to 100 days. Since I had mentally prepared for the worst, it didn't matter whether I spent one night or 500 nights. Now that I was in jail, I was destined to live here with no guarantee of when they would let me out. I had reconciled to not being released for at least two years. Some ministers, like Anil Deshmukh from our MVA alliance, got bail only after 16 months, while Nawab Malik is still inside *(at the time of the interview)*. Eknath Khadse's son-in-law has been serving a sentence for more than two years. Girish Chaudhari was finally released after two years, in July 2023.[53] In view of these cases, I was convinced I too would be in jail for a while. It is important to note that there is no evidence in all these cases, and the jail terms they are serving are not commensurate with the charges filed against them. The same is the case with Satyendra Jain and Manish Sisodia in Delhi. Just because all of us are political opponents and are seen as troublemakers by the government, the authorities have been instructed to arrest us under draconian laws like PMLA and UAPA. Look at Anand Teltumbde's case and see the observations made by the Supreme Court against the NIA. The Bombay High Court cited in the bail order that there was no prima facie evidence to prove the offence of terrorist activity levied against Teltumbde. In fact, during the hearing, the SC bench asked Additional Solicitor General (ASG) Aishwarya Bhat, who was appearing for the NIA, 'What is the specific role of bringing UAP(A) sections into action? The IIT Madras event you alleged is for Dalit mobilisation. Is Dalit mobilisation a preparatory act to proscribed activity?'[54] We have seen in other matters too how the court has rejected the NIA's objection, like in Sudha Bharadwaj's case. In the case of the poet from Hyderabad, Varavara Rao, why was he arrested? They killed Stan Swamy when he was in prison. What evidence did they have against him? Who is accountable for these breaches?

NK: Can you recall the day you were released?

SR: Of course, I distinctly remember it. We were taken to the court as we were expecting the bail order. I sat in the front row, and behind me were my wife, our daughters, and my son-in-law. Everyone was tense about the outcome. I didn't want to think too much, but I was hopeful after seeing the way my lawyer had confidently argued and presented all the facts. On the other hand, the ED's lawyers made some false claims. I felt the court would see through their false claims and realise we had concrete proof. The judge began dictating the order, and it went on for over an hour. Then he suddenly said, 'You both are granted bail.' I actually couldn't hear the judge. I asked what the judge said, and my brother reassured me that I had been granted relief. All of a sudden, people cheered and clapped loudly in the lobby and inside the court. Thousands of supporters thronged the lobby. 'Talyancha prachanda kadkadat (Thunderous applause was heard.)'. Ravish Kumar aired it that night on his programme, and mentioned how this had occurred for the first time in a court and called it historic.[55] Of course, the ED objected to the bail and urged the judge to stay his order. He refused and said he would resume court at 3pm after considering the objections placed by the ED. After the court resumed, the judge rejected the ED's objections and said he would not stay his own order. The judge allowed the ED to appeal in the Bombay High Court, and the speed with which they rushed to do it made it evident that they wanted to do everything to keep me in jail for that one night. My family, especially my wife and daughters, cried with joy, and my brother too wept. They were not sure I would get bail that day. Meanwhile, I was sent to jail even as the ED approached the HC in a hurry. When I was back in my barracks, I saw the television and breaking news flashes. Around 5pm, on a channel, the ticker flashed how the judge had termed my arrest 'illegal'. I saw the news, and it said the order was 122 pages long. The ED objected, of course, and the judge questioned the ED, asking why I should not get bail. Their lawyer also wanted to delay the arguments just to keep me back for one night. All of their demands were rejected. My lawyers and team acted swiftly; they took the bail order and reached Arthur Road Jail within an hour. They were forced to release me by 7pm. Thousands of party workers had gathered outside the jail, and there were celebrations. They burst crackers and set off in a procession for me. Their love was evident.

NK: How did your mother and the women in your family deal with your arrest?

SR: My mother is an extremely strong woman, and she told me right at the beginning, 'Sharan nahi jaayecha, turungat jayacha. Amhala baher tond dakhvayacha aahe' (Don't fall on your knees. Go to jail. We want to face the world with pride). Those were her words when the ED came to arrest me (*smiles*). My wife too had shared the same strong sentiment, and my daughters told me, 'Baba, amhala taath manena jagayacha ahe, amhi sagla traas sahan karu' (Baba, we want to live with our heads held high, for which we will bear any amount of pain).

NK: Did any of your extended family members or friends distance themselves from you all after you were jailed? Did your daughters face any consequences?

SR: Of course, some people distanced themselves from us. One of my daughters is an entrepreneur, and she has a small fashion design business with a small shop. Their business runs on credit to vendors, ₹10,000–15,000, and all are cheque transactions. Now, her business has been impacted. The vendors and clients fear the ED will chase and interrogate them. Obviously, nobody wants any agency at their doorstep. We middle-class people are scared of such things. Now my daughters must piece their lives together again and start from scratch. My wife is a teacher, and I cannot imagine the barbs she may have had to face. Though the school authorities were supportive, it wasn't easy for her.

NK: Being out on bail is one thing, but surely you must be constantly under the radar of the ED and other authorities. What is your support system?

SR: Yes, of course they are looking for something against me, as the government has said I should be put back in jail. I have lived in the shadow of Balasaheb Thackeray. We have been living with his ideals, and we don't fear anybody. My party leader, Uddhav Thackeray, is a huge support for me, my family, and even Sharad Pawar. Leaders from parties other than ours are with me. Even my friends from the BJP have extended their support to me. We are not 'lafangas' (good for nothing). Some BJP leaders who live by Atal Bihari Vajpayee's ideals of the old-school ideology and respect their opponents support me even today. All are not blind bhakts. They don't like the ruthless politics that is being unleashed against their opponents.

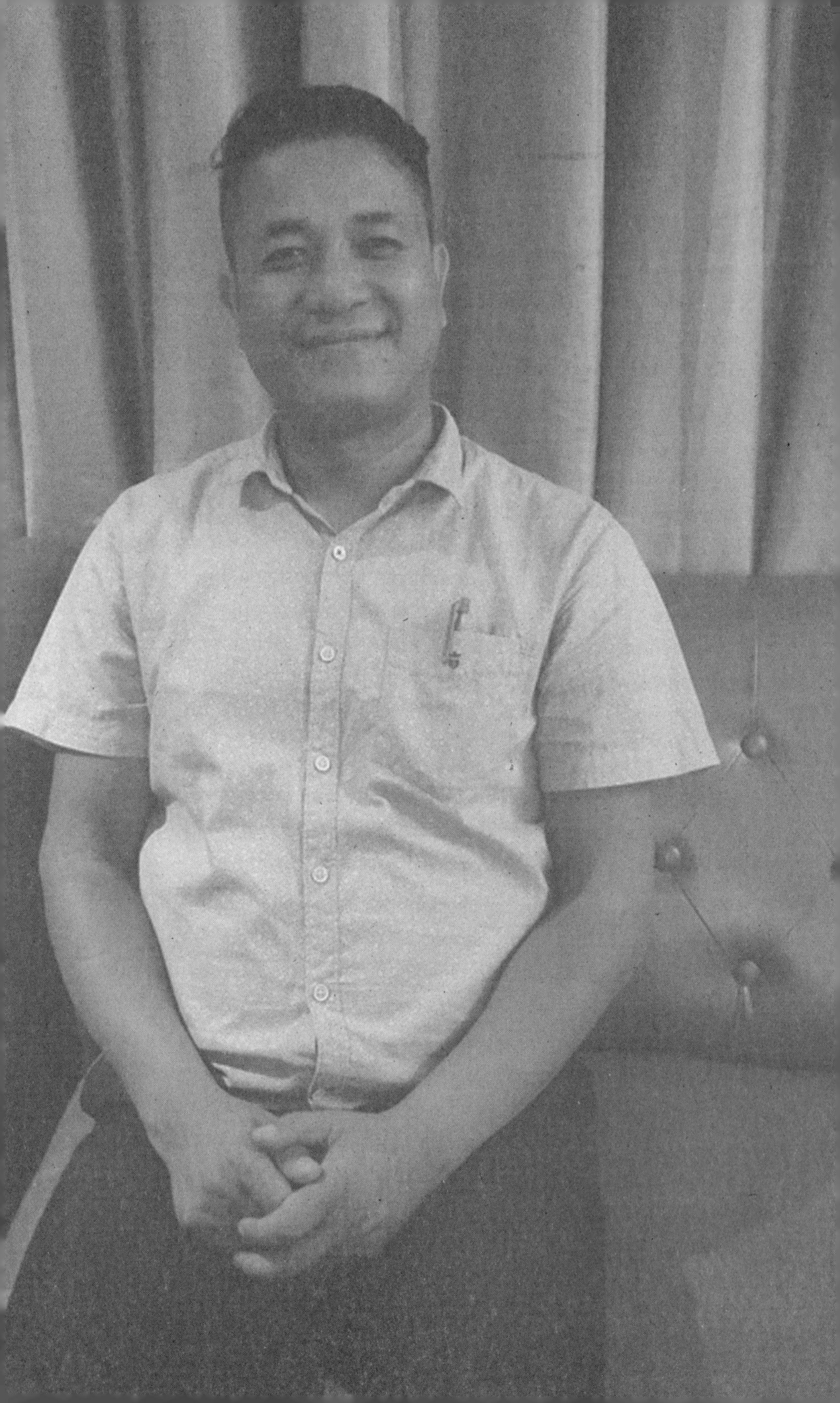

6

'They write, and wrath is wrought upon them.'

Kishorechandra Wangkhem

Manipur has been in the news since May 3, 2023, when violence broke out in the north-eastern state between two ethnic groups, the Kukis and Meiteis[56] *resulting in death, the destruction of public property, rapes, killings, and loss of homes. Tens of thousands of people have been displaced. Despite this, mainstream media and top leaders have refrained from discussing the violence and its causes. While the Bharatiya Janata Party leaders, especially the Prime Minister and the Union Minister for Home Affairs have stayed away from visiting the north east, Congress leader Rahul Gandhi launched his Bharat Jodo Nyay Yatra (Unity March for Justice) from Manipur's Thoubal region. He walked from Manipur to Mumbai and referred to Manipur as an example of 'politics of hatred by the BJP'.*[57] *The fact is that there has been a build-up to this violence for numerous years and journalists from the northeast have tried to highlight the relevant issues time and again, only to face the wrath of the government.*

Interestingly, May 3 is also World Press Freedom Day, and in 2023, India's rank in terms of this parameter slipped down to 161. Journalists in the northeast have indeed faced the worst as the BJP-ruled states in the region have become intolerant of them for speaking the whole truth.

In March 2022, when I attended a workshop on human rights in New Delhi, I met wonderful journalists from Assam, Manipur, Mizoram, Nagaland, and Manipur. They shared their experiences of how it felt to be on the receiving end of authoritarianism and urged me to speak with Kishorechandra Wangkhem, a journalist who had previously worked for a local cable channel in Manipur and was now a freelancer. Kishorechandra was arrested repeatedly in 2018 and 2021, once, under the draconian National Security Act, and twice for sedition because of his social media posts. His fight for justice has been lonely, since there is no media body supporting the revivalist movement of the indigenous people in the northeast. He says this is particularly alarming because the CM, Nongthombam Biren Singh, used to be a journalist before he became a politician. One important point that Kishorechandra raised is how working journalists gang up against journalists who are not mainstream but independent agents. They are the first to distance themselves from an independent journalist when they are uncomfortable with the work or statements of the latter. This is fine but they don't stop there, they go on to make statements against the independent journalist and worse, write to media associations asking for the derecognition of such independent journalists, like Kishorechandra. This trend of allegiance to the authorities or a government is disturbing, to say the least, and it lands independent journalists in the plight Kishorechandra finds himself in currently.

Sitting in the hotel lobby where the workshop was held in New Delhi, Kishorechandra and I talked at length. He is unassuming, funny, and a man of steely resolve. He narrated his jail experience to me and also spoke of the manner in which the state machinery is rampantly being used to muzzle the voices of those who don't support the popular narrative. As we spoke, I learnt that a vital part of his story is also about the immense troubles his wife Elangbam Ranjita has undergone to support and get Kishorechandra out of jail.

Neeta Kolhatkar: You have been arrested a few times under draconian laws like Sedition and the National Security Act (NSA). Could you go back to the time in August 2018, when you were first arrested? Was this

the case when you had uploaded a video regarding your views on observing a valour day for Rani of Jhansi?

Kishorechandra Wangkhem: The point is that we have no negative feelings about her, but you need to understand that her reference has no place in our culture. I respect her valour and her involvement in the 1857 movement, but with due respect, Manipur was not even a part of India in 1857. Manipur was a princely state. There is nothing wrong with observing something in one's personal life, but this sort of official observance will impact our younger generation negatively. My point is that the Rani of Jhansi has more significance in Madhya Pradesh, Uttar Pradesh, and some other states of mainstream India. It is pointless trying to force it on us because it has no significance in our local history or tradition. I uploaded the video with these same comments on November 19, 2018. On November 20, I was picked up from the residence of my legal counsel. In fact, I had gone to meet him to discuss the legal options I had since there was already an arrest warrant issued against me. We were planning to surrender before the magistrate, but somehow the police got a whiff of our plans, and they landed there to arrest me. I was remanded in police custody for six days. Later, I was produced before the chief judicial magistrate, the same one who had previously dealt with my case. This time, he somehow managed to give me bail and did not send me to jail. His observation was that the opinions expressed in the video were of an individual against a public leader and in street language because I had used the 'F' word. I returned home on November 26, as I was granted bail, but I don't know what transpired between the officials of our state government and the CM. The very next day, police were back at my doorstep, around 12.30pm, just as I was preparing to have lunch. Some policemen in plain clothes came and led me to a car, in which I was driven to the police station. I was made to sit in the office of the additional SP for nearly six hours without any officer speaking with me. My family waited outside for me, as they wanted to know what the authorities were planning to do with me. The police made it seem as though they were chatting with me, but I was forced to sit alone. Around 6.30pm, a police officer came with a sheet of paper and asked me to sign it. I refused, so he just went away with the paper, and then around 7pm, I was asked to go and sit in the backseat of a gypsy parked in the compound. Obviously, I had no clue where they were taking me. I wasn't blindfolded but I could not see anything outside, since it was dark. Once we reached the spot, I saw the central prison complex of Manipur, and I immediately knew I was going to be jailed. They had completed all the formalities in the SP's office. Now here is how they thought they would surprise me. Just as I stepped out, they handed me a paper that showed I was being booked for a breach of the National Security Act (NSA). Till then, I had no clue about their plans. (*Laughs*). At that time, the deputy superintendent informed me that, under these charges, I would be in jail for one year without being allowed any sanction to apply for bail. That is when I was first shocked, and I just allowed this news to sink in. After that, I spent precisely 140 days in jail.

NK: Did you receive any support from the media fraternity or other sections of society at this time?

KW: Yes, the media fraternity supported me at that time, and they lodged a protest. Many journalists came out on the third day of protests, and I was granted bail on medical grounds. That was also done in a hurried manner because the CM had directly intervened, and I was eventually released around August 10. Later, a few journalists did tell me that this was the first time they had supported me, but if I kept up with such rants, I could not count on similar support in the future because they were under pressure. I got what they were saying because they had to face their editors and management, and the government could target them too.

NK: The second case against you is very important. Again, you uploaded a video on social media, showing how the ethnic Manipuri community was being forced to fall in line with majoritarian religious views. Can you tell us about this case? Did you anticipate the severe charges, like sedition?

KW: The second case was in November 2018, when the state government forced us to observe the birthday of Rani Lakshmi Bai of Jhansi. This programme was organised by the ruling party (the Bharatiya Janata Party), and our CM inaugurated it. I was editing this news, and I wasn't happy seeing the live videos; they upset me. I posted a video on my social media account because I wanted mainstream India to understand that in Manipur and the surrounding north-eastern states, we had our own indigenous language, culture, traditions, and beliefs, all of which were assimilated into mainstream Hinduism over a period of time. In the last few years, there has been a momentum to revive our indigenous culture and traditions. Many people in Manipur took to social media platforms to oppose this move to celebrate Martyrs' Day in their state.[58]

NK: This must have been tough on you and your wife. How was this news taken by our fraternity? Is there any organisation that you or any arrested journalist can turn to in the northeast?

KW: As I said earlier, after the first case itself, my colleagues and other journalists had told me if I continued speaking up, they would not be around for me. Forget whether they supported me or not; that is insignificant. What irked me was their attitude towards my being a journalist. They simply refused to accept me as one. Shockingly, they seemed to have written to the Indian Journalists' Union that I should no longer be considered a journalist. They cut me off from the profession that I love. I was all alone in jail for 140 days. However, the high court quashed the NSA order of the government on April 8, 2019, and I was out on April 10. It was tough on my wife; she has gone through a lot, but she didn't give up.

NK: You still had one more sedition case against you, right? You hadn't learned a lesson, eh? (*Both of us burst out laughing.*) How many more cases are lodged against you?

KW: So, before I was sent to jail, I was charged with sedition, and they have still not withdrawn it, which means I have to go to court every time my case comes up. The third case was filed in 2020, in which I was accused of criticising the first wife of the CM. I mentioned the racial slur made by the second wife, who is from the majority community, against the first, who belongs to an ethnic minority group. In fact, at that time, bypolls were to be held in Manipur, but eventually, they were not held. I had posed the question: if such racial slurs were being used against the wife of a public leader, then how was she going to woo the voters from her husband's constituency? There are lots of tribal voters in the CM's constituency. This was all that I asked in my post on social media. In fact, I had spoken in favour of the first wife. Some members of a tribal union objected to the word, which was actually used by the CM's second wife, but the authorities wrongly attributed it to me. I had written it in Manipuri, and those people were not familiar with this language. They went and filed a complaint, and the authorities were just waiting to pick me up because they had been minutely tracking every word I spoke or wrote, anywhere.

The police came home, but I was not there for some reason, and they summoned me to the police station the next day. We had applied for 15 days' anticipatory bail, but on the last day, they did not extend it, and I was arrested. Again, they had charged me under Sedition and Section 504 of the Indian Penal Code.[59] I was in police custody for five days and then sent to jail, where I spent two months thereafter.

NK: Did members of this tribal union eventually realise they had made an erroneous interpretation, and have they withdrawn their case against you?

KW: Yes, as a matter of fact, they did when the matter came up for hearing. They realised they had erred, but they were unable to do anything. In fact, before I was arrested, I read out my post to them and explained to them what I had written and what the CM's second wife had specifically said. I told them those were her words, and I hadn't made any untoward comments; I had just quoted her verbatim. These people had even gone to the CM's first wife to seek her suggestion, and she had also explained to them that I hadn't written against her and that I was actually pulling up the second wife, who had spoken against her. What they told her was that since they had already filed a case against me, they could do nothing about it. They refused to accept their mistake and instead placed a condition on me. They said if I would publicly apologise in a newspaper, then they would withdraw the charges against me. I made it absolutely clear to them that I had not said or done anything illegal that needed an apology. In fact, I had supported a woman from their tribe. This is the only case against me in which the police have not framed a charge sheet, and the trial is going on. It will be over soon. Interestingly, in another case too, there was a sedition charge slapped on me (*laughs*). In fact, it was absolutely unnecessary. The court dropped the sedition charge against me, but by then, I had already spent two months in jail.

NK: Phew! What is this sedition-sedition the authorities are playing with you? Now, a fourth case has been filed against you. Unfortunately, the Indian mainstream media and people in mainland India don't seem to be aware of your fight for justice. What are your views?

KW: Yes, this is the fourth case against me. The BJP state president had been advocating cow dung and cow urine as cures for COVID-19 and other health problems on various television shows. Every time we had discussions on the Coronavirus, he would speak of these cures for the virus. He said Indian cow dung had been exported to the US, and they had found evidence of its benefits in treating Coronavirus. Every time, he got away with making such false claims. Eventually, he succumbed to COVID, and at that time, I wrote, 'Oh, you were unable to help yourself with the same cow dung and cow urine you had advocated? It's really sick.' My last sentence was: 'I will have fish tonight.' This may have upset the state BJP (*smiles*), as they seemed to have taken this as an insult. (*Laughs, as we nod in resignation.)* The police picked up my activist friend Erendro Leichombam (who had also written the same post) and me on May 13, 2021, and we were placed in police custody for five days. This time, there was no sedition. (*Oh no, what a loss! I remarked, and both of us laughed.)* The judicial magistrate granted us bail, but they did not let us go home, as they were running from one office to another to get a court order to put us under NSA. Around 7.30pm, we were finally detained under the NSA and spent two-and-a-half months in Saajwa Jail. (*Oh boy! Manipur jails must have missed you, I said. He simply laughed*).

NK: Did they finally drop the NSA charge against you both? How tough was it for you to fight back?

KW: Luckily for me, my activist friend Erendro, who was arrested with me, moved the Supreme Court. The apex court issued a really fantastic order, and my wife, Ranjita Elengbam, wrote a letter to Chief Justice Sanjay Kumar of Manipur High Court. The Supreme Court had asked the Manipur government to release my friend immediately.[60] Ranjita stated this order in her letter and appealed that since I too had been arrested with Erendro, I should also be released immediately, as stated by the SC. In fact, the order stated that he would be released by 5pm that same day. Earlier, too, my wife had written to the state home department, requesting my release based on the SC order. Somehow, they didn't respond to my wife's request, so she moved the Manipur High Court to seek my immediate release. The HC gave us a hearing within a day, and CJ Kumar listed the matter for an urgent hearing on July 23.[61] The two-judge bench led by the Chief Justice stated:

> On the face of it, we find no distinction or difference between the case of the petitioner's husband and that of Erendro Leichombam. Both of them put up similar Facebook posts, critical of the utility of cow dung and cow urine in treating coronavirus. As they stand identically situated, we are of the opinion that the continued incarceration of the petitioner's husband would be as much a violation of Article 21 of the Constitution, as it was in the case of Erendro Leichombam.

That is how I was granted bail. As for the NSA charges, at the time of the interim bail hearing, the government had written an application to the court stating they didn't want to press those charges any further and withdrew them unilaterally.

NK: How have all these prison stints changed you as a person? What did they teach you?

KW: I am a stronger person now. I have become more resilient and definitely more confident than I was prior to my arrest the first time. Initially, I did think maybe it was silly on my part to post a comment; we tend to introspect and blame ourselves. There is a lot of time on hand in jail to introspect and question oneself. (*Laughs*). However, after the harassment I was put through in jail and the impediments that were deliberately put in place to prevent me from getting bail—from the executive officers, police officers, and jail authorities—I realised it was not my fault and I should not give up. It made me want to fight on. I also realised that, because I am a journalist, stories about my case and all the details somehow got published. But as I saw those around me in jail, I thought, what about the common people who are languishing in jail? They go through the same ordeal and trauma, and in some cases, much worse. They are not as lucky as me. My stories have at least been published and read by people outside India, and eventually I got justice. The general public, who have no influence or contacts whatsoever in our systems, is completely ignored. Worst of all, they have absolutely no money to pay legal fees or their bail surety, so what happens to them? They continue to rot in jails for years. In this current political dispensation, every other day, a citizen is being arrested to instil fear in them just for expressing an opinion against the government or our CM. The kind of humiliation I was put through and the way they have tarnished my image in the world outside, and most of all, within our journalistic fraternity, I thought if I remained silent, it would be interpreted as my having given up. This would have obviously given the authorities an upper hand over me. Also, my silence would be used against the common people. The authorities would have been more forceful in suppressing the voices of those who are underprivileged. I realised I should take the lead in fighting and speaking up against the inhuman treatment meted out by the authorities, which could stop these arbitrary arrests of the general public.

NK: Were you harassed in jail?

KW: Fortunately, I wasn't harassed. Not exactly the way people would assume the jail authorities usually do. As a matter of fact, I was treated with respect, maybe because of my profession. Or it could also be out fear that I may upload something on social media again—about the conditions in prisons and the way jails function. (*We both laughed heartily.*) In fact, I haven't even commented about the conditions in jails. However, after my fourth case, the second NSA matter, I did mention about the behaviour of the authorities, the way the inmates are treated, the unhygienic conditions inside our prisons. I thought that the next time they arrested me, I would find myself in even worse conditions, for speaking about jails. I must say, the conditions are really something that nobody can see or tolerate.

7

'Prison is the centre of sadism.'

Anand Teltumbde and
Rama Ambedkar

Anand Teltumbde studied engineering from Visvesvarya National Institute of Technology, got an MBA from IIM Ahmedabad, and did his PhD in Cybernetics. He had a brilliant academic record all through. Armed with his qualifications, he entered the corporate sector and reached top positions such as Executive Director at Bharat Petroleum and Managing Director at Petronet India. After his corporate stint, he was invited by IIT Kharagpur as Professor at its B-School where he taught for nearly six years before shifting to Goa Institute of Management (GIM) to start the country's first programme in management in Big Data Analytics. At the time of his arrest, he was a senior professor and chair of the new programme in Big Data at GIM. He had a parallel career in activism right from his school days which flowered alongside his professional career and made him one of the leading civil rights defenders in the country. He was General Secretary of the Maharashtra-based Committee for Protection of Democratic Rights (CPDR), a civil rights organisation dating back to 1978. Anand is considered a scholar, activist, and public intellectual. He is particularly acknowledged for his scholarship on the issues of caste, class, Ambedkarite ideas, and peoples' movements in India. He is also married to Rama Ambedkar, granddaughter of Dr B. R. Ambedkar. Naturally, one would wonder, with such an illustrious profile and family links, why the government would want to incriminate and incarcerate Teltumbde? He was named in the Elgar Parishad-Bhima Koregaon conspiracy case that became prominent in the media in June 2018 with the arrest of five activists. His residence on the GIM campus was raided by the police on August 28, 2018. Protracted court rounds followed for quashing the case and thereafter for anticipatory bail, during which time his petition was clubbed together with Gautam Navlakha's, and ultimately both were asked to surrender by April 14, 2020, the birthday of Dr Babasaheb Ambedkar. The fateful paradox of an illustrious member of the Ambedkar family getting arrested on Ambedkar Jayanti by the government that swears by Ambedkar may haunt history. It was all these reasons that noted Kannada writer U.R. Ananthamurthy called Teltumbde a 'critical insider: fighting for change in the system as you continue to be a part of the system'. Another noted scholar, Sunil Khilnani, a professor of politics and the Director of King's College London wrote in a foreword to his book Republic of Caste: 'Anand Teltumbde's clear-eyed arguments won't bring comfort to anyone but they need to be read and engaged with by all, for they urge us to think harder.'

There is an aside to Anand's story: his younger brother, Milind Teltumbde, was a leader of the CPI (Maoist), an organisation banned by the government. The latter was gunned down in an encounter with 26 of his comrades in November 2021 when Anand was languishing in Taloja Central Prison. Whenever the news on Maoists with the alleged involvement of Milind Teltumbde makes the rounds, the media makes it a point to highlight that he was Anand's brother. Anand was not the only brother to Milind; they were eight siblings, Anand being the oldest and having rather tenuous contact with Milind because of the 16 years between them. As became evident from our conversation, all the siblings lived their lives independently. Anand spoke to me about how he always had to comfort his distraught mother and ask her to be proud of Milind. He himself extolled Milind's death as the supreme sacrifice one could make.

During our interview, he spoke very emotionally about his mother, who had contributed a lot to help her children find their paths. She naturally had fond feelings for Anand since he was the first of her children to receive many laurels. When Anand was arrested, the family ensured that the news was kept secret from his mother, fearing she would not be able to bear the shock. When Milind died, Anand sought court permission to visit his mother to console her. Similar permissions were granted to two of his co-accused by the High Court, for 15 and 10 days each. He was however granted only two days permission and with such stringent conditions that he had to eventually decide against it. Suffering from an acute spinal problem, the long train journey was too risky to undertake for him. When I requested Anand for an interview, which was the first he was to give to anyone, he was initially reluctant. But after my assurance that I would not ask anything relating to the case, he agreed to meet me at Rajgruha, the residence of late Dr Babasaheb Ambedkar, where he currently resides. It is a Grade 1 heritage building guarded by four policemen. I spoke for over two hours with him and his wife, Rama, (who is the granddaughter of Dr. Ambedkar), in their ground-floor room. Still emotionally fragile, Anand felt terrible about the distress and anxiety his wife and daughters had faced due to his incarceration. While Anand got emotional during the conversation, at times his sense of humour would surface along with occasional sarcasm about the system, even as we kept off the subject of the case itself.

Neeta Kolhatkar: Was your arrest a strong message from the government and authorities, especially to the Dalit community and Dr Ambedkar's supporters?

Anand Teltumbde: Yes, it may be. Off and on, there was a move to stigmatise the Ambedkar family, even Prakash Ambedkar, Rama's brother and a politician, as not being a true Ambedkarite. It starts from there and then goes to the extent that his name appears in letters purportedly written by Maoists in connection with the Bhima-Koregaon case. They tried tarnishing the Ambedkar family, even the extended family. I was perhaps the soft target, as people thought.

Rama Ambedkar: I keep feeling that somewhere, they wanted to tarnish the image of Dr Babasaheb Ambedkar. If they were to target a direct descendant of his family, the entire Dalit community would have gotten enraged. So, they made Anand a soft target. They have touched Anand and tested to see the extent of anger felt in our community. The next step would be to approach the direct descendants. It is a strong message sent to our Dalit community—those who believe in Babasaheb and swear to save the Constitution. We didn't see the kind of protests from the community as one would have expected. The authorities targeted Anand for his criticism of the government. Unfortunately, the Dalit community fell prey to government propaganda. My daughters and I had to fight all by ourselves during the entire period when Anand was in jail. In fact, over time, I began to feel that the Dalit members had forgotten their history—about what ensued at Bhima-Koregaon in 1818; Babasaheb said those who were killed there belonged to our lineage. When the same community members were attacked on January 1, 2018 by this government, the Ambedkarites gave in meekly. They refused to fight back. Those who attacked and instigated the violence against Dalits remain untouched and roam free. Those who had no role to play in that violence were jailed. This is the reason the community has remained backward and continues to be exploited. It is because they don't take any fight to its conclusion. Take the example of Bhima-Koregaon, the Ramabai Ambedkarnagar violence, or Khairlanji, where the community leaves the victims and those attacked in the lurch. We cannot do anything or bring about change, as the entire community shows itself to be either disinterested or available for sale. Take my example: my daughters and I were often left helpless in these two-and-a-half years. Our family life was nearly destroyed. There was no mental peace, with me worrying about what would happen to Anand and us. We would eagerly wait for his letters. Our older daughter would cry all the while; she is extremely attached to him. Both daughters hold good positions but are constantly preoccupied with the thought of their father's well-being. The older one is married, and her spouse as well as her in-laws were supportive. But the community just left us to fend for ourselves. We had never imagined we would live to see such times.

On the contrary, the community created a controversy over Anand's surrender on April 14, the birth anniversary of Dr Babasaheb Ambedkar observed the world over. They accused him of deliberately choosing that date to surrender, so as to seek the sympathy of the community. I can't understand how they could be so irrational and insensitive. They did not even care to know that it was the Supreme Court that had ordered the accused to surrender on that day. One person had the temerity to ask me why Anand couldn't have surrendered on April 13. I had to counter-question him: If a doctor tells you your father is going to die on April 14, will you tell him, 'No, he cannot die on Ambedkar Jayanti; kill him one day before?' It was not Anand alone; Gautam Navlakha, whose petition was clubbed with his in the Supreme Court, also surrendered on April 14. He was at least not seeking sympathy from these great Ambedkarites! When our family faced such a dire situation, the educated Dalits asked such foolish questions.

Another issue that cropped up was that protests were not possible due to the lockdown. A thought crossed my mind that, at least in a symbolic manner, I should protest. We carry forward Babasaheb's legacy and the values of freedom. As a commitment to our Constitution, when such an unconstitutional arrest occurred, we had to protest. So, I displayed a black flag here at Rajgruha, where we too lived after returning from Goa. The community questioned even this. The kind of forwards and questions that were circulated on social media against the display of the black flag at Rajgruha were shameful. They forget that it was our house, a private house. If they had so much concern for Babasaheb, they should have come out and protested. Rajgruha still serves as a symbol of revolution. All I wanted to do was condemn the government that had raised questions about our family. Do these educated Dalits realise that they have failed Babashaeb, who expected them to help the underprivileged people of our community living in rural areas? Every time an atrocity occurs, and it happens in numbers each day, they just stand by and watch. There is not a whisper of protest, but other times they wax eloquent about Babasaheb and their muddle-headed Ambedkarism. No wonder they continue to remain a backward community. I wonder if they have any sensitivity left any more.

AT: Indeed, people seem to forget this is a private residence. It stands rather as a symbol of their inaction that they could not make it a national monument.

NK: Rama, do you feel you were left all alone during these two-and-a-half years? How were the first few weeks after Anand's arrest?

RA: Yes, we were absolutely lonely, all by ourselves. Every day I was tracking his case, going to court, and meeting him during mulaqats. I will only say that his coming out was nothing short of a miracle. Despite being mentally prepared for his arrest, the first few weeks were the worst for me. I was allowed to visit him at the NIA office on Peddar Road. I used to go between 4pm and 5pm every day for the 11 days that Anand was kept there. We were permitted to meet for 30 minutes, but they would not mind (if we wanted) more time. They would keep their distance from us—which may be because of social distancing norms—and one policeman would stand close to us to ensure we did not exchange any notes or papers. However, after he was moved to the Taloja Jail for 12 days, there was absolutely no communication. The pandemic was at its peak (at that time), and we were terribly scared about his health.

AT: Yes, I pitied seeing her come every time for mulaqat. You have to experience it to understand how torturous it is. She had to travel for an hour and a half, register her name, and wait for hours until her number was called. She was all alone.

NK: Exactly. Being mentally prepared is one thing, but being moved from NIA custody to a prison in the midst of a pandemic, what was your state of mind?

RA: It played complete havoc on my mind. We couldn't speak, forget meeting face-to-face. It was around April 23. I went to the NIA office in the morning, and I overheard them speaking. They had detected one COVID case. They tried to hush it up and rushed Anand to court on the 25th to demand judicial custody. He was taken to the hospital in Taloja to be quarantined. For almost two weeks, we did not hear anything from him. We had no clue about his condition at all. Then, around that time, Anand made a special request to the superintendent to speak to us. Finally, I received a call for only five minutes. The first three minutes were wasted saying 'hello, hello' because of the bad network. We could barely speak for two minutes, whatever one could think of at that time. Moreover, it would be extremely noisy on his side, so we could hardly hear what the other was saying. The only consolation was that the person was alive. At the peak of the pandemic, when Anand's health had deteriorated and he was put on a saline drip, I feared the most because they refused to take him to a hospital outside of the prison.

NK: Anand, do you really feel free since the time you have been out on bail?

AT: Since the time of my release, I have been trying to recover from the shock of this horrific phase of my life. This was not something I had ever imagined in my worst nightmare. We laughed when the police read out a letter on TV in their press conference about what they found on the seized computers of people arrested in June 2018. But then they raided our house on August 28, along with nationwide raids on five more people. Rama had left for Mumbai a few days before, and I took an early morning flight the same day to go to Mumbai for some official meetings. When the news came, we were shocked. More shock came when they forcibly opened our house and obtained the keys from the guard. Fortunately, they could not arrest me then. They could easily do that if they wished, but for some strange reason, they did not. My wife took the next available flight to Goa and filed a complaint at the Bicholim Police Station that our house was raided by the police in our absence and we would not be responsible if they planted something in the house. She went and checked the house and did not find anything untoward. But the incident shocked us to our bones. After looking at the first chargesheet they filed, we filed a quashing petition in the Bombay High Court. It was rejected and the case reached the Supreme Court. The Supreme Court advised that I seek anticipatory bail and gave me protection for four weeks. Thus, the new round of courts began, this time starting with the Pune court. My request was rejected on February 1. I had gone to Kochi for some lectures. I took a return flight and landed in Mumbai by 2am when the airport police waiting for my arrival took me to the airport police station and handed me over to the Pune police.

My ordeal thus began with police custody, which fortunately did not last longer as the court pronounced that my arrest was illegal and termed it contempt of the apex court by the police. Further court rounds began, and eventually the Supreme Court ordered us to surrender to the NIA, which had in an intervening period taken over the case. Thus, I surrendered to the NIA on April 14, 2020, at 2pm.

After my release from jail, we planned a full body check-up, which had been pending for three years. Fortunately, there aren't any significant issues. We had a series of friends visiting from various parts of the country and abroad. Now, we have started our new routine here. I began keying in my handwritten stuff and working on the books, whose publication was paused because of my incarceration. I have written four books in jail. Partly it was a survival strategy, and partly it was making use of my time. All these books will need work to be completed.

NK: Can you tell us about the books you propose to write?

AT: One is my memoir. When I went to Taloja, I learned that one of our senior co-accused, Dr Varavara Rao (VV), was penning his memoirs. It appealed to me as a task to engage myself with. As such, I had not told my daughters about my past. Down the line, I changed the format and wrapped it within the socio-political context. Hopefully, it will be an interesting book. The second was an intimate letter to Babasaheb Ambedkar, as my role model and as my grandfather-in-law. I wanted to tell him how our lives were impacted by the Constitution he wrote. And, of course, we discussed many things as though he were alive and listening to me. It is interesting as it juxtaposes contemporary reality with the various visions he expressed throughout his life. The third one is on nationalism, an abstract concept that has perhaps taken more human lives than any single cause since its inception. It extends to theorise how all such abstractions serve the ruling classes to keep the ruled ones in subjugation. And the fourth book is one of interviews conducted with me by my co-accused in jail. It covers 49 questions asked without bounds, and my responses run over 300 pages.

NK: Did the co-accused interview you? Can you please elaborate on this?

AT: (*Laughs*). This interview happened when I was shifted to the anda cell. I had one of my co-accused in my neighbouring cell who began asking me some questions during our open time, i.e., when our cells were opened: from 7am to 12pm and from 3pm to 6pm. As I responded, he would take notes. Some of his questions were about a doubt that surfaced from one of his readings, but others emerged while interacting with the Ambedkarites in Pune. I proposed that he list down all the questions so that I could also address them in writing. This mode could also accommodate questions from the other co-accused in the anda cells who had a similar grassroots interface. Later, two more co-accused from other quadrants contributed to the question banks. The answers run to over 300 pages and may be useful to activists.

NK: This format has never been done before and sounds most interesting. Didn't the jail authorities stop you from interacting or circulating a sheet of paper?

AT: No. As I said, the inmates interacted freely with each other within their quadrant. There was no restriction on what we discussed, read, or wrote. Yes, it may be quite a novel format because, usually, people are familiar with prison diaries or memoirs. There may be some other genre, like poetry, novels, etc., but never an interview.

NK: Were you allowed to take steam for your Asthma? Didn't the jail staff prevent you from doing so?

AT: No, they allowed me, as well as the others. There may not have been any restrictions on it, but they dictated when it was allowed. Also, even if it was allowed by the officer, every time you had to ask the guard, who would go down and check and then only permit you to go. Such restrictions on your movements are normal. It is because of the logic that people should not meet each other using that excuse. We had to go down to the first floor to the front office and take a break.

NK: Do you remember April 14, 2020, the day you were arrested?

AT: We were prepared because we had actually had one-and-a-half years to reconcile with the eventuality of my arrest. I had gone to the courts seeking relief, and of course, learned how the law and the courts operate. It is an educational experience to understand the character of our democracy. The process ended with the Supreme Court rejecting our bail (in the process, the petition of Gautam Navalakha was tagged with mine).

RA: The police arrested Anand even though he had protection from the Supreme Court. After the horrendous experience of 13 hours in the police lockup, when he was produced in court, our lawyer pointed out to the court that not only was it an illegal arrest, but it was in blatant contempt of the Supreme Court. And that if the court did not concede it, this court itself would be in contempt of the apex court.

AT: The court did concede. It pronounced my arrest illegal and in contempt of the Supreme Court, copying the judgement and bringing it to the attention of the Supreme Court. This was perhaps the first and last judgement in favour of the accused from the court in the case. Of course, I was then freed. There was no accountability of the police, who committed the illegal act on purpose. There is no compensation for the indignities my family and I suffered or for the damage to my reputation. Such is the rule of law in India. There is absolutely no accountability of the state functionaries to the people who are supposed to be sovereign, paying them their salaries.

NK: Could you describe your experience in police custody after the first arrest?

AT: Yes, I was aghast. If they had to arrest me, they could have done so from my home or Rajgruha where I lived in Mumbai. After all, they were tracking my location. But they would not do it; they arrested me at the airport in the wee hours, as though I were a dreaded fugitive. That day, I was returning from Kochi and I had two valid tickets, one to Mumbai and another to Goa. I couldn't cancel either of them. They may have been tracking me until I boarded the Mumbai flight. My flight landed at Mumbai at 2am. There were two policemen standing at the entrance. They let me walk past and then followed me. As I was booking a cab on my phone, they came closer and asked me to follow them. Despite the SC's protection, they acted in this manner. The policemen at the police station would not let me use my phone. But when I shouted, they relented and let me inform Rama that I had been arrested. At that odd hour, she would not get anyone on the phone. She ultimately took her brother and his wife and reached the police station. After some time, the Pune police arrived. After doing some paperwork formalities, they checked my bag and took me inside a rickety car to Pune. They kept me in a lockup for 13 hours. It was clearly illegal, as pronounced by the court. The police did it because they did not have to worry about the consequences. Effectively, as I wrote way back in my book on Khairlanji, in this country, you lived at the mercy of an ordinary policeman. If he does not like you, he can take away your dignity and reputation and ruin your family. This is not hypothetical; it has happened in hundreds of thousands of cases and continues to happen with impunity. In one way, it was a good experience to see what people face in this country. As a civil rights activist, I was not completely unaware of this, but experiencing it is different from knowing it.

After a journey of three odd hours in a rickety vehicle from Mumbai airport to Pune, my spondylitis got aggravated. I was feeling miserable due to lack of sleep, a severe headache and the humiliation. The feeling of losing control over yourself is so horrific. You are simply driven around by a constable. They first asked me to get down when we reached a police station in Pune. He led me to a dingy room where policemen lay like dead sardines. I found a bench and coiled myself on it to steal a wink. But after just ten minutes, the constable came over and took me to the car. They took me to some hospital and talked to a fellow sitting behind a table on the veranda. He took papers from the police and asked me, 'Koi taklif hai kya?' (Do you have any problems?), and before I could answer, he signed and handed back the papers to the police. Thereafter, they dropped me into a lockup at some police station. Horrible—I can't even describe it. It was a dingy, dark room with no light at all, with six fellows huddled up inside. The constable guard sitting at a table took all my things away, placed them in a plastic cover, and asked me to dump my shoes in a corner. A police guard asked me to go and find a chatai (a coir or plastic mattress) to lie down on. They were all torn to shreds and so dirty that ordinarily you wouldn't even touch them with your hands. (*Shudders*). I just told him, 'nahi chahiye, dekhenge baad mei' (I don't want it, I will see later). (*Laughs*). He asked me to get into the cell and locked the door from behind with a big clank. The cell is a dingy, dark affair. For a few seconds, I could not see anything. The only light that entered was from a small bulb outside. I did not know what to do. I had to take the support of the wall to sit on the floor and straighten myself. Within a few minutes, the door opened again with a big clank. The entire lock-up section had a main steel door that was kept locked all the time, but even inside, the cells were kept locked, and each time it was opened, it would create a big metallic clanking sound. The police shifted all those men to a different cell. After all, I was a dangerous terrorist, right? (*We both laugh*). One hefty fellow was ushered in, and the door was locked. He began speaking with me, cleared a spot for me, and helped me sit down. The first question anyone asks is what case you were in for. He did not know Bhima-Koregaon but recalled saying, 'Woh jai Bhimwalla?' (*A colloquial for Dalits*). He told me that he was caught in an extortion episode, but was confident that he would be released within a few hours. After some time, the police guard shoved in our breakfast, two idlis wrapped in newspaper and a tiny cup of tea. So I guessed it was morning. I wanted to go to the bathroom and was shown it at the end. It was a dirty, small closet with a stinking Indian toilet and a small tap in the corner. I did not know what to do, so I just wet my eyes and came back. I tried eating idlis but gave up and drank the tea. I asked for more of it but received no response. My companion ate his breakfast. He advised me that I should not sulk in prison and to eat regularly. He was a professional offender and was familiar with every bit of the process. He would stand, clasping the door, and shout at the police with all kinds of swear words and the choicest abuses. He told me, 'These police take haftas (money) from us. Woh kya, unka baap bhi mujhe kucch nahi kar sakata. (They and their bosses don't have the guts to do anything to me). I made a small mistake and got arrested, no problem, I will be released by 3pm.' And really, the police kept quiet. He sounded absolutely confident that he would be out after a few hours. In that short time, he taught me their terms like khoka, peti (*slang for crore and lakh*), how they operate, and how the police help them. After some time, the guard came and asked us to have lunch. My companion went out, took a plastic plate from the heap, served a plateful of rice like all the others, sat on the floor, and gulped it down with watery daal. I just went out, saw the condition of the plate and the food and came back. My cellmate told me that I should have eaten. The food was much better, he said, than what they serve in jails.

I shuddered at whatever was in store for me.

After some time, the door clanked open, and my companion was taken out. I was alone in the cell when the door was locked. After some time, the door opened, and I was called out. I saw Rama sitting with a policeman. She looked completely distraught. She told me that people had put up posters everywhere protesting against my arrest, and a huge crowd had gathered outside. Furthermore, she requested that the police permit me to sit in a chair, but the policeman declined. He also did not permit me to eat some chocolates she brought for me. It was very cold, so I asked her to send me some jackets. The jacket arrived after some time. The police guard checked it thoroughly, just short of tearing it apart, before giving it to me. (*Laughs*) I annoyingly asked him, 'Should I tear it for you to convince you there was nothing there? He said, 'Nahi saheb asa karava lagta' (No sir, we have to check it)'. He did not seem to realise that he was overdoing it. Then, after an hour or so, the door opened again. I was taken by two policemen to a vehicle standing at some distance. Due to a large posse of media and people gathered in the front, they brought the vehicle to the back gate.

I was seated between two policemen, and our baaraat (wedding troupe) headed for the court. As the crowd in front saw the vehicle, they ran after it, but in vain. Some enthusiastic journalists followed on bikes and went on clicking pictures all along the road. They persisted and reached the court with us, and shouted, 'Anand, Sir, are you well?' Anyway, they were all stopped outside, and I was taken up by the lift to another floor and conducted into the witness box. The courtroom was full of friends. Somehow, I was confident in my mind that I would be out. My lawyers met me and reinforced my confidence. But the way things were going, one could not be sure. During the proceedings, my lawyer threatened the judge that it was not just the police, but his court would also commit contempt of the apex court if he were to not release me. The judge eventually declared the arrest illegal and in contempt of the apex court. He copied his order to the SC. My things were left in the lock-up, but I did not care to collect them and headed for Mumbai.

NK: Can you recollect the humiliation of your first day in jail?

AT: The humiliation you go through in jail is indescribable. I left at 12pm from the court and reached Taloja jail thereafter. I had to stand in the circle drawn (on the ground) before the table as the person behind it took down my details. My bag was taken away. They took me to the place where we are checked. They made me empty all my belongings from my backpack onto a platform. Not only that, they curtly said I wasn't allowed to take my bag. When I asked them how I should carry my things, they asked me to carry everything in a towel. Some fellow standing there got me a sack. Then they asked me to strip completely behind a makeshift cloth partition as their CCTV camera looked on. Anyway, I took it in my stride and mentally braced myself for whatever I was to face.

NK: How did you deal with your emotions when you went through these processes?

AT: A prison is a different world altogether. You have to get acclimated to it before you can react. The NIA treated me relatively well in their lock-up, compared to my experience with the police lock-up earlier. But it does not mean it is free of humiliation. There was not a single relevant or meaningful question asked, but they still kept me there for 11 days. Sometimes, they would take me to some saheb (senior) who would do some typing or clerical work. Then suddenly, he would take me to the SP, who was heading the investigation. He would ask me some silly question, and after my response, he would keep quiet. They had photographs of me from all possible angles and also my fingerprints. This repeats itself everywhere, despite the fact that all our biometric data is always available to the government. No one ever reviews the processes, and as a result, they create a cobweb of redundant procedures.

RA: That still doesn't diminish the humiliation. That is how their processes are built. In court, we were asked for our Aadhar card, PAN card, ration card, electricity bill, bank passbook, etc., as proof of our identity and address. Do they not have the identity of a prisoner? Naturally, all these documents obtained over the years might have some discrepant details, which would create further complications and harassment. Then another process would begin, asking for affidavits, notarisation and court orders. Ridiculous.

AT: After that, they took me to the doctor in the hospital, who was seated behind the closed door. He just scribbled something on a piece of paper. Later, he would become quite friendly with me. I was then taken to a big, empty hall. I didn't know what to do. I kept strolling there and looked for someone to ask for water and a bed to sleep on. Till then, I had never slept on the floor in my life. A guard appeared, so I asked him for water, and he showed me the bathroom tap. He pointed to some folded durries (mattresses) in a corner for me to sleep on. I spread one and sat leaning against the wall. I hadn't carried a bottle, as I thought they would not allow it. Thereafter, I went and surveyed the lavatories and bathing places. Both I found rather filthy. There were either no doors or they were broken. There was a huge drum with a big puddle around it, emitting an immense stench. After some time, suddenly the door opened, and an emaciated old fellow came in. He went over to the drum, inserted the plastic mug, and gulped down water. He shouted aloud 'Yeh gutter ka pani hai' (This is sewage water). I asked him in Hindi, Kahan se aaye ho? (Where are you from?) He retorted, 'You look educated. Then you should converse in English with me.' (*Laughs*). He told me nonchalantly that he murdered a fellow. I didn't feel anything, because once you are inside, you imagine such people would be your friends. (*Chuckles*). There were some steel containers. I put my hand in them to check, as there was no spoon. One had rice, and the other had vegetables. I smelt it and didn't dare to eat it. I ate some snacks and tried to catch some sleep. For many hours I couldn't, then I just fell asleep.

NK: How was your experience thereafter?

AT: The next morning, the guards came shouting to wake people up. I heard that in the barracks, people had to line up to be counted. The previous night itself, the jailer had come, and I had requested that he shift me to some proper place because of my health condition. He sounded positive and asked for some time. The next day, nothing much happened except for some more people filling the barracks and my experience with the food, which I did not eat. On the third day, we were taken in a file to the checking hall and asked to take off our shirts and sit on the floor. I was spared the ordeal when I told them I could not. I stood against a wall. They took our pictures in that position, one by one. After about an hour, the superintendent, accompanied by over a dozen officers and guards, entered and took positions. We were presented before him. I was the first to tell him about my ailments. After that, I was asked to step outside and wait at the edge of the road. As I stood, I heard the lashing and screams of people from the hall. Later, I learned that on a signal from the superintendent, the guard would give them as many lashes as possible with a special device made of a thick leather belt, which the guard held with both hands and whacked on the bare back of the prisoner with full force. I did not know this still happens in our prisons. I could just hear 'rap, rap' sounds of whipping and screams. Back in the barracks, when I asked the fellows who underwent it, they told me the police beat them regularly. It made me wonder, what law was this? It is supposed to be judicial custody, and which law permits such things? Of course, it is a message to the rest of us, such a thing could happen even to us, theoretically speaking. One more aspect, everything in the prison is conducted in a parade. The Superintendent doesn't come alone, he is accompanied by a posse of 20–30 policemen, and he moves around with this baaraat.

NK: Was life better thereafter—like new barracks, better environment?

AT: I had requested that the jailer shift me to a better place because of my ailments. Whatever transpired, they shifted me to the first floor, to a self-contained room. They provided me with a steel cot, a cotton mattress, buckets, etc. I felt such great relief. I took a bath after two days and tried to eat some snacks. I just threw myself on the bed and had a nice sleep until the next morning. Furthermore, I had a round of floor time and had brief introductions with some inmates. Then my proper routine began.

A few people were housed on the first floor, a so-called gangster, a serial killer, and another murderer. All appeared quite humane to me if you did not touch their egos. They shared good food with me, as they used to get it from the kitchen called BC, by paying (bribe) money. It was a nice experience. There were two barracks supposedly meant for patients, but they were very crowded. Those people were also quite humane and helped each other.

NK: Could you meet the other co-accused?

AT: When I was in the hospital, and they happened to come to meet the doctor, they would send a message, and that is how I could meet them. It was not permitted, but it could be managed. The first one who came to see me was Arun Ferreira, around the time I was being shifted to the first floor. The second person I saw was Varavara Rao. He was quite sick when I was brought in. In the first three days itself, I met a few of them.

NK: Rama and Anand, how did your families deal with the arrest?

AT: My father's side of the family, my brothers and their families are simple, and they would not understand these issues. For them, as for us, it was all unimaginable. I was like a towering figure in our family and the entire village. Nobody would have ever imagined that I would end up in jail. I was most worried about my mother. My brothers, Rama and our daughters told her that I was abroad and that because of the COVID-19 lockdown, I was unable to come.

RA: She believed us. Both our daughters are living abroad and she easily believed that he could have gone to meet them. As such, she was familiar with his foreign visits. The story worked very well during the pandemic.

NK: While you were away in prison it has been the toughest time for your mother. Very few know of her background as a labourer, she has gone through a lot too. First your brother was killed by the authorities and then your arrest. How did she take it?

AT: Few know we were the poorest of the poor, you can't even imagine. We had no assets. (*Chokes*). Yet, I tell you, my mother had tremendous confidence. I did everything to ensure she did not know of my arrest; otherwise, she would have died of shock. (*His voice cracks, and we pause for a while*). There was a TV on our floor. I would generally go and catch the headlines on it before getting into my daily routine of reading and writing. The day Milind was killed, I saw the breaking news of an encounter wherein some 27 Maoists had been killed, among them a top leader. They had not named him, but I suspected it might be him.[62] Every time we got news of encounters against Maoists, we feared he would be one of them. I cannot describe my mother's grief (*chokes*). Over the years, my family had reconciled with the idea of not seeing him again. He lived his life for the poor and made the ultimate sacrifice by dying for them. He was no thief, dacoit, or murderer. Every time my mother would inquire about his wellbeing, I would tell her that she should not worry about him. He is living his life. I only told her to be proud of him. (*Chokes. Pauses*). The State had also made him an accused in the case I am implicated in. We then had to ensure my mother would not get a whiff of my arrest.

NK: In Maharashtra we are still to see prison reforms while other states have adopted them. What was the protocol for mulaqats?

AT: Although Maharashtra, perhaps more than all the states, flaunts its prisons as reform centres. Prisons are very opaque institutions and do not generally figure on the agenda of democratic rights organisations like the Committee for the Protection of Democratic Rights (CPDR). Basically, there is no information that comes out of jail unless something leaks to the press. Prison reform has been on the agenda for years. The Supreme Court has expressed concern from time to time on the sub-human conditions in Indian prisons. It has been universally conceded that prisoners do not lose their human rights except for freedom of movement by virtue of them being confined to a bounded space. The apex court in the Ramamurthy vs. State of Karnataka (1996) case had brought to the fore an urgent need for uniformity in laws relating to prisons and had directed the central and state governments to formulate a new Model Prison Manual. Such a model prison manual has since been created and has been approved by the current regime. But unfortunately, it has not been adopted by many states. Not unsurprisingly, Maharashtra, which keeps patting itself on the back for being a progressive state, still follows the manual from the British colonial era. People who were transferred from Taloja to Sabarmati (Gujarat) and Cherlapalli (Hyderabad) jails found them far better in every respect. They could communicate with their families every day. Family members were even allowed to meet them three times a week. We used to hear that in Tihar jail, people got to speak with their contacts every day for 5 minutes or so. And here, it was for 5 minutes every seven days, which could extend to 10–12 days because of the muddle-headed handling of the jail administration. Midway through my stay, it became 10 minutes. During COVID-19 times, we were really at our wits' end trying to communicate with our families. The prisons had bought smartphones during the pandemic, and video calls were allowed. After the pandemic, these were withdrawn. Taloja has prisoners from all over India, and a few are from abroad too. It is obvious that their relatives cannot come for mulaqat. What was the problem in extending the video call facility to such people, and even to the locals? It is pure sadism that makes them disallow it.

RA: Once the jail people had made a mistake and we were made to suffer. A jail guard who was in charge of placing calls pressed the video call button instead of the audio button. It was not recorded in their register as a video call, and still the Superintendent made an issue of it and stopped providing phone facilities to all B-K people. We, the family members, had to write numerous letters, visit the higher-ups of the prison administration in delegation, to resume the facility. It was only after a month or so that they restored it. It was not only irrational but illegal, but they persist with such behaviour because they know that information would not leak out of jail and even if it leaked, nothing would happen to them. We had our basic worries to take our people out, and we would not spend our energies over these petty matters.

NK: Did the situation ease after the first lockdown in 2020? Were you allowed regular mulaqats?

RA: Yes, they allowed weekly meetings after they lifted the lockdown. I had to travel for nearly three hours, as I also had to carry my own water and protect myself from the sun. There was no proper shed to wait in, and there was no toilet for women. There was only one toilet inside the premises, which was common and extremely filthy. I used to leave at 8am in my car and would return around 2pm. As soon as we reached, we had to register our names between 9 and 11am. They claimed for some time that we could register our visit online, but that never worked. If you get delayed, then you are kept in the second half slot, which means you end up spending the entire day at Taloja, if you are lucky. Otherwise, you have to return another day. The mulaqat is anyway only from 11am, so even if you reach early, you waste your time waiting there. Also, even if you take a car, you are forced to park it rather far away, again for security reasons. It was not easy to travel by public transport. You had to get off at Kharghar then take an autorickshaw, to reach jail.

AT: That also works in such a complicated manner. Rama was allowed only ten minutes, for which she had to spend six hours. This meant she had to wait in the hot sun, sometimes without even being able to sit, until her turn came. Even for this basic right, Sagar Gorkhe, one of our co-accused, had to sit on an indefinite fast. All of a sudden, they took away our mosquito nets, saying they were a security risk. All these nets were permitted by the previous administration, but they would not listen. Taloja falls in the malarial zone as per the World Health Organisation (WHO) and yet they chose to risk our lives. It was quite scary, and if someone had falciparum malaria, he would have certainly died because of the lethargic responses of the jail administration to take people to outside hospitals. Sagar sat on the fast for these common public causes like the provision of sufficient water, waiting shade for visitors, etc.[63] The legislator, Kapil Patil, intervened and mediated with him to end the fast. The superintendent accepted all the demands in front of him but did nothing except for providing shade where the visitors waited, which was anyway under construction at the time.

NK: Once you came face-to-face, for how long were you allowed to speak?

AT: Only for 10 minutes.

RA: When they say face to face, it means you can only see faces through a glass barrier. The communication took place only through phones. Actually, there was no need for physical mulaqats, which could be easily substituted by video calls. They had already invested in buying the phones. Even local people like me would prefer it. But the authorities would not see the point. It (in-person meetings) was a huge task for them to manage, but they would not mind so long as it harassed prisoners and their families. There was coordination problem during mulaqats. Sometimes they would call Anand and make him wait, but my name would not be called. Another problem was that in the mulaqat room, there were ten people talking simultaneously, and most of the time it created a cacophony.

RA: Another big problem we faced was that on some days that we had mulaqats, Anand and other co-accused had their court dates, which the authorities would not convey to us. We would end up wasting our entire day coming all the way to the prison. Then we would rush to court.

AT: I used to feel bad for her. She had to suffer unnecessarily (*chokes*). I had reconciled to my fate that I would never come out alive from jail. With the way they behaved, I wasn't sure I would survive the ordeal because my health had always been frail. Surprisingly, after I survived the COVID-19 infection, nothing significant about my health troubled me. Otherwise, I would have to visit a doctor every six months. In jail, they would not take you to any hospital. If you approached the court, the jail authorities would claim they had a well-equipped hospital in prison. The fact is that they did not have doctors with prescribed qualifications, and they did not have any nursing staff. They did not have proper instruments and equipment. When I suffered from COVID-19, and was quite scared, the superintendent kept trying to assure me I did not have the infection. There were no tests carried out until then. And when the tests started, many people were found to have the COVID antigen. The jail doctor who counselled us would simply say that we had Corona, but now it is gone. What if I were to die of it? Father Stan Swamy, one of our co-accused, actually died only because of the delay in taking him out of prison. Those days, he, Arun and I were housed on the same floor. We were alarmed as his Oximeter readings fell below 80 for two consecutive days. I had to shout at the doctor. Only thereafter, on the second day, was he shifted to the Holy Family Hospital, where he ultimately died. The main cause of his death was the delay in giving him medical treatment on time.

In fact, during the COVID-19 outbreak, many inmates died. There is no human dignity for the dead in prison. They didn't even have a stretcher. They would dump the body on a bedsheet and take it out of the hospital. The doctors in jail did not touch patients; they carried a big torch (like a railway guard) and would focus their torch beam on patients to diagnose them. Dressings, injections, administration of saline, etc., were done by the prisoners themselves. I had a first-hand experience of this; fellow inmates inserting needles four times into my hand to take my blood sample. If you had any emergency problems, there was no guarantee of your survival. There was no way they would shift you out of jail. They had several excuses. Even after filling out their forms, they would say that the guards (police escorts of Maharashtra Police) did not turn up. This happened to me on several occasions. The doctor would keep the forms ready, which were a requisition for the guards to take me to Sir J.J. Hospital. The next day, you would expect the guard to take you to the hospital, and you are all ready to go. Then the guards would not come. This would happen week after week. Of course, you would lose appointments given by the JJ-doctor. If you filed an application in court, the judge would ask the prison staff to explain. Who would admit his fault? This process for the application to reach a conclusion would take many months, and mostly the applicant would wear out and give up. This is in the context of health problems. Rama and I submitted an application to court, saying our letters were being scanned and circulated among authorities, which was an infringement of my constitutional right. The rule, as explained by the court, is to scan the letters just to ensure there are no code words or messages that would cause problems for security. These fellows would read every word, take days to read it, and thereafter hand over opened letters. In our case (Bhima Koregaon inmates), our letters were digitally scanned, stored, and sent to the NIA, ATS and other agencies.

This is absolutely illegal. Our petition is still pending in the HC on this issue.

8

'I will not come out alive if I am jailed again.'

Binayak Sen

Binayak Sen completed his MBBS from Christian Medical College in Vellore with distinction, and he chose to stay back in India to make a difference, despite his father's wish to send him to the United Kingdom.[64]

He completed an MD in Paediatrics from Vellore and then joined JNU (Jawaharlal Nehru University) as an Associate Fellow as he desired to study for a PhD in public health. He left his academic position and joined the TB Research Centre and Hospital run by the Friends' Rural Centre at Hoshangabad (MP). Thereafter, he went to Chhattisgarh, where he joined Shankar Guha Niyogi, a trade unionist. Dr Sen worked with the mine workers and their families at the captive mines of the Bhilai Steel Plant at Dalli Rajhara and Nandini, and later in the 1990s with the daily wage labourers in factories at Bhilai and Raipur. He helped set up a health centre for the mine workers at Dalli Rajhara, which was run by the workers themselves. It grew into a 25-bed hospital and was called Shaheed Hospital. He then left Dalli Rajhara to join his wife, Dr Ilina Sen in Raipur to start an NGO called Rupantar.

On April 13, 2006, then Prime Minister, Dr Manmohan Singh, stated in his speech in a meeting of Chief Ministers for tackling Naxalism, 'I came here with the primary purpose of listening to your views and the strategies you are adopting to face the challenge of Naxalism. It would not be an exaggeration to say that the problem of Naxalism is the single biggest internal security challenge ever faced by our country.' His speech also spoke of Naxalism having spread to over 160 districts of the country. He talked about the police response recommended by CMs, 'We may need specialized force on the pattern of Andhra Pradesh's Greyhounds. This investment is essential if we need to turn the tide in favour of the Government.'

Since then, every government has targeted the Naxals, also called Maoists (by government agencies). Among the first intellectuals to be arrested in this regard was Dr Sen, whom the authorities alleged to be a Naxal ideologue. The Chhattisgarh government arrested Dr Sen on May 14, 2007; he was charged with acting as a courier between jailed Naxalite leader Narayan Sanyal and businessman Piyush Guha and was accused of having Naxal links. In July 2007, the Chhattisgarh High Court rejected his bail application. Later in August 2007, the Supreme Court bench of Justices Ashok Bhan and V. S. Sirpurkar sought a response from the Chhattisgarh government after senior counsel Soli Sorabjee claimed that Sen had been illegally detained since May 14, 2007, on fabricated charges of supporting Naxals; they later rejected the plea.[65] *Finally, on May 25, 2009, Dr Sen was granted bail by a vacation bench of the Supreme Court, comprising Justices Markandey Katju and Deepak Verma.*[66]

However, on December 24, 2010, the Additional Sessions and District Court Judge B.P. Varma of Raipur found Dr Sen, Narayan Sanyal, who was accused of being a Naxal ideologue, and Kolkata businessman Piyush Guha guilty of sedition for helping the Maoists in their fight against the state.[67] *Dr Sen was held under the Unlawful Activities (Prevention) Act and the Special Public Security Act (2005) and was tried under Section 124A of the Indian Penal Code (for sedition). He was taken back into custody.*

The conviction was severely criticised both in India and abroad on the grounds of reliability of the evidence and the interpretation of the sedition law. This was highlighted by B. Raman, Additional Secretary (Retd), Cabinet Secretariat, Govt of India, in his article on October 26, 2010, and continued on February 3, 2022.[68] *Dr Sen applied to the Supreme Court for bail, and on April 15, 2011, the Supreme Court of India granted him bail after questioning the sedition charge against him.*[69]

Since May 2022, the Supreme Court has allowed the central government to reconsider the provisions of Section 124 IPC, Sedition. It is the first time since the Sedition Law came into effect that operation of this section has been suspended. Reliefs granted to the accused by courts are continuing and the challenge is still pending before the Supreme Court. However, the IPC has been replaced by a new Bharatiya Nyay Sanhita Bill in the meantime, which in fact is severe than the existing sedition section.[70] *Under the new Bill, Section 150 replaces the 124A of the old IPC. Legal experts say it is more stringent than the existing one.*[71]

Even though the relief continues for Dr Sen he is under immense pressure as he has not yet been cleared of the charges. He fears being re-arrested and, during our interview, he commented that if he is arrested again, he will not come out of prison alive.

I planned to interview Binayak Sen as part of this book because the entire effort to highlight the experiences of political prisoners would have been incomplete without his interview. I have met and spoken with him previously when he was released and residing in Mumbai with his wife, the late Professor Ilina Sen. In fact, I had interviewed their daughter Pranhita prior to speaking with them which was published as a feature article titled 'When dad is labeled a Naxal', for a newspaper in May 31, 2009. After a few telephonic conversations, we decided on a date and time. I went to Kolkata to speak to Dr Sen. His mobility is a bit more restricted than before, and we both gladly agreed that his daughters, Pranhita and Aparajita, would be present at the time of the interview. Both of us felt it would be helpful for him in case he forgot anything. Interestingly, both his daughters learned an important point pertaining to Dr Sen's arrest for the first time during our interview.

Now, I was meeting Dr Sen after a few years since my last meeting with him. Though Aparajita had mentioned his fragile health, I wasn't prepared for how he appeared. I wasn't prepared to see him frail, losing words while he spoke and his loss of memory. Prior to this meeting, every time we had met, he was cheerful and looked healthier. After we greeted each other and caught up a bit informally, we waited for everyone to settle in. Our conversation was peppered by a lot of laughter amid all the serious talk.

On a serious note, I could see the toll two jail terms have taken on Dr Sen, though he is still sharp in his observations and warm and sensitive in his understanding of larger issues. Both his daughters have moved cities to be with their father. One has taken on the huge challenge of becoming an entrepreneur; the older one has given up cinematography to take care of the elders in the family. We met over two consecutive days, which must have been difficult for Dr Sen, who truly exerted himself to recollect and share the experiences of the work Ilina and he did in the Bastar region.

Ilina was a professor, a human rights activist, a feminist, and a trade unionist. She taught at the Mahatma Gandhi Antarashtriya Hindi Vishwavidyalaya in Wardha and later she was Professor at the Tata Institute of Social Sciences in Mumbai. She died on August 9, 2020 in Kolkata.[72]

Neeta Kolhatkar: How is your health, Dr Sen?

Dr Binayak Sen: It is not good. In addition to various other problems, like cardiovascular issues, I also have early stages of dementia, which has been diagnosed by a psychiatrist. It is a neuro-disorder that is being treated, and I'm on various medications. Yes, they slow me down, but I am much better than before because of the care my daughters have taken of me. My friends have also been helping me in moral terms. With the help of my friends and family, I am better now than earlier. I realise that is an issue that can complicate our lives more and more as time goes by.

NK: Does it worry you?

BS: So far, I haven't reached that stage. I am coping with the realities of the illness, but I haven't had time to get worried. At some stage, I will not be as able. Between these two stages, there will come a time when I am worried and I can't do anything about it, and that is going to be something difficult.

NK: How are you coping with the loss of Ilina? She was the pillar for you three. You also have the pressure of the conviction charges not being dropped, does that scare you?

BS: Firstly, Ilina was intellectually far ahead of me. There is no comparison. Doctors think that they are very clever, but they don't have the apparatus to understand whatever is happening around them. Apart from that, she was the one who structured our reality. We saw reality outside, with lenses that were not restrictive but interpretive. She was able to see reality and interpret the world as we saw it. That was something very difficult for us. There is no question of substituting for it, but even to get over the reality, that was very difficult. I think slowly we are learning to compensate to some extent. I am not sure, but I think so.

(*As I turned to the daughters, they promptly said: We think he said what we feel.*)

NK: How did the two jail terms affect you, both physically and psychologically?

BS: One of the diagnoses detected in me was post-traumatic disorder, which was due to jail. Jail was not only a negative experience. People were really kind to me . People understood my condition and helped me to spend my days there. Except for the time I was kept in solitary confinement, a lot of the time was spent in the ward, and the people were very helpful. I must also say that the jail staff is distinct from the police. The jail staff was helpful and they hardly ever treated me badly. When I came to the jail, at that time the Director General of Police called for a meeting with the jail staff, which he had no business doing because he had no locus standi in the jail. He told them they should cooperate with the prosecution in securing a conviction against me, otherwise, they would face consequences. In spite of his insistence, the jail staff didn't adhere to the orders of the DG Police, Chhattisgarh. Basically, they were asked to cook up some evidence for my conviction, which they didn't. A lot of people didn't have a good opinion of this DG and the police administration in general. Some of them even faced harassment and informal punishment (was) meted out to them; they were transferred suddenly.

NK: Do you recollect the day you were arrested the first time?

BS: Yes, I remember. I wasn't expecting the arrest. I was in Calcutta, as I had gone to spend time with my family.

Pranhita Sen: Yes, we had come to spend time with our grandmothers. Baba left for Raipur before us, because he had to attend the village clinic, with which he was regular. Patients would come from as far as 100 kilometres, so he was always there for them. There were rumours that the police were going to arrest him. Even though he had a ticket for Raipur, he went to Bilaspur and met Sudha Aunty. *(Advocate Sudha Bharadwaj, who lived and worked in Bilaspur.)* The police however were tracking Baba's mobile phone, so they reached Sudha Aunty's house. Baba was told that the thanedar wanted to meet him, so he should come to the police station. Baba and Sudha Aunty went together to the police station and the thanedar informed them that a team from Raipur were on their way and they would be arresting Baba.

BS: I had got up to fetch some tea, I wanted to have something and they stopped me. Initially, I didn't suspect anything. At that time, their whole body language changed. All of them kept making me sit in the police station under some excuse. 'Aap abhi kahin mat jayiye' (Now you please remain here, don't go anywhere), the thanedar said to me. Once his body language changed it was clear that something was happening. Then they took me to the Hospital for my medical examination. The doctor told me during the examination that he can arrange for medical admission to the Hospital. I refused and made it clear I will go to jail. That is a bit I haven't told my daughters till now.

(*I turned around and asked the daughters for their comments.*)

PS: We didn't know of this! I don't think Ma knew of this either. Yes, I am surprised, but I think he did the right thing. I was 22 years old at the time, when Baba got arrested.

Aparajita Sen: Oh. He shouldn't have said no. He should have taken medical admission. I was 16 years old when he was arrested. At that time, I was with Ma in Wardha. While Didi was in Raipur, near Baba.

(*I said, 'there speaks the lawyer.'*)

NK: Then what happened, Dr Sen?

BS: Sudha (Bharadwaj) was there throughout and was a big source of strength for me.

PS: We two sisters were with our Dadi, and Ma had promised her mother a trip to Murshidabad. My Nani had not seen the Murshidabad palace and the places around it, so Ma had planned this trip with her.

BS: Both Ilina and her mother had a passion for history, and it was a long-term promise Ilina had made to her mother. She was confronted with the dilemma, and she finally took her mother to Murshidabad. Then she rushed back. The events from the beginning to the end are not known to me. Apart from the facts that were told to me, even the stuff that I remember is uninformed compared to what these people have witnessed and recorded in their consciousness.

NK: Where did they take you finally?

BS: They took me from Bilaspur to Raipur, which is 125 kilometres away.

There were several policemen in the jeep, and one had a big, fat belly. The police were angry with me because I had constantly pointed out the contradictions in their human rights reports. One of my proudest moments was when Pranhita came with me to record the Golapalli incident; she was just 14, and she did the videography. We travelled in the dark.

Coming back to my arrest, I was lodged in the Raipur jail.

NK: How was your entry to the jail? What did they do to you?

BS: They took me to Raipur Central Jail. They did not strip me down, at least. I don't remember the rest in detail. I was not alone; there were people around. Nobody interfered with me, and nobody even recognised me. *(He said it as a matter of fact.)* They found out about my reality much later. I was allowed to talk to people who were nice to me. Some of them were very kind to me.

PS: Initially, Baba was jailed in 2007 and released in 2009. The second time he was arrested in December 2010 and released in April 2011.

AS: There was one dedicated person who took care of Baba during that entire period. He was a young man who looked after him.

PS: That young man was serving a murder sentence. He had killed his own father because the latter had tried to strangle his mother.

BS: That young boy was good to me. He would cook food for me. By then, many prisoners had gotten to know of my situation—that I was jailed for being a 'Naxal' as I was termed by the government. They didn't judge me and, in fact, helped me in jail.

NK: How did you occupy yourself during your incarceration?

BS: I would read newspapers in detail. They allowed me, though the jail staff would cut out some of the news items from these papers.

NK: No way. You'd get newspapers with big holes in them? *(I laughed aloud)*.

BS: Yes (*nonchalantly*). More important than that, I received a lot of letters in jail. Most of these were in English. One member of the jail staff who knew English told me after a few days. 'Dr Saab, aap chitthiyon ki sankhya toh kum kar dijiye' (Doctor, please try to restrict the number of letters you receive). (*Laughs*).

(*We were all in splits. I exclaimed, 'As if it was in your control.'*)

PS: Finally, when Baba came out of jail, he had six bags filled with letters. There were 3000 letters from citizens around the world.[73]

NK: Can you tell me a bit more about these letters and the news the prison staff would cut or not let you read?

BS: There were a number of schoolchildren who had written to me. I received letters from schoolchildren in Sholapur. They sent postcards with paintings on them, which they had drawn. In those days, they would write the address on one side, some drawings on the other, and sign it with their name. There were many who sent letters written in English. It kept this particular jail staff person so preoccupied that he came asking me to temper the flow of letters. *(Both Pranhita and Aparajita giggled aloud).*

They cut news (items) that they thought I should not be reading, which would not be about the court case or such news. They only wanted me to read news which they thought I should be reading. I also asked for a radio for shortwave radio programmes. They gave it to me after a lot of deliberation, which lasted for two months. I asked the jail staff, why did they take so long to give it to me? They told me they had to test it to ensure there were no messages being transmitted.

NK: You are not serious, are you? Wasn't this whole drama made by the authorities rather filmy?

BS: Yes, I am telling you this is what the jail staff told me.

AS: I remember Baba's lawyers filing an application in court. There was one hearing that took place on the radio issue, and even the court was not in favour of him keeping a radio.

NK: Were you finally allowed a radio, and could you listen to music?

BS: Yes, I got a radio and I would often listen to music. I would listen to news on All India Radio and I developed a taste for new music. Eventually, they didn't try to restrict me from listening to the radio.

NK: Was your family allowed to meet you, and did you get a lot of visitors in jail?

BS: Yes, a lot of people came to meet me. My family would come to meet me, but they faced a tough time.

PS: Every time we would go to visit him, the jail authorities would come up with excuses and ask us to come the following week. At that time, I was at University, while Aparajita was living with Ma in Wardha. They had to travel a long distance, so they would leave on Friday night and reach Raipur on Saturday morning. Then we would go to Raipur Central Jail to meet Baba. Often, it was as per the whims and fancies of the police. Sometimes they would just not allow us to see Baba and would make us wait for nearly a full day. We would argue and fight to meet him, at least for a few minutes. In those few moments, the jailor was made to sit close to us to eavesdrop on our conversation. Actually, he was a nice man; he would tell us to continue talking while immersing himself in his work and not listen in.

AS: We used to go every weekend, and the staff would create problems.

We would be made to sit for two to three hours until they relented. Sometimes we would sit under a tree; if we had a vehicle, we would wait for our turn; or sometimes we would make someone wait, and the three of us would go home, hoping to get a slot for that day. All this was done even after we followed the procedures for writing applications regularly and submitting all our personal details.

PS: Every week we would give some potatoes, onions, and other food ingredients to Baba because that boy would cook for him. The sentry at the jail gate would try and take some of our ingredients. Most of the time we had to persuade him from doing so. We'd tell him it was for Baba; he needs to eat properly, and at least they would listen to us. Once, we met a young woman with a 3-month-old baby, outside the jail premises. She had come to meet her husband, who was in jail. She was put through the same ordeal of waiting for long hours, and the sentries had taken half of her food contents. She wept as she narrated her ordeal to us. Ma asked the constables why they'd behaved cruelly and made her weep by taking the food she had brought. She had come four times, and each time the police had refused her a personal meeting. Ma requested the police to let her meet her husband. They dilly-dallied and they also told Ma that they confiscated some of the food ingredients because they had to fend for themselves too. Such are the conditions in the jail.

NK: How did you have the courage to take on the police? Or were you scared?

PS: It was Ma. She wouldn't take anything lying down. She gave us that courage.

AS: Oh! We fought hard. *(Both smile).*

PS: Once, Baba was brought to court and the police did not behave properly with him. Baba wanted to drink water while he was still in the police van. He asked me to bring some. I gave him an unopened Bisleri water bottle.

The Investigating Officer was quite nasty. As he saw me giving Baba water, he came running and accusingly asked me, 'Zeher pila rahi ho kya unko?' (Are you giving him poison?) I said why would I poison my own father? Wouldn't I poison you instead?

NK: Any other memories of your time in jail? Was Dr Sen in good health in prison?

PS: Baba had a fall and injured his elbow when he was in solitary confinement. We couldn't get a date to meet him during that time, and we could only see him after a fortnight. Then we saw his bandaged elbow. Ma asked him what happened, and that's when he told us he had had a fall. He had fallen off the stone slab on which he slept. *(Inmates are given rather narrow stone slabs to sleep on.)*

AS: Once he had a rash on his face.

NK: Did you ever feel scared of falling ill in prison?

BS: I continue having this fear. If I go back to jail I won't come out alive.

PS: Yes, He still has that fear.

(For a few minutes, we were all quiet.)

NK: How damaging has been the period of solitary confinement and long-term incarceration for your Baba? Have you daughters been able to see the damage to his mental health?

PS: When Baba was imprisoned, initially when we visited him, everything seemed fine. After his fall, Ma asked Baba how he fell. Was there not sufficient light? What happened? He told her he was in solitary confinement when it happened. Apparently, solitary confinement cells are dark rooms. The only source of light or air is through one vent. They have to stay in that room for most of the day. Imagine if any person is kept in such a solitary confinement cell, where there is no light and only brief interaction with others for a few hours, while most of the time one is by oneself and not able to see the world, it makes the whole situation rather depressing. That took a toll on him and we have seen a change in him after that. After he was released, he would have sleepless nights, or wake up screaming at night. Several times I would wake up because he had woken in his sleep screaming, 'Usko mat maro, usko chot lag jayegi' (Don't beat him, he will get injured). There were other issues. See, the jail authorities couldn't beat him, but there was mental abuse. From what Baba would tell us then, the authorities would beat prisoners to make him feel scared. Our Baba is extremely soft, kind, and caring. For him to witness another prisoner being beaten tormented him. He would take that torture personally. Those things impacted him severely and he would wake up every night screaming after his release and we sisters would feel frightened seeing what had happened to our father. Thankfully Ma was there and being an extremely strong woman, she would reassure him: everything will be fine, just go to sleep. She would tell him that we were all with him now, he was safe. Along with this, he suffered from depression. The Baba we had seen in our childhood had turned into a different person. He used to be extremely friendly, and would love to speak to everyone. The tribals, his patients and others would come to meet him and would sit to talk with him. If he could not go visit them, they would travel long distances to get medicines from Baba. He was friendly and loved to meet people. However, after he came out of prison, he was a completely changed person. He couldn't find the bathroom or restroom, he couldn't find the kitchen, and he would fumble forgetting where the vessels were kept.

Till Baba was imprisoned, he would wake up at 5.30am and make chai for himself and coffee for Ma, after which he would wake her up. Once he came out of prison, he stopped making chai and coffee because his memory was impacted. He couldn't find the utensils. Everything changed after that. We realised that the solitary confinement experience had left him disoriented even after his release.

NK: How did it affect you mentally and emotionally? Did you need to take any help, like counselling, or medication?

PS: We were young at that time. As I mentioned earlier, I was in the final year of University and my sister was younger. What we witnessed with Baba was something that I had seen only in films till now—a person being jailed and their condition in prison. We sisters have seen our father's work since childhood and he has never done anything that he was accused of. He was a brilliant doctor and the government just ruined his medical career. We would feel scared and worried for him wondering what would happen. As I stated, I was also threatened, though that didn't deter me. Yes, one thing that scared us was regarding our Baba's safety and our future. We would be mortally worried wondering if the government would kill our Baba, would they attack Ma? I started watching films back-to-back and I never judged whether they were good or bad. Every night I would watch a new film; my sister tells me, 'You can watch any film, be it Govinda or Mithun's.' (*Laughs.*) I watched international films—Iranian, Spanish, any language films. I am not good at articulating or writing well, I simply love watching films. That was my coping mechanism or medicine if you can call it that. Also, I have this fascination for watching horror movies. So, I would get an opportunity to let go of my emotions while watching these films. One thing I must confess, I would get angry a lot, which was out of control. Beyond any explanation, I still don't understand how or why, but I would be enraged ever so often. Now when I look back, I realise anything would spark this anger in me and on top of that I would bluntly say things to a person's face, like a mooh fut (bluntly). I would tell people in authority they are the cause of my father's problems and if I could I would want to hit them. Maybe it was a result of watching too many violent films, I don't know. Things have of course changed; I am extremely calm now. Maybe time mends a lot of things, I don't know. Yes, I do feel frustrated, that I am not able to do what I want to do. I feel I am stuck at home taking care of sick and old people. I feel like I have nowhere to go. I mean even to go for a coffee I have to think ten thousand times because I have to take care of Baba or take him along. His dementia has increased, so it is tough. I never contemplated or needed to take medicines.

NK: Dr Sen, what are your memories of your jail term? Did you believe, then, that you would be released?

BS: After a point, I stopped thinking about it. I stopped anticipating the outcome because it was very painful to build up expectations for a hearing and then have that hope smashed. That was painful, and so after a while, I stopped thinking of the possibility of getting bail.

NK: Did you read about the global campaign for your release? What are your views about it?[74]

BS: Yes, I read about it in the newspapers. The police had not cut out that part. (*We all laughed*). You know, there is a lot that I don't remember.

NK: Do you see a concerted effort to stop political opposition and dissent?

BS: The whole discourse in politics has become so criminalised. The thing is, there is no agency that people can experience through their ordinary political activity. People need an alternative, a form of political activity that gives them legality to articulate their agency; otherwise, it is difficult to engage people's energies. The trade union movement in Chhattisgarh, with the idea that the movement comprised the energies of large sections of working people in the iron ore mines, was formed on March 2–3, 1977, when the Chhattisgarh Mines Shramik Sangh—Chhattisgarh Mine Workers Union was founded by Shankar Guha Niyogi.

After a few months, in June 1977, a whole gathering of workers—men, women, and children—were fired upon, and 12 people died, including a 16-year-old youth.[75]

On September 28, 1991, early in the morning, Niyogi was shot dead.[76]

His windows were big and had been left open. The same picture is repeated all across the country and the globe. Unless we are ready to find a legitimate form of political activity through an agency, as ordinary political workers, how do we hope to survive?

NK: From being a renowned a paediatrician and health worker to being a security threat to the nation. Did you ever imagine you would be in such a situation?

BS: No, I never thought I would be in such a situation. Never in my remotest dreams did I think I would end up being jailed twice on sedition charges. It was not even a quality I aspired for. One of the fact-finding reports we jointly published about the Salwa Judum was entitled 'When the State Makes War on Its Own People'.[77] It is very difficult, and it goes on and on—a continuous reality. It is a reality that the State is waging war on its people, and large sections of our people have to face that reality. The huge gaps, the rising inequity, the rising malnutrition levels among certain sections of people, and whatever happened during the COVID-19 pandemic forced certain sections of our people to bear the consequences. The World Health Organization (WHO), along with the Institute of Health Equity, came out with a report on COVID-19 and the social determinants of health and health equity.[78]

Michael Marmot said that social inequity is killing people on a grand scale.

The history of famines, and the analysis of the Great Bengal Famine of 1943, shows that it was caused not due to a scarcity of food but because food was sent to the war front and common people were left in the lurch. The Bengal Famine of 1943, as it had already come to be known, had not resulted from any 'calamity of nature', but instead was the result of shameful and prolonged government bungling. The understanding that the Bengal Famine was man-made has, ever since, met with few detractors. This is a global phenomenon, and the challenge is to confront this reality.

PS: When we speak of sedition, I want to ask: what did my Baba do, that they slapped sedition charges on him? He hasn't done any harmful work. Baba was one of the first people to be charged with sedition during that period. Now it has become common.

BS: Well, it took a long time to file the chargesheet. The conviction was something unexpected and surprising.[79]

NK: What do you both feel about this entire case and the charges against your father?

PS: I know and have seen my father as a paediatrician, who was working among the unprivileged and marginalised people. I used to often wonder why don't I get sick? Like my classmates from school or any of my friends, I came to a conclusion that maybe because I am the daughter of a doctor, that's why I don't fall sick. He is a very good doctor, apart from being a human rights activist. We knew our lives wouldn't be easy or normal. Baba had explained to us many years before his arrest that he may be harassed, jailed, or killed. We had begun hearing rumours and had also seen the authorities creating problems. There have been many fact-finding missions in Bastar and investigations for which Baba used to go. Once there was an attempt on his life, our driver saved Baba's life. We would get scared, but we never thought he would be charged with sedition.

AS: It was unfair because I think the state (Chhattisgarh) failed to see Baba's contribution to society. There seem to be vested interests that have driven their actions. It can't be seen from only one angle.

NK: Is there anything that you have missed in your life now that you look back?

BS: Among my regrets is this one. The kind of pressure my case put on Ilina and our daughters is something I regret tremendously. Also, how the system limited their potential even though they are two exceptionally intelligent daughters. I need to have a reason for this. Comparing it to others is the only way to justify it, but that is a weak and unpersuasive argument.

NK: What are your thoughts, please be honest with me—unintentionally, you've all been drawn into his case. Did you really think you would end up trying to clear his name for more than ten years?

PS: I've even had threats since Baba was incarcerated and Ma and Billo (Aparajita's nickname) moved to Wardha. My university was 100+ kilometres away from Raipur, I made the decision to stay home and make the commute.

Ma said I could stay back if I was ready for the 'Trip'. The handling of the letters and court documents that would be sent home required someone to be present. And even Baba would require someone from the family in case of any emergency. After a month, I started to notice that flyers were being sent home and placed within the newspapers. They were essentially telling me that they were observing me. These individuals who were threatening me were aware of the timing of the buses I would take to University, and they were also watching me in court. The threatening letters said that our mother would also go to jail and our lives would come to an end. They threatened to kill Baba as well. My HoD and my friends' parents asked Ma to let me finish my last few months of the university even though Ma wanted me to leave University because of the threats. I was so happy and grateful that they took my responsibility for those few months, so that I could finish my graduation. We initially felt that people were turning away from us after Baba was arrested.

The media acted in a very unprofessional manner. We knew he was going to be convicted even before the court made its ruling. The media extensively detailed his arrest and called him a hard-core 'Naxal'. Such news has an impact on ordinary people. Fortunately, people who really knew us were not swayed; Billo's friends were not influenced.

AS: My friends helped me out, so everything was fine. Didi wasn't as protected as I was. Being the younger one, I was in Wardha with my mother. One of the reasons I chose to study law was because of his arrest. Since 2007, a lot has happened, programming me to become less emotional and more mechanical. I also try to compartmentalise things in order to deal with these problems. Ma also made an effort to minimise the significance of his arrest and to give us a normal life. Yes, but that did not turn out to be the normal life we had planned for each other (*chokes, tears welling up*). I was sixteen years old at that time and I was attempting to make sense of my life. I had to make a big decision at that point, and my mother told me that Baba would have helped me more if he had been present. Regretfully, he was absent when we accomplished our goals.

BS: That's true.

AS: Most importantly, having people around all the time meant that our family did not have any privacy. Many of his patients who required medical attention but lacked the means would be kept at our house.

PS: Our home has been crowded with people since I was a child. That doesn't just refer to intellectuals; even villagers or sick people would often be at home under Baba's watchful eye. We were never alone as a family.

NK: Is there something about him that is not known to others?

(Both the daughters laugh…my eyes widen: 'Tell me.')

PS: Baba was a good cook. Ma was a vegetarian who only enjoyed eggs and fish. We (the daughters) would both look forward to his non-vegetarian food, which we could only get when Ma would go out of town for conferences.

There was this one occasion when we knew Baba would get chicken because Ma had gone to Delhi. None of us will ever forget that particular gourmet meal

(*laughs*).

AS: It was extremely traumatic (*laughs*).

NK: What did he do?

(Aparajita threw back her neck, rolled her eyes, and said, 'You must hear this.' As I turned to face the trio, it appeared as though Dr Sen had resigned to his fate. The two daughters began regaling me about Dr Sen's culinary prowess.)

PS: Baba asked us to do our schoolwork and said he would drop Ma off at the airport and head to the bazaar to get the ingredients. We were elated; now that Ma is going, we will get chicken. He came back carrying two dozen eggs and a large bag full of spinach. Wow, I exclaimed. He intends to create something novel. I asked if I could help him in the kitchen out of pure curiosity. Baba declined, telling us to continue studying while he quickly cooked. Our tests were approaching. Baba is a very laid-back guy who takes his time chopping and cooking. The two of us sisters were curious about what was being cooked and were hungry. I requested that Aparajita peek inside the kitchen to see what he was doing. She noticed that there were two enormous pots: one held boiled spinach, and the other held boiled eggs. We had anticipated eating some egg curry. Since Baba has always enjoyed soups, we also expected palak soup. After an additional hour, we were growing restless. I asked him if he needed any assistance as I entered the kitchen. The eggs were cooked by then, but I could not see any yolks. Baba had eaten twelve yolks while cooking, we later discovered, leaving only the egg whites. (*Laughs*). After being cooked, spinach was being ground in a mixer. Even though we believed something strange was being cooked, I noticed a green paste in a container.

Afterwards, we observed green paste in one vessel and egg white paste in another. I then went and said to Billo: who knows what he's cooked up with these ingredients? We were served large bowls of soup which had the colour of pistachio after all those hours of cooking. After this first soup, we still felt that there was something exotic. When Baba asked if we wanted anything more, I said, 'No.' We want to go on to lunch. He then said, 'This is lunch.' (*They both started laughing*). As if this wasn't enough, he asked us if we would like to take it in our tiffins the following morning! We simply said no. (*They both chuckle loudly*). He is a good cook, but that was the only occasion we didn't enjoy what he had made.

AS: This was fed to everyone who visited Baba that day at the house. Everyone found it extremely difficult to finish that soup of egg white and spinach. (*Leaps into giggles and rolls her eyes*). Yes, he cooks well otherwise.

(Dr Sen just grinned and gave a resigned shake of his head.)

NK: Any other unknown facets about Dr Binayak Sen?

PS: He was a very good photographer.

AS: I was told by people that he directed plays in his college days.

BS: (*smiles*) I directed Agatha Christie's Mousetrap.

NK: So you like fiction and murder mysteries? This sounds exciting...

PS: Not anymore. Things have changed after his jail term. He likes poetry and he can sing.

BS: I now enjoy poetry. I like the work of W. H. Auden.

AS: His mother was a singer.

BS: Yes, she was a good singer of the calibre of professional singers, but she didn't get opportunities to showcase her talent.

NK: What was the reaction, particularly from the general public, when you were released?

BS: There were many who held talks, one such was at Kolkata University to felicitate me and celebrate my release. There was a huge crowd and many years later, several people would come up to me and tell me they were there.

PS: The public, along with numerous institutions and peoples' organisations, contributed significantly to Baba's release. Protests occurred outside the Raipur jail and participants from several states met there once a week. Residents from Maharashtra were scheduled to attend one specific week. The train they had taken to Raipur came to a lengthy stop when it arrived in Nagpur. Some went outside to buy food or drink, or they just stepped outside to stretch their legs. At the station was a banana vendor who spoke with one of these visitors, whose name escapes me, he was a friend of Baba. This uncle was asked where they were going by the vendor. He explained that one of their friends, Dr Binayak Sen, had been imprisoned, so they were travelling to Raipur to protest the arrest. This vendor told him that either his father or he had received treatment from Baba when he was a little child. They were now residing in Nagpur. He took out Rs 300 from his pocket and said he would like to contribute personally if any money was being raised. Even though Rs 300 was a significant sum for this vendor, he remembered Baba and made a contribution.

BS: (*Humbly nodded*). One time, on our way back to Kolkata after my release, there was an octogenarian wheelchair user on a flight. He was waiting on top of the stairs. He asked me if I was Dr Binayak Sen as I walked up and reached out to shake his hand. He said, 'I'm 80 years old and today is an important day of my life.' It is significant that thousands of people believe that a new society needs to be built, and that makes one feel humble. They're attempting to put these feelings into words.

AS: People used to recognise him everywhere we went, and wait for him to get closer. A few people would touch his feet, and once a pilot declared how happy they were to have Dr Binayak Sen on board. Many people tell me they were at the lecture at Kolkata University and consider him to be their hero.

(*After over two-and-a-half hours of interview and informal conversation, we decided to call it a day. Dr Sen was exhausted and moreover he had to go back. After some deliberation, we decided on meeting again at the same café the next day. We chalked out the talking points, as Dr Sen wanted to speak of the Anjan tree, Ilina's work and his in Rupantar.*)

NK: (*As he talked about his memories, he reminded me to ask him about the Hardwickia Binata tree in Raipur, commonly known as Anjan*). **Could you tell me about that Anjan tree research? It seems to have been the only one in Raipur.**

BS: Much of our work was based in Nagri Sihawa, in Dhamtari district. Hardwickia Binata, a botanical name for Anjan trees, used to be another notable feature of this region. Rupantar was the organisation we had founded. An eminent Botanist, Gautam Sengupta came to Nagri to look for the Anjan trees, which used to be common in this area. A meter gauge line ran from Dhamtari to Nagri, but it was used by the British to move the

wood of Anjan trees. The British abandoned the entire region after removing nearly all the Anjan trees. My friend looked for Anjan trees all over the area because he was keen to learn more about this history. He went back to Raipur after failing to locate even one Anjan tree. Together with us on our way back, the superintendent of Shivpur's Botanical Garden suggested that we go meet the Raipur forest official in his bungalow. When he entered the bungalow's courtyard, he at last noticed the lone Anjan tree standing in front of him.

NK: What do you recall, Pranhita?

PS: We simply started laughing. I still recall how we searched for that tree for hours, walking deep into the forest, but we were unable to locate even one. Well, now it's unclear if the tree is still standing.

NK: Can you tell us about the work you did through Rupantar?

BS: Shankar Guha Niyogi was assassinated in 1991 and in July 1992, people who had been sitting on protest on the railway tracks, were fired upon by the police, in which 16 people died.[80]

Following that, we worked to offer the tribal people health care services. Our work began in Nagri Sihawa, which is now in the district of Dhamtari. We were experiencing a famine at the time because the crops had failed, and this was a forested area. We made rice stocks, or 'stocks for four', known as 'char Jhaniya'. People would engage in a variety of developmental activities in exchange for payment in grain. They would construct because we needed to build a small shed. The recipients and distributors were all primarily women.

The people found this idea appealing. It also gave the people more power to make decisions. The decisions were not made by us. We established health centres and clinics. Although I was the one running them, they selected the medical personnel whom we trained. There were several diseases endemic to the area and also a cerebral malaria outbreak. During the outbreak of this epidemic, many people perished.

We set up facilities for testing and treating blood slides. To ensure we don't lose time, these were set up in the villages to treat the patients closest to their homes. On certain days, I used to be able to identify every family member who had cerebral malaria by name as I strolled down the village street. Because we had established these village clinics for diagnostic and treatment facilities, we were able to prevent an enormous loss of lives. We also set up facilities for the diagnosis and treatment of Tuberculosis.

The government acknowledged the training programmes we had established for the women health workers in the villages called Mitanins (word for a woman friend in the Chhattisgarhi language). To create the training programme for these village health workers they established a committee. At the time, we had a relatively understanding bureaucracy, and Ajit Jogi was the Chief Minister.

However, no one discussed how to oversee the work of these health workers or how much money should be paid to them. There was no concept of standardising the work. At that time, I had written an article in the Medico Friends Circle journal about the health workers having raised pertinent questions at that time about[81] remuneration, control, how their work relates to the power structures in the villages, etc. It sparked much debate in the medical community. This begs the question of how Mitanins, referred to as ASHA workers in other states, would ensure knowledge transmission, have access to infrastructure, and obtain knowledge. Rather than offering a means of emancipation from healthcare disparities, they have evolved into the government system's lowermost ancillary health bureaucrats. After all, the Mitanins kept Chhattisgarh safe during the Covid-19 pandemic.

9

'I was wondering whether I would ever come out alive.'

Kobad Ghandy

After Dr Binayak Sen's arrest, the authorities thought they had made a significant breakthrough with the arrest of Kobad Ghandy. He was not an activist strictly speaking. However, the fact is the authorities were targeting even Maoist sympathisers.[82] *Kobad has indeed been a sympathiser of the Communist movement including its radical wing, the Communist Party of India (Maoist). Kobad, along with his late wife Anuradha Gandhy worked for many years in Vidarbha. They dedicated their lives to this cause, even giving away their worldly possessions and money for the same.*

Kobad was arrested in 2009 by the Delhi Police. In June 2016, Additional Sessions Judge Reetesh Singh acquitted Kobad in charges under Sections 20 and 38 (member of a banned outfit and furthering its activities) of the Unlawful Activities (Prevention) Act (UAPA). He was however convicted of cheating, forgery, and impersonation under provisions of the Indian Penal Code, for which he had already served. In October 2019, a court in Surat gave bail to Kobad in the sedition case on grounds of parity with other co-accused who had been released on bail.[83]

After his release, Kobad wrote his memoir, Fractured Freedom: A Prison Memoir,[84] *which has been translated in various languages and which received flak from many in the radical left circles. On a monsoon day in September 2022, Kobad finally got time to sit down with me for an interview. We decided on a café in Bandra. It was a bit noisy, but that is now the norm in any café. Kobad cycled to the café and sat with me for nearly two hours, speaking at length. I had just finished reading his book, and had pasted scores of post-it notes in my copy. Initially, I thought oh dear he has written it all in that book, yet as it emerged, there was still a lot to explore about an individual who had been incarcerated for over 10 years.*

Neeta Kolhatkar: Have you tasted true freedom, Kobad? How difficult has it been to adjust to the new way of life, being outside?

Kobad Gandhy: My last jail term was in Surat and I knew nobody in Gujarat. I got bail because the others were granted. The people handling my case and those of the others were mostly human rights lawyers. Actually, my sister has been there for me and she paid my bail. She brought me to her house once I was released. In Surat I knew I would be out soon, but my biggest worry was once I come out where would I go? I had sold all my properties and I didn't have any place (to stay). I was wondering who would keep me. Not one of my left associates offered me their place. They all have big flats, extra flats but not one of them offered me place. Till today, not one of them has asked me about my well-being. Anyway, my sister suggested I stay with her and she has been cooperative. Since then, I've been living in her house even though she doesn't agree with our ideology. I also found it difficult to adjust to such an upper-class atmosphere, but without her help I would have had no place to stay. This was around five to six months before COVID, when the lockdown was declared. It was first pure freedom immediately after release and then semi-freedom, locked in our houses. In these three years, the Parsi community and especially the *Parisiana* magazine and other community members have been extremely supportive (of me). The editor of *Parisiana*, Jehangir Patel, is an extremely nice person. On a few occasions, he has taken the trouble to send me medicines, and chlorine tablets and has been of much help. Such type of a nice feeling is there. Like I have mentioned in my book I have raised questions on philosophical aspects of the Communist movement regarding values, freedom and happiness. I found I am getting support, which has been refreshing. One didn't realise that ordinary, old, Parsis wanted to meet me. I never expected that.

NK: When did the idea of writing *Fractured Freedom: A Prison Memoir* take shape? Were you surprised by the support you received from the Parsi community along with that of your friends from Doon School?

KG: When I was arrested in Surat, I began to think of writing a memoir. Initially, I didn't have the intention because nothing was sure regarding my release, bail and all these issues. Where would I be staying? All was unclear. When I saw the possibility of getting bail, from then I began to conceptualise it. Around January 2020, I began looking for a publisher because I know nothing about the publishing industry. A few friends put me in touch with some publishers and soon the lockdown was declared. The lockdown was a boon for me, as I could focus on my book and there were no distractions. In fact, this book came out around March 2021 which gave me a lot of confidence as it has done well. Even my publisher Roli Books has promoted it excellently. I'm told it is still a bestseller on Amazon. The way it has sold, people do seem interested in reading about the possibility of a better future. I have kept the translation rights as I knew I could get it done inexpensively, so it has already been published in Marathi, Bengali, Punjabi, Hindi, and Kannada. It will soon be coming out in other languages as well. I've been told the Bengali version of my book has sold well in Bengal, though there is strong opposition from many of the Maoist circles. Marathi has sold the maximum, especially after the awards controversy and the publicity it got.[85]

I believe that the Maoist Party has written a 100-page paper attacking my book in English, Hindi, and Telugu. I am told it is sub-standard. It seems they have nothing better to do. I'm persona non grata in these circles. I have been in jail for 10 odd years and cut off from any civilisational contact let alone political. In fact, for 15–20 years I haven't been in touch with any organisation. I just find it pointless.

NK: Do you feel the authorities have kept track of you since the time you have been out?

KG: I haven't noticed anything as such. On the other hand, I feel they don't have the need to do keep an eye on me. They know everything. I am doing everything legal: I go to the courts and attend to all my case dates. If at all they want to watch me, it is if I was doing any organisational work. That they would want to know, but I am not interested in that. I am interested more in research, study and analysing what we have done and not done in the last many years. I want to dwell on those concepts. My talent was writing, even when I was an activist. I don't care whether they (*party people*) are disturbed by my writing because what is more important is the future: the future of humanity and our work. I feel that Dialectical Materialism and Communism is the best and there is no better alternative to it. The fact is, it has faced a setback because of the reasons outlined in my book, and I have given an example of Anuradha as the ideal Communist in my book. I had presented her as an example to be followed. Then I posed the concepts of freedom, happiness, and the question of values of simplicity, truthfulness, straightforwardness, etc; these model values were seen in Anuradha. I found these values missing at lower levels of the party; this must be worse at the higher levels throughout the Communist parties of the world. This has resulted in setbacks.

NK: The Parsi community is not known to revolt yet they have supported you. Does that come as a surprise? Also, do you think because you belong to an elite Parsi family the community has supported you? Is it typical of class and caste that exists in all our Indian communities?

KG: Yes, to some extent it could be, because class and caste is relevant in our entire society. A person who comes from an elite background is given support when he/she sacrifices everything for the poor and oppressed. But a poor person who joins the cause has nothing to sacrifice. It is another matter that most do not sacrifice and keep their wealth while also following Communism. I found this even among the police officers; they all respected me for this sacrifice which they said is rare these days. Maybe because I have been living by the ideals and because the Intelligence Bureau and other authorities knew that I had given away all my property and had nothing in my name. From that point of view, I got support from all jail authorities except those in Tihar. The officials expressed surprise and respected me from this point of view; in this day and age few individuals live by ideals for the poor. Now I've found this respect even among my Doon School alumni.

As far as the Parsi community is concerned, well that is also divided. Many years ago, when we used to live in Colaba, my neighbour, who is a Parsi, told me that while some people are against me, many are sympathetic. I think *Parisiana* has made a huge difference in influencing the community. In fact, I have personally sold 150 copies of my book, mostly within the Parsi community. There is a section of the Parsi community who are anti-Muslim and pro-Narendra Modi—some of my relatives too are like that. But there is a large section of Parsis who are ethical. My father was sympathetic towards us. The Parsis are sympathetic because of their ethical values and honesty. These are still prevalent among the general Parsi community. During my incarceration also I got a lot of support. Jehangir, the editor of *Parsiana*, in fact, came to Tihar jail, despite being nearly blind in one eye. Since the time I am out of jail, he continues to be extremely supportive of me. So, the community is supportive, because write-ups (about me) are being carried in *Parsiana* regularly.

NK: Speaking of your school mates at Doon School—Kamal Nath, Naveen Patnaik, Sanjay Gandhi, Ishaat Hussain, Gautam Vohra—it is a long list. How many distanced themselves? Are there any sympathisers?

KG: (*Laughs*). Actually, earlier on, I wasn't in touch with these people. First, college and then till 1972, I was in the UK. I wasn't in touch with all of them. After I returned, I was involved in my activism work. The only person who was in touch with me and even came to visit was Gautam Vohra. He is a maverick Leftist who has met Castro, Che Guevara and went on a march against the Vietnam War; he still has this spirit. He was one person who has throughout my entire stay in different jails, kept in constant touch with me. Practically every week I would get a nice postcard from him. Once he came all the way to Jharkhand to meet me in jail. He has been consistent in his views. To some extent because of him, others have come forward to support me. He tried contacting Kamal Nath and a few others who didn't respond; the others have. He even gathered money for my eye operation when I was in Tihar. He helped build the atmosphere of support for me. Ishaat initially wasn't in touch with me though he was my closest class friend. As I have written in my book, he said he pursued CA because of my father and me. Later he met me often in the UK and that was all. We lost touch since. He apparently asked Gautam if I would be willing to meet him. Since then, we meet every month. He is cooperative and sympathetic.

Gautam initiated a class WhatsApp group. Everyone is extremely well-read and progressive. Even though some are pro-Modi, there is no negativity. They are open to discussions and I had a lot of progressive discussions. Of course, there is a lot of humour too. Navzer Taraporewala is always sending us jokes. He lives in Malaysia and is extremely well-read. He has read Noam Chomsky and all. Where being a Parsi he has read all this, I wonder (*laughs*). I must say they are very sympathetic and nice. My classmates are positive, Parsis are sympathetic. The book is selling well and most are not Leftists and that is interesting.

NK: Had you at any time expected to be arrested and that too for such a long period?

KG: Yes, I was expecting to be arrested for the kind of work I was involved in. It was a possibility; it was collateral damage that one expects in this kind of work. We (he and Anuradha) were in Nagpur for many years and we didn't face much trouble then. But after that, things began to get tense. Anu went to stay in the forest for three to four years. It affected her health a lot. She returned to Jharkhand which is where she got a dangerous bout of malaria. That apart, the pressure was getting to all of us. We could see people getting arrested. The Andhra IB (Intelligence Bureau) people were overly active. People all over the country were getting arrested. Andhra IB officials, who detained me illegally for three days, said they were waiting to arrest me and thought they could do so when Anu died.

NK: How were you treated in prison?

KG: No one dealt with me badly actually. They all had some sort of underlying respect. I was kept in a special cell, but otherwise, it wasn't that bad. When I was taken for interrogation, the senior officer said he was looking up what 'Urban Naxals' meant on the Internet (*laughs*). I had been sharing a room in Delhi before my arrest with a Hindi speaking man who was an avid reader. There were books by Prem Chand and other authors lying around which they got from my room. There were many literary people in the interrogation team and they told me they were reading those books (*smiles*). They were mostly Hindi books. I got decent treatment in most jails, except the jail authorities in Tihar who were rough. I even got good judges. My lawyer, Rebecca John, is an excellent lawyer. She is a tough person who did everything for my cause, extremely warm and nice. And still, it took 10 years for me to get out on bail.

NK: That is a long wait to taste freedom, 10 years. Did you ever believe you would be released?

KG: The way things were dragging on, I was wondering whether I would ever come out alive. Only when I reached Surat did I have some inkling there could be a chance of me getting released. But then I was re-arrested at the gate. I first came out in 2017 and was re-arrested after three days and put in Jharkhand jail. Here too the superintendent was decent. I got a lot of time to write articles in that jail and I had the opportunity to write for alternate media, like Nikhil Chakravarty's *Mainstream*. They printed everything I wrote.

I tried to keep myself mentally fit and not get depressed.

NK: You were sent to different prisons, including Tihar. Can you tell us a bit more about the conditions of Indian prisons?

KG: At one time, Tihar was terrible; it has come a long way. Yet, it is no patch on the jails in Hyderabad, Vishakapatnam, Kerala or, I believe, even the Bengal jails. The rest are still run mafia-style, especially in Delhi. Everything in Delhi is like that, I suppose, even the politics. When Arvind Kejriwal came to power, I wrote two or three letters to him regarding jail reforms.

He didn't bother to respond. Everyone thought he (Kejriwal) would do something different because prior to him (Delhi chief minister) Sheila Dixit was a terror. I believe she never released anyone. I have a few memories of jail in London. They gave me a two-month term. All I remember was that I was given a room in a dark kind of chamber. I was given hard labour and had to carry potato sacks. You can't compare Indian jails. In fact, you can't compare the jails in the South (India) and for that matter in Jharkhand to the ones in Delhi. Tihar is the worst. In fact, when I moved to Hyderabad and Vishakapatnam, it almost felt like a hostel. The food was good of course because Andhra is respectful of Naxalites. Even in other places, they were nice, except Delhi.

NK: How did you ensure that you did not break down?

KG: I've seen almost everyone break down. From the beginning, I made it a point to have a regime for yoga and exercises in the morning and maybe sometimes a little bit in the evening. In Tihar, we were locked up practically the entire day. We were isolated, but I had Afzal Guru with me. He was extremely helpful and cooperative because it was my first jail experience. I spent most of my time studying and writing. I was not allowed, but I got an outlet to publish my work. I made it a point not to break down and keep my sanity intact. I ensured I was physically and mentally active all the time. I had a lot of health problems. I still managed. I had to fight to get certain things and towards the end, I was getting a bit frustrated. In Jharkhand, my case was going on and on, and I was not getting bail. That time I was getting a bit upset, but I made my mind strong. Delhi was bad. We got the court dates only after four months. So that really put me off. I would then divert my mind to studying and writing. I got an opportunity to study a lot in Tihar. Even though the Tihar jail officials didn't allow me access to the library, there was a good person there who got me books. Being a Naxalite prisoner, the jail officials didn't allow me to read books. Dreaded dons were allowed to read books, but they didn't allow me. It is as per the whims of every Superintendent. He was originally quite decent, but when he came back the second time, he was really nasty. Maybe at someone's instigation or what, I don't know, but that's when he transferred me and got me nearly beaten up. The dons were fine, decent people and respectful of me. As I have stated in my book, they are more decent than our politicians. They had no problem with me. They have other issues; they would carry or plant blade bars to attack us. They didn't do anything to me or Afzal Guru, but they planted blade bars inside the HRW (*the High Risk Ward where Kobad Gandhy and Afzal Guru were imprisoned*). As far as Gujarat was concerned, there were strict rules in the jail there. If I had stayed there longer, it would have got quite problematic for me.

NK: A decade of incarceration is enough to take a toll on one's mental health. Are there counselling facilities for prisoners and how are they?

KG: I have written on this issue. I have said that particularly Tihar jail is designed to break one psychologically. I noticed the same in Gujarat jail, and also Jharkhand (to a lesser extent). In AP we were given political prisoner status so it was different. But even without that, in the south, jails are said to be more humane. The Hindi belt and Gujarat were the worst. I was lucky to be able to keep myself occupied with my writings in *Mainstream;* these articles were smuggled out (one is not allowed to write in jail). Also, my strict regimen of yoga and exercises helped maintain my sanity, to some extent. Being in the high risk ward, though cut off from other prisoners, I was able to get a table and chair in the cell due to a court order, which helped me focus on my writing. In fact, a table was uncommon in the entire history of Tihar. Imprisonment, I have found in West Bengal, sufficiently breaks a person and most when they come out, prefer to take a nonconfrontationist approach, by allying with the CPM. In fact, the CPM cunningly uses a person's vulnerability to entice comrades into their fold creating the fear threat of re-imprisonment. The CPM acts as the defacto agent of the State, and radicals who have been softened in jail realise the CPM is acceptable to the State, and so convenient to associate with, as they can also thereby maintain their 'Marxist' tag.

Gujarat authorities and even Tihar do not allow writing material inside. Even reading books is only allowed in the jail library. I was fortunate to have managed to get both books and writing material, and even able to smuggle out my articles to be published in magazines and newspapers. We are not given a political prisoner status and are treated as ordinary criminals. In Tihar, I met the 2G Scam people who were put in the VIP ward. If one pays sufficiently, one can get any facility in jail. It is exceedingly corrupt from the ordinary guard to the top officials. Every benefit comes at a price.

NK: Can you elaborate a bit more on your interactions with the late Afzal Guru? You have written about your interactions with him in your book, like he would make chai for you and about your discussions with him.

KG: Everything served in jail is watery, the food and chai. From the very first day, when the gates would open, the jail staff would come with chai, and Afzal would call me to his cell. He had a white thermos. I had asked for it (after he was hanged), but the authorities refused to give it to me. I said give me that at least, if not his writings, but no. So, in that watery chai, he would add tea bags and milk powder. He would then make an excellent cup of tea. He hated Pakistan and the ISI, but felt strongly for a free Kashmir and he believed in it. Afzal Guru was well-read and he was sympathetic to Communist ideas, unlike all the other Islamists who were with us in the HRW. The others were all lumpen types.

Their only purpose of talking to you was to convert you to Islam. Afzal Guru was humane. He told me he was treated very badly in the first few years after his arrest. However, he would talk about it with no sense of grudge or bitterness. He talked about the people who were dealing with him and he felt betrayed by them. He was trying hard to get his case to Kashmir, which was his right. His wife was a teacher and couldn't come all the way to see him because it was expensive. He wanted to be closer to his family, which was his right. That is a right for every prisoner in jail, which he could have got had the lawyers tried. Probably the plan was to hang him, which they could not have done had his case been transferred to Kashmir. Afzal was angry with them because he saw what they were doing to him. He had an inkling the night before he was hanged. The jail authorities were preparing the cell. The night before, we saw things being prepared. We were all scared for him, but nobody wanted to say it. I felt I should have kept his diary at least. But how to ask him? It would have impacted him psychologically. We hoped for the best, but...(*pauses*)

NK: You have spoken of the reasons for the failure of Communism in India, that it has not taken cognisance of the caste conflict, especially the atrocities on Dalits. Can you elaborate?

KG: It is the Brahminical outlook that predominates. The kind of behaviour I'm seeing among party people is Brahmanical—a kind of cunningness, manipulation. There is more democracy in western society. Just like the relationship between any couple is more democratic. Here it is Brahmanical in the Indian context. It is a feudal ideology. Now, identity politics is dangerous. I'm opposed to identity politics. Even when we worked among the Dalits, we never blamed a particular caste. We said that the enemy is the ideology. The ideology which dominates the upper castes is everywhere in society. It is even prevalent among the poorest castes. India has very strong people traditions: Lokayatas, the

Buddhist tradition, the Bhakti movements. We have had leaders like Periyar, Dr Ambedkar, Jyotiba Phule. People's democratic traditions are deep-rooted in India, dating back 3,000 years and it has been continuous which is seen in non-Brahmin castes. Till now, not one Marxist has spoken about this. We have replicated Marxism directly from Russia or China, that's all, but we haven't Indianised it; which is to build on this non-Brahmanical tradition and peoples' democratic traditions. There is also a lot of folklore. At one time, the CPI had very good folk artistes like Annabhau Sathe and others, but they never theorised on these issues. The CPI has even written a book on caste, but not one word have they written on the Brahmanical ideology which dominates even subtly Left circles. Like one-upmanship and extremely bourgeoisie lifestyles (*laughs*). To Indianise Marxism is to take it to the people and also to fight the Brahmanical ideology within us. When I see comrades, they are so patriarchal, and it is all subtle. They won't beat their wives, but they will expect their spouses (women) to do all the housework. There is politics in it. The husbands will be doing the party work and the wives will accept domestic roles, even in a place like Mumbai. It is extremely deep-rooted as I see it and I am developing on this concept. This is seen in psychology where a thought is parked in the conscious mind; it is all scientific, but we are not paying attention to the subconscious which is ingrained in feudal and bourgeois thinking. In the West, there is more individualism. I found with my long association with the Left, we talked about values, but we never define them—proletariat values like simplicity and living with the masses. I don't see any other values being talked about like the declassing and criticism of leaders. It worked for some, but not across the board. That's why I talk of freedom and happiness as a concept. It is necessary to talk about them, and particularly in relation to Communist leaders.

NK: Do you have any regrets? Do you feel you could have spent more time with your wife in her last stage of illness as you have mentioned in your book?

KG: I don't have any regrets. Since I had so much experience, I can now write what I feel and I am not apologetic about it. Else I would have been defensive if I were bitter. Even after the criticism from the Left party, the boycotts they called for, all of which was reported in the newspapers and later I was expelled from the party. My lawyers in Hyderabad asked me not to get depressed. I told them nothing of that sort as I am not attached to such things. My attachment is to the future and to the youngsters. If we have done anything wrong, then hopefully the young will do better than us. I did feel in her last stages, I should have given Anu more time. In fact, I had made a decision in my mind but it was too late, by then she died. She had various ailments and also very bad arthritis. In those days there was no knee replacement or it was not so common. Otherwise, we had spent a lot of time together.

NK: Right from Father Stan Swamy, then Pandu Narote, Prashant Rahi and many others, including you.... Why do the authorities resist giving treatment to political prisoners? Is it deliberate?

KG: It is deliberate in a way. It is exactly like what we see even outside jails, everything is corrupt. If you have that kind of money to throw around, you can get best of medical attention. The prisons are extremely corrupt in the north, even in Maharashtra I'm told. In South India, it was much better. In Andhra I experienced this myself, and I've heard the same about Tamil Nadu and Kerala. In Andhra, the officers were decent people. In Jharkhand too, I have seen good officers. Even in Hyderabad I got good medical treatment. In Tihar I got good medical treatment as well, because basically I got good judges. They specified it in their orders. Maybe, I don't see that sort of due diligence being done in the Bhima Koregaon case. Now it seems more vicious and personal out here. In spite of the fact that the state and jail authorities were under a non-BJP government till a while ago. One thing is, they are portraying Naxals as terrorists in their circles and the jail authorities are also cruel. Their bosses tell them to do things and these men don't seem to take a different approach. Most importantly they are corrupt. Even in the Bilkis Bano case, the question of revision of arrested accused and releasing them, it made me angry. First it was 14 years for life imprisonment and some laws changed after a Supreme Court decision. It said the board has to sit after the arrested criminals completed 14 years of their sentence. This board has to sit every three months and they decide the total number of prisoners to be released. All those who had money would be released while others, mostly the poor, languished for 30–40 years. In Tihar jail, I remember the prisoners hated Sheila Dixit because she'd meet the board only once a year and hardly released anyone. I don't think Kejriwal is any better. However, things are different in the South. There, after 9–10 years, prisoners are released from jail. That's how it should be and not arbitrary as we are seeing today. This is not reflecting in any of the articles which talked about the release of the rape accused in the Bilkis Bano case. It is an arbitrary decision.

NK: In all the prisons you were kept, did the jail authorities know who a Parsi is and that you were a Parsi? What were their reactions?

KG: Interestingly, only in the Gujarat jail did they know what a Parsi is. (*Laughs*). They would ask me, a Parsi and a Naxal? You are in jail? There I was given very good treatment. You see, in jails we had to fill 'caste' in our forms at the time of entry. They'd ask what caste I belonged to and I'd say I don't believe in caste. Yet they would insist. I was forced to write and I ended up writing Parsi. None of them understood it. They were only concerned with filling that section and they would not bother beyond that. Even in Andhra, people don't know who a Parsi is. Only the police in Surat knew it, because that's where the Parsis first landed. Though it is Modi's heartland I still get respect when I go for my court dates there.

10

'There seems to be some sort of a central direction being given to all the prison authorities to act tough with the Maoist prisoners.'

MURALIDHARAN. K

Muralidharan was born in 1953, at Chitrapuzha in Ernakulam district in Kerala. His father was in the Indian Foreign Services and, as a result, Muralidharan lived abroad till the age of 11. He completed school and college education in Kerala and went on to pursue engineering. He left engineering in 1975 and became a full-time activist in the Maoist movement. He was mostly involved in its propaganda activities. His is a unique case of a political prisoner. He has been arrested twice: the first time during the Emergency.[86] *He was arrested again by the Maharashtra ATS in 2015 and charged under UAPA.*[87] *He has been out on bail since 2019, and till the time of writing, his trial is yet to start.*

Muralidharan was part of the editorial team of Comrade (a Malayalam bi-weekly) and MassLine (English monthly). He has also contributed articles to A World To Win, an international Maoist journal, and published a few books in Malayalam and English. Critiquing Brahmanism and Of Concepts and Methods were written while he was in Yerawada Central Prison. Some of his books have been translated into other languages too. Against Avakianism a polemical work, has been translated to Italian, Persian and Spanish, and Critiquing Brahmanism into Telugu and Tamil. Another book, Bhumi, Jati, Bandhanam (2002) (Land, Caste and Servitude) in Malayalam is a study of agrarian relations in Kerala, critically assessing the outcome of land reforms. Its second edition, with an English translation, is under preparation currently.

Muralidharan has to come once every three months to mark his presence at the ATS Kala Chowkie office in Mumbai. For this mandatory five-minute process, he has to travel back and forth, make arrangements for lodging, boarding, and food. He stays in Navi Mumbai and travels from there for his appointments. We decided to meet on one such day when he had to register his presence. We met at a café close to CSMT and what followed was a mix of alarming (for me, not for Muralidharan) and hilarious anecdotes that he narrated. By the time I reached at the specific time, Muralidharan was already seated and noticed who had followed him and the specific number of places he had spotted the same plainclothes person.

Neeta Kolhatkar: What have you been doing since your release?

Muralidharan K: I have been reading and writing; sometimes I give talks, attend seminars, and also have a podcast, on various topics like politics, and current affairs, but of course all of this is in Malayalam.

NK: You are out on bail, but of course you must be watched? Like do you see them at your talks or the seminars you attend? And how do you know you are being watched?

MK: Yes, of course (*laughs*). More than attending the same talks, they keep a watch on my home, I think they have infiltrated my cellphone, they have put a malware like Pegasus. I got strange emails, like one I got from the income tax department, saying I will be prosecuted if I don't pay my tax, with an attachment of course. (*Laughs*). It wasn't authentic. I contacted the income tax office, sent them an email and informed them I don't have any income to pay, as in taxable income. That mail I received was of course spam. Why should they send an email with an attachment?

NK: Do you think the authorities can get back at you, for your writing and political work?

MK: Oh, yes. They can always get back at me. (*Smiles*). That shouldn't stop me from what I am doing.

NK: Apart from what you stated earlier, are you being followed? Like today?

MK: Yes, even here. Even in Mumbai. From Vashi to here, I spotted the person following me, thrice. Actually, I will tell you (*smiles*), I had gone to the Centre for Development Studies in Trivandrum. I had gone to their library to read something. After calling up a friend who is a professor there and talking about it on the phone, we fixed a date and time. After I reached there, some officers from the Intelligence Bureau or the Special Branch contacted the director. It was absolutely unnecessary. They asked the director, what was the purpose of me being there and who was I talking to, etc.? The director asked the professor who informed him that I was sitting and reading in the library and he could go and verify with me if he wanted to. Then she (the professor friend) told me if she had such 24x7 bodyguards following her, she would be wearing all her jewellery (*laughs*). She asked me to recommend her name to these guys (IB officials). (*Peals of laughter*).

NK: What about in Kerala, do the officials keep a watch on you even there? The political environment is not against your ideology. That government seems sensible, even then?

MK: Yes. They keep a watch on me even in Kerala. Yes, they have killed eight comrades over the past few years. Yes, they are sensible (*laughs*). They were killed in encounters. Altogether there are some 70 UAPA cases in Kerala and a good majority of them are for people who were sticking posters on walls. It is done by the UDF government which is led by Congress and CPM. Both the parties are equally active in that matter.

NK: You have to come to Mumbai every three months to register your presence at the Anti-Terrorism Squad office in Kala Chowkie. Can you tell me more about it? Especially the kind of travel you have undergo, the expense you have to bear?

MK: As part of my bail conditions, I am expected to appear once in three months here. In fact, one of the bail conditions was that I had to come once a fortnight, twice a month, to Kala Chowkie. When I came out on bail, I didn't have any identity papers, you need those to travel. So initially, I had to take someone along with me, who had identity papers with them. It was pretty expensive, because I had to pay for the travel of two people and also for the stay. After one year, it was put in the bail order that I have to come once a month. Then we saw the outbreak of the COVID-19 pandemic. I filed an application in the Bombay High Court, to allow me to sign my presence in Kerala instead of Kala Chowkie, in order to avoid train travel. I made that application citing my age and health. The HC quite graciously amended it saying I could stay in Kerala for two months and then come to Mumbai every third month, risking Corona (*laughs*). That is how this once-in-three months business happened. Every month, I have to go to the local police in Kochi and the third month to Kala Chowkie. I also have all the required identity papers or cards. Now again, when you compare my bail conditions with what others got, the court was quite considerate. The seven Reliance workers who had formed a union and were charged under UAPA, they had to sign every seven days. They are all workers from another state. Not local residents, which meant they were forced to stay here in Mumbai. Or the conditions imposed on Varavara Rao, Sudha and others, that they can't leave Mumbai and go anywhere. I have been spared that.

NK: You have to undergo quite a lot of travel for this five-minute mandatory signing? Do you stay in Kerala Bhavan?

MK: Yes, so it is over a day's journey from Kerala to Vashi, where I stay. Then I take the harbour train and I have to sign between 10 and 11am, but all that is not a problem really.

NK: The day you were picked up from Talegaon, where was it from and were you aware that you were being followed? What were the officers like when they picked you up?

MK: I would go for morning walks every day and I was out early in the morning on that day too. I wasn't aware of being followed. It was unexpected when suddenly many of them pounced on me. There were quite a lot of them. They grabbed me and threw me into the car. They told me I shouldn't feel tense and they even told me, 'We are all on the same side' (*laughs*). In that case, I shouldn't have been sitting there in the first place. I just simply listened, because they were rather a humorous lot. They followed the usual standard practice drill, of blindfolding me and I had no clue where I was being taken. They said the only difference of opinion between them and me is on the use of violence. So, I told them they had put me in this car in a very non-violent way (*laughs*). After that there was no further conversation. *(We both laughed for a while).*

NK: Where did they take you finally after they removed the blindfold? Were you told which city or anything?

MK: In a room, in some interrogation centre, and I had no idea where I was taken. The following morning, I was produced in Pune court. Then I told the court they had kept me up late at night and interrogated me till 2am. That is a problem because I am a heart patient and I should be allowed to take rest. Accordingly, the court instructed the police, after which every day, the interrogation would end around 7pm. They would take me to the cell and keep me there till 8am. I was in custody for some nine days. I was produced in court again and then sent to Yerawada prison.

NK: When were you brought to the prison? Tell us something about Yerawada. Was this your first jail experience?

MK: I was taken to Yerawada around afternoon. No, this wasn't the first time. I was in jail during the Emergency. Jail conditions are not different largely. Only difference was around that time there were large number of CPI (ML) prisoners in the jail where I was kept in Kerala. That was quite helpful because it was my first experience and one gets support when there are other comrades there. Here in Yerawada, there was one comrade who had been arrested a year before, Arun Belke. His wife (Kanchan Nanaware) was killed due to medical negligence by jail authorities.[88] She was a heart patient and developed a brain ailment. She passed away in jail. He was in a separate barracks. In Yerawada, the cell was not shared. The entry to the prison and the process thereafter was similar to what I had experienced in Kerala. There are a lot of unnecessary things here in Maharashtra.

NK: Can you please explain this in detail?

MK: Say for example, according to the jail regulations in the prison manual, a prisoner is allowed to keep their personal belongings. If the person has a little more than what is specified, the prisoner is allowed to keep it in the storeroom with a record and he/she is allowed to collect it on the date of release. The jail authorities in Yerawada refused to let me take any extra belongings. I had a change of clothes and few things in my bag. They said the bag and a few other things would not be allowed and they told the police who had brought me to take these back. Somebody must have taken it or they may have even thrown it away. Another important thing, we are supposed to be provided with brand new bed sheets and towels, etc. They didn't give us brand new sheets. They gave laundered but old ones. We were not allowed to carry toiletries, so they gave me soap. The cell was quite convenient compared to my first experience. Those days it was crowded, like four of us in one cell. Here one person was in one cell and everything was within it. There was tap water, it was good, except during summer when they would ration the water supply; we would get it every alternate day. This became challenging later. When I went to jail, there were only 3000 prisoners in Yerawada and when I was released in July 2019, there were 6000 prisoners. Also, to keep up with so many prisoners, only one new barrack was constructed. So, you can imagine the amount of overcrowding and the natural stress on resources like water supply. More than the jail, I would blame the judiciary. They are simply sending people (to jail) without any rhyme or reason. Also, the number of kids that are being put in prison under the Protection of Children from Sexual Offences Act, 2012 (POCSO)! I met some 17-year-olds, 19-year-olds, who had fallen in love with girls. Then the parents of the girls caught them, put up a charge of rape against these boys and they were sent to prison. Only because the parents of the girls claimed they are minors. With the POCSO charge, it is tough to get bail. There are quite a few right now in jail. Then there are people who have been arrested for not repaying a debt on time. A large number of people are languishing in jail and it is totally unnecessary. As per the regulations of the Prison Manual, if male prisoners have completed more than half the period of their sentence, without the prisoner's case coming up for trial, they should be given default bail on his own personal surety, which has to be referred to the court by the jail authorities. This is not happening. A lot of prisoners don't even know of this law. Another issue is the jail staff comes under a lot of pressure due to the high number of prisoners. Especially the lower-level staff, they are not at all happy with the conditions in the jails.

NK: Were you allowed to interact with prisoners closely?

MK: Yes. The jail authorities tried their best to keep us (comrades) from interacting with the other prisoners, but we would get opportunities to speak. When we would go for regular check-ups to the hospital, or some would come to work in our barracks, then we'd chat.

NK: How was your day in jail? What all would you do?

MK: Oh! I was quite busy. In fact, I was most concerned that I won't have the time to finish all the things that I wanted to. (*Laughs*)

NK: Do share with us, like what all?

MK: Things I wanted to write. I would get up at 5am and do some yoga, exercises, and breathing exercises. Around 6/6.30am our cells would be opened. I would walk for around an hour, then tea would be brought. In fact, during the period when I was there (in Yerawada), the quality of food had greatly improved. The Superintendent who was in charge of the prison at that time, he was particular that the food quality should be good. He was absolutely dictatorial on a few other matters, but regarding the food quality, he was good. It was even tasty. It all depends on the person in charge. You see, this gives a lot of opportunity for corruption, but he wasn't corrupt in this matter. Now another thing, we were kept in the anda cell. It was a high-security cell inside the central prison. The quality and quantity of food served to the prisoners in the anda cell is much better than what is given to the other prisoners. Interestingly, when somebody from the barracks is put in the anda, they go in with a lot of fear because of the reputation the anda cells have. They feel they will have a horrible time and after a day, they come to realise that anda is the best thing that has happened to them. (*We both laugh heartily.*) The amount of food that they can eat in addition to having one cell completely to themselves, unlike the barracks where there is no space because of the number of people put there. The anda cell experience is like a five-star hotel one for the other prisoners. They sometimes want to find ways to come back to the anda cell.

Later, I was shifted to another cell, called 'Suraksha 3' barracks. Earlier, Suraksha 2 and 3 were the high security barracks. Prisoners who were to be sent to the gallows were kept here. If you have heard of the Chaphekar bandhu.[89] In fact, I learnt some interesting things in the jail. There is a Gandhi barracks.

NK: Oh! Interesting, are there are such barracks still in Yerawada?

MK: The interesting thing is that the Gandhi barracks are where the prisoners are taken to be beaten. (*What an irony!*) There is no camera there and it is called Gandhi barracks because there is a museum centre on Gandhi over there. Schoolchildren are brought to Yerawada jail to visit the Gandhi Museum. Obviously, their trip is usually conducted after these guys have beaten the prisoners.

Honestly, I respect Gandhi. Then there is a Tilak barracks and a cell where Sardar Vallabhbhai Patel was kept, that is maintained with a lot of honour. And the place where the RSS chief Devras[90] was incarcerated during the emergency is being preserved as a museum. But all the martyrs of India's freedom struggle like Chapekar bandhu and so many others who were hanged by the British have no mention there. There is not a single plaque or board commemorating them inside the barracks where they were kept. Outside the barracks on the flag pole there is something to the effect that a lot of people during the independence struggle were lodged here and something to that effect. What I am saying is that in the barracks where these people were kept before being taken to the gallows, there is no mention of them. There is another aspect to it, a popular myth among the prisoners and wardens, the morning bell when the cells can be opened, that rings seven or nine times.

NK: What is the myth? Can you tell us?

MK: The specific number of times the bell is rung is related to another hero martyr, Umaji Naik. Now Naik led a peasant uprising against the British in the Lonavala-Pune area. He was finally caught and hanged by the British. The story is that the British tried to hang him three times and every time the authorities failed, which meant he didn't die. Finally, they asked him what could they do to kill him. He gave them three conditions to fulfil. First, he said, there is an armlet or bracelet he had worn which was blessed. He told them to cut it off, but for that to happen, they had to first tell him who had betrayed him. They had to bring that person before him and then only the British would be able to hang him. Last, he said, the bell should toll nine times. The British readily agreed and it turned out his own sister had betrayed him. She was brought there and he killed her right in front of the British soldiers. After that, he allowed the British to cut off his armlet, the bell tolled nine times and Umaji was hanged. That is why the bell rings nine times in all of the state prisons. The interesting thing is, Yerawada did not exist at that time and this man wasn't hanged here. He was hanged in Katraj in a public place, yet nine bells ringing is a phenomenon which is prevalent in all jails across Maharashtra. It is only an urban tale among the prisoners. See how the prisoners honour the martyrs of our independence struggle while the authorities and governments have ignored them. It is a typical fairy tale, wherein a prisoner doesn't die three times and then he tells the authorities the method to hang him. (*Laughs*). People really believe it and some of the jail staff repeat this story often and say it really happened. I did some investigation about the bell ringing nine times in prisons across Maharashtra and then found that this man was hanged in Katraj and not Yerawada, because this prison didn't exist at that time.

NK: So, how would your day unfold after the walk? Did you get enough books to read? I have been told the women prisoners would get a rationed number of books and that too mostly in Marathi.

MK: After the walk I would eat breakfast and sit down to read or write. Aah, now that was one nasty thing about of Yerawada for some time. In Kerala, they never tried to keep prisoners from getting literature, be it novels, research or even political books. Except those that are banned formally, all books were given in jail. There have been several court rulings regarding this and specific regulations in the prison manual state that a prisoner can read whatever material they want, as long as it is not material that is banned. In fact, even a convict prisoner can keep 12 books with them, but in Yerawada they simply refused to allow that. They say only those books which are on their list can be made available. It is illegal to deny the prisoners the right to read. They would not just refuse books, they even prevented us from getting money orders until the person who sent it was verified by the authorities. It caused a delay and as a result, one couldn't even buy newspapers to read, except of course for those who would share their newspapers. I asked for a Marathi grammar book and dictionary and it was given only after a court order.

NK: (sounding appalled) You had to apply to the court for a Marathi dictionary? Now I want to know, does Yerawada have books in other languages, like English or Hindi?

MK: No, absolutely not. They don't keep books in other languages other than in Marathi, which is why I wanted a Marathi grammar book by Walimbe as well as a dictionary. Imagine, the jail authorities denied me permission to get even these two books. I was compelled to move an application in court after which I was allowed books from the jail library. Obviously at that time, I couldn't read and write in Marathi, so I asked for English books. Well, we got English books from the library which date from 1870. You won't even imagine, I got a first edition of a Charles Dickens book. I told the Superintendent this is a collector's item, he shouldn't keep it in the library and instead he should keep it in his office (*laughs*). This went on for three months and luckily the list of publications I was allowed to read included *EPW (Economic and Political Weekly*) issues. That was the only serious reading available and of interest to me.

NK: Were you given newspapers to read and did the jail authorities cut any articles which they didn't want you to read? Some others have shared such stories.

MK: Oh, yes, I got newspapers from which sometimes they would cut out a few articles which they didn't want me to read. That is the standard practice. But actually, it is meaningless because when you see something is cut out, you know it was important. I asked the warden what were the rules regarding this. If the warden was friendly, it usually depends on your equation, they will tell you. Most of the time, they cut out news items on jails because that is something they pay extra attention to. Like somebody jumping bail or jail or a fight reported in some jail. Otherwise even important news items like about something occurring in Dantewada is not edited or cut. Either they did not notice it or didn't realise it was important; I learnt of that incident from the papers. These prison employees also get bored, so one can understand their state of mind.

NK: Eventually did you get your books in Marathi? How was the progress in reading and understanding the Marathi language? Please tell me more about this?

MK: Yes, I got *EPW*s regularly; later, I was given the two Marathi books that I had asked for. Then I began learning the Marathi language. It was easy since I already knew Hindi and the Devanagri script was the same. I started getting Marathi books from the library. I mostly got literature books, autobiographies, and historical novels. I read an interesting novel, on the third Battle of Panipat, wherein the Marathas were defeated by the Afghans. It was different because it was written from a Dalit perspective. Interesting thing is at the end, the Maratha chief ran for his life and was saved by a Dalit who had been actually sent to kill the former. He was seeking revenge because the Brahmins of Pune had killed his father. The Dalit informs him of this and the Maratha chief, when he learns of the incident, commits suicide out of remorse. It is a very interesting novel. I would recommend this novel to all those who understand Marathi. At that time there was a Maratha man (in Yerawada) who discouraged me from reading it (*laughs*). I asked what was the problem, he defended himself saying it was not a good novel. He had read it and didn't like the Dalit perspective of the Peshwas and Marathas. I also read P. L. Deshpande and other Marathi authors. Another interesting book I read was on Lakshmibai Tilak. I am trying to translate that into Malayalam. It is called *Smritichitren*. I liked this novel because first, her way of writing is really humorous and sarcastic. She recounts her relationship with her husband Narayan Wamanrao Tilak, whom she has described as a short-tempered man. She ends the chapter with 'Zala, amchi ghari jayacha kshan ala' [Now it is time for me to go back home (maternal) home]. Wamanrao was a renowned kirtankar (those who sing praises of gods or eulogies) and they lived together and he didn't force her to convert to Christianity (Narayan Tilak had converted to Christianity). Much later, she converted of her own free will. He had suggested they should divorce because she wasn't willing to convert. Lakshmibai said she will not divorce because they had a son and he needed a father. They lived separately for a few years and then again, they decided to live together. At that time in one house, they had two separate kitchens and then out of her own will, she converted to Christianity. She had, in fact, till then practised Hindu traditions and rituals strictly. So much so that during one of her journeys, travelling on a train, she stayed without food and water for many hours as she wouldn't take it from the hands of another person, who of course wasn't of her caste. Once she had to eat food cooked by somebody from another caste; she learnt of this later. She thought over this incident and realised she needed to overcome her caste inhibitions. Once she did it, she converted to Christianity. Then, after converting, she adopted a Dalit girl whom she had seen on the streets. Later when she took the girl to meet other Christians, they chastised her for adopting a Dalit girl. It is ironical (*laughs*). I started reading Marathi books with Tilak's *Gita Rahasya* or *Karmayog Shastra*. I used that as a foundation to learn Marathi, apart from the grammar. It uses heavily Sanskritised Marathi which is easy for me to understand because even Malayalam has a lot of Sanskrit words. You get the gist of what the person is trying to say and later I began picking up even the nuances. That was critical and I began focussing on various Brahmanical philosophies, ethics and things like that. When I read P. L. Deshpande, he is quite similar to one of our Malayalam authors, VKN. He is extremely sarcastic and humorous, and made fun of everything on this earth, especially the higher-ups. Deshpande is quite similar in his *Batatyachi Chawl* and such books. While going through the library catalogue, I saw a *Marathi sahitya charitra* book, or the History of Marathi literature. I thought it would be interesting and I got it from the library. It turned out to be a thin volume. I was rather taken aback, a volume on Marathi literature and so thin! I began to read and the first thing that caught my attention was a sketch by Jyotiba Phule. We have a person hammering away at a rock. That is the first person who has written in Marathi. From there the story starts and the last sketch is of one of the Bhakti poets of Maharashtra. It is a family portrait, the Bhakti poet, his wife, and the number of abhangs they have all sung. All the way behind them on the wall are photographs of Vithoba and Rukmini bai. It is an altogether humorous take on Marathi literature. I could not understand much of it though it is written in Marathi. Interestingly, I read a word in it and I checked it in the dictionary I had. It is a standard dictionary and that word was not there. Then I got another dictionary which indicates the etymology of words. This word showed the origin was in Prakrit. Phule used to write in original Marathi words and not the Sanskritised version. The other interesting thing is, one of the mastermind killers of Narendra Dabholkar, Govind Pansare, MM Kalburgi and Gauri Lankesh, Dr Virendrasinh Tawade was in the adjacent cell. I asked him the meaning of those words but he couldn't explain them. He could get a sense of it, but couldn't tell me the exact meaning. In the other adjacent cell, there was a Dalit boy and he was one of the accused in the Kopardi rape case. I asked him and he gave me the exact meaning. I asked him how he was so sure. He told me they commonly used that word in their village. Then I realised why I could understand Tilak and not Phule. The interesting part is this phenomenon has repeated itself in all the South Asian languages in more or less the same period. In Maharashtra, you had Vishnushastri Chiplunkar and in West Bengal you had Ishwar Chandra Vidyasagar. Bengali is also a highly Sanskritised language and the person responsible for it was Vidyasagar. In Kerala too, we have these Brahmins who always tried to trace Malayalam to Sanskrit instead of Tamil. It is interesting to study the role of colonialism in the re-promotion of Brahminism in the usage of languages. Another thing I realised was that autobiographies and biographies written by women in Marathi are far more interesting than those written by men. In both the style of writing and range of topics they have covered—the inner world and outer world and their links—as compared to the male authors. I'm a fast reader so I read many books.

NK: Did you have any conversations with Dr Tawade?

MK: Yes, we did have a few. He was kept in the anda cell and he would be locked for nearly the whole day. He was let out only after we were sent back in our cells. We were quite an assorted lot of people. In one cell, there was Pappu Kalani and a Muslim man from Hyderabad. While he was religious, he was broadminded in most other ways. Then there was a don of Pune, Bapu Nayar. His parents were originally from Kerala, he was born in Pune, and went on to become one of the top dons of the city.[91] Coming back to Tawade, we were the ones who assisted him by giving him water, food and other things. Then both of us, Tawade and

I were shifted to Suraksha 3. I think they wanted to shift Tawade out, but it would be easily noticed, so they first moved me out and then followed up with Tawade. He did have issues with my ideology. Once other people started coming into the barracks, he tried to vigorously dissuade them from having any relations with me. (*Laughs*). *(I was shocked, asked why?)* Because I'm a Comrade.

NK: Arre! He ate your food, drank your water and what gall he does this to you?

MK: (*laughed*) So what? Those are different matters. I would say that was a typical Brahmanical way of doing things. But it would rebound, because I was friendly with everyone and was helping them in whichever way I could. I've even gone against the authorities if anyone of them were to be attacked or when they were beaten. Naturally when this person went around telling the other prisoners, don't talk to him, don't discuss matters with him, they would ask him why? He would tell them some things about Communism and instead they would get more attracted to Communism (*we both laughed*). It seriously boomeranged on him. I call them hypocrites for all their claims. Actually, the whole theory they have is based on explicit beliefs that Brahmins and Kshatriyas are born to rule.

NK: Did you boycott him and stayed away?

MK: No. The other prisoners strongly wanted to isolate him, but I opposed it. It is generally our (Communist) policy that we shouldn't create conflicts among prisoners. Prisoners should stand united against the authorities whatever may be their personal contradictions. I would never encourage conflicts towards one another.

NK: How did the authorities behave with you?

MK: I felt harassed when they refused to give me literature and books. Till the very end they continued to do this. Apart from this there was no harassment. From what I learnt, after I came out on bail, the atmosphere inside the jail has changed. For example, the Superintendent of the Taloja jail was a better officer than in Yerawada. But he was the one who refused the straw/sipper to Father Stan Swamy. The fellow Comrades were treated rather badly in Taloja and Byculla. See, what is happening in Kerala jails where the prisoners are being refused books, the harassment they face and if they complain they are put in solitary confinement. These things never used to happen in Kerala earlier; there seems to be some sort of a central directive being given to all the prison authorities to act tough with the Maoist prisoners. It cuts across all states. Now prisons are a state issue, but we see prisoners are being harassed. Though there is a court order that the prisoners should not be stripped and searched, and instead X-ray and scan machines should be used, the officials refuse to do it. They claim that order is only for one person and not for all prisoners. There is a visible change in treating Maoist prisoners in jails compared to when we were there. In Hyderabad, there is a huge prisoners' struggle on various issues and there have been historic uprisings against prison officials. Prison guards have been severely beaten by prisoners. Conditions in prisons in Hyderabad have been greatly influenced by such incidents. In Kerala, as I said, during the emergency, there were two types of (political) prisoners: those who were arrested under MISA, Maintenance of Internal Security Acts, and others like us who were arrested as mandate prisoners; we were locked most of the time in our cells. MISA prisoners and convicted prisoners were left out most of the day. Once the emergency was lifted, slowly prisoners were let out. During the emergency, literature was freely available and we were allowed to write letters every week to magazines and newspapers. There was no holding back; of course, you couldn't write about prison conditions. But if you wrote about other things, they would pass it on. Also, if we wrote to the publishers in Kerala that we wanted certain books they would send them to us. We had the jail library and within the high security barracks there was another cell which was our library and we could keep our books there. There was no hindrance like what we are seeing now. I am told in the high security jail in Thrissur, prisoners are not allowed books and they don't allow the prisoners more than five books at a time. One prisoner was interested in learning about Islam, to counter political Islamic ideology; his request for reading books was refused and when he raised the matter in court, he was put in a solitary cell as punishment. This, despite several court rulings to the contrary. As I said, there seems to be some sort of instructions from the Centre on this matter because there is no reason why such developments should take place in Kerala.

NK: The philosophy of a prison is to rehabilitate a person. However, we are seeing authorities continuing to place impediments and deny basic rights like allowing simple things like literature, books and other such things. Or do they deliberately give only Marathi books if you ask for English?

MK: I don't think that is happening. For example, I also read a book on emotional intelligence in English, which was recently published. If somebody gets a book like that, reads it and contributes it to the jail library then one can get it. Prisons accept books. The copy of *Gita Rahasya* I was reading, after completing it, I handed it over the Yerawada prison library and they accepted it. It is interesting that the jail library didn't have a copy of Tilak's book. (*Laughs*). That too in Yerawada, Pune, though there are Tilak barracks. The other aspect, of making prisoners suffer, that is certainly happening. Like those prisoners serving the death sentence: according to the Supreme Court rulings, the prisoners who haven't exhausted all the appeals, they have all the rights like any other prisoner. He should not be put in isolation. He should not be given any other work, alright. But everything else should be equivalent to other prisoners. A number of my students; I taught a lot of prisoners English and Hindi so that they could read and write these languages. I was put in the barracks where there were death row prisoners. Few of them wanted to learn Marathi, I taught them the Devanagri script. One of them was a graduate, some were tenth pass and one was less educated. I suggested they can enrol for some external course and pursue higher studies. They insisted I should request for them. I said, no. They had to make up their minds and write to the prison authorities themselves. The Superintendent didn't reply so they asked the jailor and he told them it wasn't allowed. When I had an opportunity to speak to the officers individually, I asked them why they weren't allowing the prisoners to study as per the law. The reply he gave was revealing. He said if they allowed that, they would get a favourable remark in their appeal. That is the mindset of making people suffer for the crime they have committed. Now, the officer who gave me that reply was also a Dalit, so he was not suffering from a caste bias. There was a caste conflict there in the Kopardi case, the girl was a Maratha and the three were Dalit boys. The officer believed they should suffer and there was no question of letting them complete their studies and using that in a later appeal.

NK: Do you have to be rich to get things moving in jail? Like new caste lines in prison?

MK: Aah. Yes. Money speaks, but not just money. You have to be a don. Dons are very useful in jail to control other prisoners, especially in the barracks. The don decides who sleeps where and who gets what. If anybody tries to assert their rights in whatever limited way, it is the don who intervenes before the prison authorities. The dons treated me well. They think we are bigger dons than them. (*Both of us burst out laughing.*)

NK: You are not serious?

MK: One of them actually told me, we deal in crores, you guys deal in billions. We, as in, our party. He said we are super dons, walking around with AK-47s and guns. An interesting experience I had was when I was put in the lock-up at the time of my arrest. There was a gang of Dalit youths who were in jail for a murder. It was a supari job and each one got Rs 5 lakh for that killing. I asked them what did they do with the money? How long did it last? They said, out of that total amount, they were spending Rs 2 lakhs in engaging a lawyer and getting out of jail. Out of the remaining Rs 3 lakh, they said, 'Goa jayenge, thoda ghumenge, phir dusra job lenge' (They will go to Goa, travel around for two-three months and take up another supari job). 'Aisa doh, teen kaam karega toh don notice karega. Phir uske gang mei shamil honge' (After taking up a few such hit jobs, the don will notice and induct us in his gang). That was their goal. But the moment they got to know I was arrested as a Maoist, the first thing they asked, 'Ghoda hai kya?' (*Ghoda is slang for a gun*). I asked, what have I got to do with horses?

NK: Hahaha, don't tell me...that was your answer? You asked what have you got to do with horses?

MK: Yes. I said, 'Nahi. Mere paas koi ghoda voda nahi hai' (I don't have any horse). I didn't know it is a slang for guns. The Hindi I know, ghoda means horse. They were pretty disappointed when I denied any knowledge of guns. It also could be that they thought I wasn't revealing information, who knows. But they were very helpful. They told me, 'Give us your family's phone number, because most probably you will be finished tonight. 'Aapka encounter hoga Naxali ka encounter karna hai' (You will be killed in an encounter). Naxals are often killed in encounters. That is understood. So give your family member's number we will inform them. I told them I didn't think they were going to kill me otherwise they wouldn't have brought me here. I thanked them for their concern. After this, our interaction was over.

Now, the next day I was put in another lock-up where there were two other youths. One was arrested in a fraud case and the other was caught for smuggling ganja. One of them asked, 'Abhi bhi khada hota hai kya?' (Do you still get a hard-on?) 'Haan khada toh hota hai, kya hua? Abhi khada khada hoke aya. Kya problem hai?' (Yes, I still stand. Why? What is the problem?). The other one said, 'Aisa nahi hai. Khada hota hai kya?' (Not like that. Does it stand?)

NK: Means?

MK: They were asking whether I could get a hard-on. I asked why do you ask this? One of them said, this question was on his mind for a long time since he was sent to prison. He wanted to know if he would become impotent when he got old. Now that I had walked in and was an older person, they said they could ask me. Who else could they ask such a question? Here I was in front of them so they found the courage to ask me. I said, 'Abhi bhi khada hota hai, koi problem nahi hai' (I'm still potent there is no problem, don't worry). He actually asked, 'Sach bolta hai kya?' (He wanted to ensure I was telling the truth). I told him I wasn't lying. 'Haan abhi bhi hota hai. Tension mat lena.' He was quite happy after that.

NK: With all that is happening in our jails, there seems to be such a dire need for education and sex education. Also, it is said that the dons treat rapists extremely badly in jail. There is some unwritten rule among them, have you heard of it?

MK: Oh yes. I have written about it in my memoir, *Yerawada Smaranagal* which is in Malayalam. There was a don in our barracks. He was the sort who belittled men who had raped women. He would say a rapist is not a man. The same person was sexist in his remarks and would boast of the number of women he had used and discarded. That was his mindset. I asked him how this squared up. It was a contradiction, that on the one hand he was talking about women in a derogatory manner and on the other hand he would get angry with the man who had raped a woman and treat him with disdain. He responded, 'Aisa koi mard karta hai kya? Phukat mei kaun karta hai?' He said the rapist had taken advantage of a woman, not paid and not given anything to her, like protection, money or any such thing. If he were to seduce a lady, then for that period she was with him, he would have provided security to her. It means he had brought some value to her life. He said no man rapes, because it is making use of a woman for free. I felt this attitude simply emerges from a patriarchal outlook; it has nothing to do with sympathy for women.

NK: Do they torture in jails?

MK: Prisoners are beaten up. First at the entry point and often in the lock-up, they would beat prisoners. On two occasions we had to intervene and stop it. We shouted and created a ruckus after which the prison authorities had to stop beating an inmate. One of these Kopardi boys was beaten inside the jail. When I shouted, they stopped. They came and tried to explain to me. I said, whatever case it may be, you have no right to beat a person, let the court decide. They do that often (beat prisoners). In the barracks, like I said, it is the dons who first carry out the punishment. Kopardi was a political issue and a caste conflict, so in their case, the dons couldn't interfere. If they had, then it would have been blown out of proportion. In fact, when the boys were sentenced, they were kept in an inside cell by the Superintendent, which was unlike the usual practice. Usually, they are taken to the holding barracks where they are beaten up and then produced before the Superintendent where again they are beaten. This is the usual drill. Maybe just a slap, but that was standard practice; especially for those convicted of rape, they were always beaten. In this case, due to the political repercussions, the dons and the jail staff didn't beat the accused.

11

'His bail is jail for me.'

P. Hemalatha

After Varavara Rao, known as VV, was charged under the UAPA in the Bhima Koregaon case and arrested on November 17, 2018, he was initially kept in Yerawada prison, in Pune. He was later moved to Taloja jail in Mumbai, where VV's health deteriorated. He suffered tremendously, which his fellow comrades and inmates, Vernon Gonsalves and Arun Ferreira brought to the notice of his wife, Hemalatha, and their family members. In response, Hemalatha wrote an open letter to all the authorities, and also held a conference online. She received considerable international support, which helped put pressure on the Indian authorities. She finally approached the National Human Rights Commission and later, she also moved the Bombay High Court wherein she said that VV's rights under Article 21c of the Constitution of India have been violated by the prison authorities. She stated that her husband's health had worsened in prison and that he needed to be shifted to a private hospital. He was eventually moved to Nanavati Hospital, where he recovered and his family believes this helped him to stay alive.

VV was given bail on medical grounds by the Supreme Court on August 9, 2022 for six months initially, but this condition was deleted later. One condition that continued to be imposed on him was that he had to live in

Mumbai. Today, VV and Hemalatha are forced to live in the distant suburbs of Mumbai. Like Sudha Bharadwaj, they are in a completely new city, where they are not mobile as they would have been if they were living in their home town. They are mostly housebound. Hemalatha speaks broken Hindi which she picked up living in Mumbai and interacting with her domestic help. Both of them are unable to commute frequently and their main concern is about whom to call in case of any emergency; they wonder who can come to help and where would they go?

In Mumbai, they have been forced to shift houses four times and are still struggling to adjust in this unfamiliar city. Hemalatha, who has in the past travelled late at night from Warangal to other cities to meet her husband in jails and courts, finds it difficult to find her footing in this new large city now. At 83, VV is not allowed to publish his writings, or speak freely and most of all he cannot interact with people, something he loves doing the most.

Hemalatha, who comes across as a silent supporter of her husband, is also a fighter. She accepted VV's proposal when she was in her teens, completed her education till Grade 10 and then settled into family life. Initially, this naïve young girl knew her husband to be a romantic poet and one who wrote on general issues. As VV got influenced by the Naxalbari movement, he began to include Hemalatha in his activities, explaining the concept of social justice to her. During 1973–74, she even became the editor, publisher and printer of Srujana (Creativity), a progressive magazine started by VV. At quite an early stage in life, Hemalatha got to learn about prisons and court procedures. In fact, she too was charged under MISA and the sedition law for publishing a few poems and writing an editorial on the Indian Railway strike of May 1974.

Varavara Rao's long poem 'Samudram' and 30 other poems translated into Hindi were published as Sahas Gatha. This collection was edited by Shashi Narayan Swadheen, Nusrat Mohiuddin, and published by Vani Prakashan of New Delhi. While Varavara Rao was in jail at the time of this book's release, Vikalp Samskrutik Manch, Bhagath Singh Vichar Manch and All India League for Revolutionary Culture conducted a conference titled

'Attack on Freedom of Expression' in New Delhi. I have reproduced below the text of the speech delivered by Hemalatha on December 3, 2005, at the Sahitya Academy meeting hall in Mandi House, Delhi.

Companionship in a Journey of Courage

Before Valmiki transformed into a Maharshi, while he was still a hunter, he hunted and killed animals for food. Apparently, his wife had to share the consequences of his sins as she cooked and ate the food with him. However, it seems like she didn't get a share in his fame or the fruits of his tapasya (penance).

VV and I have been married for four decades now and our life together started here in R K. Puram, Delhi. Jawaharlal Nehru University (JNU) did not even exist at that time. He was well known as a passionate poet but neither he nor I had firm political convictions at that time. We had no one here in Delhi. Friends back in Telugu land were urging us to go back home.

The *Srujana* magazine experience solidified VV's political beliefs as well as mine. *'Sahiti Mitrulu'* (Friends of literature) founded the *Srujana* magazine in November 1966 in Jadcharla town. *Srujana* picked up revolutionary fervour and momentum as it moved to Warangal town in October 1968. The formation of Virasam (Revolutionary Writers Association) on July 4, 1970, and its first conference in October 1970; the ban imposed on 'Jhanjha' and the *March* poetry collections in 1971 and; the arrest of *March* magazine's publisher Pendyala Kishan Rao precipitated the police interrogations, harassment and surveillance on us.

Our political beliefs have been under constant threat since 1992 and it was a long period of repression prior to that as well. In the last 15 years, VV was in jail only for a few days until August 17, 2005. But the sense of threat and insecurity has haunted us in Hyderabad since 1993.

The enthusiasm of Virasam members and their families who participated in the Virasam literary classes in Warangal in October

1973 evoked a feeling of a literary commune in everyone. Soon after that meeting, VV was arrested under the MISA Act, along with M.T. Khan and Cherabandaraju. I took over as the publisher of the *Srujana* magazine, which was the beginning of my active involvement in his political responsibilities. *Srujana* published 200 issues and was discontinued in May 1992. During that time, a Sessions judge charged me with sedition for publishing the issue supporting the Railway strike and while sentencing me to two years of rigorous imprisonment declared, 'In spite of being a mother of three daughters, she has no remorse.' VV responded by penning my feelings as a poem, 'If the sun rises in the West, I will express my remorse, My Lord!' I was in jail until the High Court struck down the case in 1977 and in police custody in 1984 and had to endure the experience of plain-clothes policemen attacking our house with axes. My three daughters and I lived under persistent pressure and duress during 1974–90. VV was either travelling across the country or imprisoned during that time. To quote VV's favourite Bahadurshah 'Jafar', 'If these four decades were four moments, two passed by in longing and two in waiting.' The period that my children and I lived in Kumarpally, Hanmakonda from 1974 to 1990 is comparable to the beginning of Charles Dickens' *A Tale of Two Cities.* Our home was not only the centre for literary creation but also for radical student and youth movements. Our home was known as the 'Swarna Mandir' for conflict, tension, surveillance, and security. The radical students all over that street and town addressed me as 'Akka' (sister) and were always there to support me.

Even though the circumstances were not tense, I had a similar experience during our life in exile away from home in GTB Enclave, Delhi from 2000 to 2004. The Hindi-speaking brothers and sisters also called me 'Akka' and took wonderful care of us. Because of my limited Hindi, most of my communication with them was only through heartfelt emotions. The world of radical student youth who stole our hearts with their love and affection brought me here today.

Our life in Hyderabad for the last 15 years felt like a kind of an exile too. VV is probably a poet in exile. He wrote most of his poetry, published in 10 collections including *Swechha* and *Muktakantham*, while he was in jail. His poetry, whether in *Samudram* or *Unnadedo Unnatlu*, is a poet's battle cry in his internal and external conflicts. My connection with him, however, is not similar to that of a reader with a poet or of a people with an activist. It is a connection of life that has witnessed his innermost and outer worlds. Poetry is a small part of it. The movement is a big part of it. My children and I have witnessed a huge aspect of his life that no one else has. A loving relationship shares dreams and hides secrets within itself. It hides its cowardice with smiles, weaknesses with generosity, lies with profundity, and separation with anticipation. Poetry, on the other hand, reveals them. Thus, poetry is a confession of wounds.

VV's world is vast and multidimensional—Literature, politics, people's movements, friendships, acquaintances, prison, journeys, reading, writing, etc. My world is with him, when he is with me and mostly when he is not with me. So, I cannot view his poetry as separate from that world. Our struggle alongside him for better times has brought us close to all of you.

On the morning of August 19 this year, when some people in civil clothes attempted to kidnap him from our house, my youngest daughter Pavana and I resisted them for hours until the media arrived at 5.30am. Then the police in uniforms arrived. After he was arrested, I accompanied him in the police van to the Chadarghat police station, made certain that he was being legally arrested and met him in the court that evening. Just like I did 32 years ago, I have been meeting him in the Chanchalguda jail which is just a stone's throw away from our house. This imprisonment is a free security for his life in this adventurous journey, for now. We have been walking hand in hand with poetry so far.

Incarcerations, bans and censorship, attacks on our house, threats to life and living in exile because of *Srujana* magazine, Virasam and our political beliefs—these sum up the last 41 years of our life. A life that I shared with him with 'Love alongside all its sorrows and joys' in VV's own words. His life, which has been dancing on the edge of a sword for 35 years. Our well-wishers, our children and I who have been constantly vigilant and agonising through the years. And all of you who have been by our side. This courageous story is a collection of all these experiences.

I met Hemalatha along with her brother Venugopal, who is the author of The Making of Varavara Rao: An Intimate Portrait by a Nephew. He is also a poet and journalist.

Neeta Kolhatkar: You mentioned in that speech in Delhi, how you have been called Amma and Akka by many youths. What are your memories?

P. Hemalatha: My thought process completely changed after I became actively involved in the publication of *Srujana*. A number of intellectuals, fearless fighters and well-wishers had become my trusted friends. They treated me like their sister or their mother and called me 'Akka' (elder sister) or 'Amma' (mother). I learnt a lot from them. What still bothers me is that the youngsters who called me 'Akka', whom I fed with my own hands and who were helpful to me in times of need, have lost their lives in fake encounters! My eyes fill with tears when I recollect those incidents.

NK: How were the early days of your marriage? Were you aware of your husband's Naxal leanings?

PH: In 1970, VV was one of the founder members of Krantikari Lekhak Sangh—Revolutionary Writers' Association, called Virasam in Telugu, an acronym of Viplava Rachayitala Sangham. When we married, he wasn't influenced by Leftist ideology. His family was mainly Congress. He wrote progressive poetry and also wrote romantic poems. In 1966, VV founded a group called Saahithee Mithrulu (Friends of Literature), which started a literary journal called *Srujana*. It was published till 1992, for 26 years. Initially, it was a quarterly but from 1971, it became a monthly. It was a Telugu magazine for modern literature and went on to become the unofficial voice of the revolutionary literary and cultural movement. In 1966, there was a cultural revolution in China and this had a huge impact on the youth in Bengal, Andhra Pradesh, and other states. This was a turning point in VV's life. He was first arrested in October 1973, for his writings. He was in jail for 36 days under MISA (Maintenance of Internal Security Act, 1971) which was repealed by the Janata Government in 1977). I was allowed to meet him twice a week and they would let us sit at a table face-to-face, in the jailer's room.

NK: Can you tell me a little bit about yourself, Hemalatha?

PH: I was born in a different environment. It is quite different from the way I am now travelling. Ours is an orthodox family from Rajaram, which is situated in Warangal district is our village. Varavara Rao's native village is Chinapendyala. My father had great affection for me. He believed that I was born as a divine gift from God in whom he had great faith. My mother's family directly participated in the anti-Nizam struggle. The feudal ideology was prevalent in my father's family but, after establishing relations with my mother's family, my father held a high regard for their ideas and feelings. He never discriminated against anybody on the basis of their caste or creed. He used to treat everyone's faith with great respect. But my father believed in the existence of God. In fact, my father's name too is Varavara Rao.

NK: Tell me something about your marriage.

PH: My marriage was a sensation... My marriage with VV was a turning point in my life. VV is my maternal uncle. When he expressed his interest in me and that he wanted to marry me, it created a big sensation in our family since getting married to one's sister's daughter was against our family tradition. My grandma was not in the mood to accept this proposal. My father consulted several experts who were thorough with our traditions and customs. He had a strong feeling that his son-in-law should be an educated one and a well-behaved person. Our people did not find any strong reason to reject the proposal put forth by VV. After being completely satisfied, my father performed the marriage in a grand and traditional way. Since I was young then, I did not have any fixed opinion about marriage. I did not say no to this proposal because my uncle was good.

NK: Were your parents supportive, since your political journey hasn't been an easy one?

PH: My father was well versed with the Vedas and other scriptures. He had a clear understanding of his chosen path of theism. With the same commitment he respected our (VV's and my) atheism too. Our mother and father wished that their girl-children should be well educated and accordingly they helped and guided our education. They donated a piece of land in our village to start a school to provide educational facilities to all the children of our village! My father never questioned our concepts and our ideology. When VV actively participated in politics, or when he was arrested and taken to jail, my father used to take care of us. In times of severe oppression, when the authorities would raid our house and when we were required to attend at courts, my father and mother stood by us solidly. My mother once told us that sometimes her neighbours insisted on commenting, 'Does your younger brother not love his wife and children? You ask him to swear on his children that he should leave his politics hereafter.' She would reply promptly, 'My brother is not doing any wrong thing. He loves his wife and children more than his life. I will never instruct him to take such a vow.'

NK: Venugopal, VV's family had been politically connected and close to the Congress government, yet he was arrested. Isn't that an irony?

N. Venugopal Rao: Hahaha... He was arrested many times during 1973–83, which was a time of Congress-governed Andhra Pradesh. In 1983, for the first time the government changed. Initially, VV wrote romantic poetry. No political writings. VV's family had literary and political influence. His three older brothers were writers prior to 1946. When VV was four years old, his older brother had published a book of short stories. Politically, his family supported the Congress Party. Two of his brothers were in the Congress party during the Nizam's time in 1938, even though the Nizam had banned the party. In fact, his eldest brother was a mentor of our two-time Prime Minister, the late P. V. Narasimha Rao.

In 1964, after the death of Pandit Jawaharlal Nehru, VV wrote a poem on him. Thereafter, VV moved away from Nehruvian socialism. He wasn't influenced by the Congress Party and they too knew of his political leanings, so in that sense what followed was no surprise. At that time, as Hemalatha mentioned, the youth were influenced by the Cultural Revolution in China. VV too was influenced by this revolution. It gave rise to the Naxalbari movement in India. In 1968, VV and Hemalatha came to live in

Warangal. Here, VV began interacting with students and he was influenced by Naxal politics. Initially, Hemalatha wasn't aware of his interests. As VV got more involved, he began making Hemalatha understand the politics, the fight for social justice and the work he was reading about. He began treating her as an equal. She began understanding his concepts and slowly, she got involved as well. In July 1970, VV was instrumental in founding two writers' associations that actively engaged in politics; the Tirugapadu Kavulu (Rebel Poets) in Warangal, and the Viplava Rachayitala Sangham (Revolutionary Writers' Association), popularly known as Virasam, in 1970. In fact, at this time, I saw my sister transform from a housewife who had quit studies after tenth grade, to a partner who supported the ideology of her husband.

NK: Hemalatha, was VV's first arrest in 1973 unexpected? How prepared were you from 1970 till 1973? How did the magazine reach the stands on time?

PH: Prior to his arrest, in 1970, the Superintendent of Police called him and interrogated him for over two hours. They asked him why he had named the Revolutionary Writers' Association as Viplava. VV tried to explain how the name exists in literature and that he hadn't conceptualised it. That interrogation shook me a little but I began to understand; after all, VV had started supporting the Naxalbari movement intellectually and in his writings. Now, this incident of 1970 is not isolated; police surveillance started from then and continues to this day. In 1973, he was arrested under MISA for 36 days. We had two daughters, eight years and five years. My parents were there for us and we also received support from friends and his colleagues at college. It did sort of prepare me, but there was always a little fear—how are the conditions inside the prison? He should be treated as a political prisoner and not as a criminal. We were allowed to meet him every week. It was good he was kept in Warangal Jail, as people knew about us. People know of VV and his work, so we receive a lot of sympathy. In fact, when he was released, there was a huge procession. It was fascinating to witness that moment. It boosted my morale that we were not alone but had the support of many people.

One important development took place at this time. Till his arrest, VV was the publisher, editor, and printer of *Srujana.* Along with him two other writers—Cherabanda Raju and M T Khan (executive committee members of Virasam)—were arrested. At this time, the November 1973 issue was yet to be published. The entire focus of this issue was on these arrests. This meant we needed to replace the publisher. I approached the District Collector because he could give me the permission to publish. I told VV I would take on the responsibility. From November 1973 onwards, till 1992, I remained the editor, publisher, and printer of *Srujana.* I took on the responsibility of publishing *Srujana* while he was in jail because I felt it was my moral responsibility. My association with *Srujana* literally started with VV's first arrest and it happened officially. I got more involved and interested and I began participating in his activities after May 1974. I took on the responsibility of calling and conducting the meetings of Sahiti Mitrulu, Friends of Literature, as they contributed regularly to the magazine, even after VV came out of jail. We would meet and discuss ideas, which I would share with VV. Besides those who were already working with VV, three radical students from REC (Regional Engineering College), Warangal, were also engrossed in building a bond of attachment with the new revolutionary literary cultural wave, which I started carrying with me. This could have been the reason why I may have been implicated in the May 1974 case.

NVR: Prior to his arrest on October 10, 1973, there was a three-day conference of Virasam. The mood in Warangal was euphoric and Hemalatha saw it closely. She learnt of Naxal politics and the Naxalbari movement. After two days, VV was arrested. So, it was a bit of a shock. Now, till this arrest, VV was the publisher, editor and printer of Srujana and the next month's issue was slated to be published, that is when Hemalatha stepped into his shoes. This also marks her entry into politics. Our family took it well in their stride. My father was a strictly religious person and when he learnt of VV's arrest he told us, even Lord Krishna was jailed, that is how life is. Since then, my father stood surety and would get bail for VV. The whole family supported him.

NK: How did *Srujana* come into being?

PH: At the time of our marriage, VV was not politically involved in any way. But because of the inspiration he drew from his brothers, he was overwhelmed with ideal views. At that time, VV worked as a lecturer for a few years in Jadcherla before we shifted to Warangal. The publication of the literary magazine, *Srujana* was started in the year 1966 while VV was working in Jadcherla. The 1968 Naxalbari Struggle and 1969 Telangana Movement had quite a powerful impact on VV. He started his journey in that direction. The left-oriented revolutionary ideology was reflected in the magazine.

NK: How different was the 1974 Secunderabad Conspiracy case from the 1973 case? Again, VV had severe charges against him.

PH: There was a lot of difference. In 1973, he was put away under MISA. Here, he was a political prisoner and the background was totally different. Earlier too, he was involved in the Telangana statehood movement, in 1968, 1969 and in 1972. Before 1973, VV was the founding faculty of Telugu literature at the Chanda Kanthaiah Memorial College, where he later went on to become the principal. That lent him a lot of prestige. I could go to the jail and meet him because there is a lot of social status even inside jail for the principal of a degree college. The 36 days in jail made him a star overnight. By this time, I had taken the role at *Srujana* to heart. The difference in the next case was that it involved conspiracy against the government by CPI-ML party leaders, Naxal workers and six writers. However, the chargesheet said: K G Satyamurthy and Varavara Rao and Others versus State. Later, in the telephone directory too, it was written as the Revolutionary Writers' Association v/s State. This case went on till 1989. They wanted to implicate the writers in a conspiracy case. Naxal leaders had gone underground. I asked VV then, why were he and other writers being targeted? I saw his point of view, that he and others being writers, their work was popular and well-appreciated by people, especially the youth. This made the State fear them.

NK: What were the circumstances in 1974 under which VV was arrested? How difficult was it for you to visit him in jail?

PH: On April 26, 1974, my third child was born and VV was not in prison at that time. He would travel a lot for meetings. Later, in May, the national railway strike began, called by George Fernandes. We received a poem from a railway worker titled, 'Can jails run rails?' This poem was published along with VV's editorial with the same title of the poem. At that time, while I was down with fever, VV was arrested. He was taken to Secunderabad jail. By May 18, I was running 104° fever due to a post-natal infection. I was unconscious for a day. I had to leave my one-month-old baby with my parents and rush to Secunderabad jail to see my husband. I went with high fever and infection. He was in jail for 11 months. I had the full support of my parents and siblings. Our friends, colleagues from college and youth from Kumarpalli (location where we lived) and writers' families would drop by and help my children and me. It would take four hours to reach the jail; we had to be there before 11am. We were forced to wait till 2pm for our mulaqat. We would finish meeting him and then go back to the station by 6pm. The train would leave at 7.30pm and it would be midnight by the time we got home.

NK: This must have been tough; how did you manage?

PH: What could I have done? It was majboori (compulsion) (*laughs*). There were many youths who would come and wait. Many students and writers would accompany me and wait to receive me when I'd be at the station, so in that way I wasn't absolutely alone. They would call me Akka (elder sister). The bus conductor had observed this and he too began calling me Akka. Sometimes if the conductor would see me running to the bus stop, he would call out, 'Akka, come board the bus.'. He would wait till I boarded the bus. All these people were very helpful and cooperative. I would go once a month because it was quite costly—Rs 100 at that time for the entire journey and food for our two daughters and me. In this case, he was in jail till April 1975.

NK: The Andhra Pradesh government banned the magazine *Srujana* in May 1974. How did you cope with this and did you move the High Court to challenge this ban?

PH: The government banned *Srujana* for the issue of May 1974, which was a special on the Indian Railways strike. I challenged this ban in the High Court because the police alleged the first poem exhorted people to break open godowns and kill those preventing it. The poems, in fact, spoke of Naxalbari and there were pieces by renowned authors supporting this ideology. The police also alleged that the last piece in that issue spoke of an armed struggle during the railway strike and there was a reference to overthrowing the government with the use of arms. The High Court upheld the ban. Taking advantage of this ban, the police filed a criminal case against me as a publisher under sedition charges during the Emergency. VV was released in April 1975, on conditional bail. First, he was in Hyderabad and later, he was moved to Warangal. But he was re-arrested in June 1975, when Emergency was declared, as many writers were arrested in that period. Now, during the Emergency, he was first put in Warangal Jail but was later shifted to Hyderabad. By then, it was the third time VV had been arrested and I had got used to travelling alone to visit him in jail.

During this period, they arrested me and produced me before the court. A journalist friend helped me to get bail. The trial was held in 1977. I would often go to court to attend the case. I would take the toddler along and the court clerk would announce 'Haazir hai' and my toddler too would repeat aloud, 'Haazir hai' (*laughs*). Everyone in the courtroom found it funny.

NK: Were you allowed mulaqats during the Emergency? How was the atmosphere during the Emergency?

PH: This case was different. In other cases, you could apply for bail in the Sessions court, High Court and one could also approach the Supreme Court. During the Emergency, there was no court that you could approach, because courts did not allow any writ petitions. All our fundamental rights were suspended and only when he was released we learned of the conditions he was in. Till then, all we could do was to wait with bated breath. We were allowed to meet in person for 30 minutes to an hour, once a month. But it was not possible for me to go every month due to various responsibilities. Now, in the Secunderabad Conspiracy case, there were six writers who were arrested. All our families became close and we became each other's support system. During the Emergency, along with these six writers, there were 30 more jailed in our state. We got each other's support.

NK: Were you able to publish *Srujana* during the Emergency period? How were you impacted during that period?

PH: On June 26, 1975, after the first day of the Emergency, I had to go to the Collector's office where I had a surprise waiting for me. I had gone to get the Collector's approval for the July issue, which was to be published. I had gone to submit the content, as that was the rule during the Emergency and only after the Collector's approval could we publish the magazine. When I reached there, he informed me there was a warrant in my name under MISA. Now, this warrant had to be signed by the Collector. He told me, the police had brought that warrant as they wanted to arrest me. The Collector informed them since he was waiting for me to reach his office with the magazine content matter, he would deal with it. The Collector then asked me if I wanted to go ahead with publishing the edition, in which case, he would have to arrest me. However, if I wouldn't publish that edition, he would spare me. So, that July and for the entire period of the Emergency, *Srujana* couldn't be published.

NK: Were you able to cope with the system and the lacunae every time VV was arrested? How scared was the administration of writers?

PH: I began to understand politics more with every arrest of VV; yet, I never went to the leaders of any party for help. From 1973 to 1985, Warangal district collectors were sympathetic towards VV and me for two reasons. First, the Collector was the Chairman of the college committee. VV was the first member of the Chanda Kanthaiah Memorial College and though he was no more the principal, he still was the first member. Moreover, VV's reputation as a lecturer was well-known in the district. People knew how college discipline had been maintained by VV. The Collector had been apprised of these positive reports. Moreover, VV was known as a prolific writer and was extremely popular among the youth. The only person to give a negative report about VV was the Superintendent of Police, which was expected. As regards VV or other writers, all those who were arrested during the Emergency were seen as heroes. In fact, the former Governor of Maharashtra, C Vidyasagar Rao and M Venkaiah Naidu, were both arrested during the Emergency and were put in the same jail as VV. Till 1985, I was only interacting with the collectors and I had no idea about the politics of various parties. Between 1985 and 1989, there was severe repression in Andhra Pradesh called 'Ata, Mata, Pata bandh' (No speech, song and dance). This was started by N T Rama Rao, then Chief Minister, who was an actor himself but ironically, he put a ban on all cultural performances, speeches and songs. At that time, I was in Hanumakonda with our daughters, and VV was in jail for the Ramnagar Conspiracy case where he was charged under TADA. Whenever the police came to our house for a raid or search, we would open the doors even if it was midnight and even when VV was not around. But, in 1986, at midnight, unknown people came and broke our door with an axe and ran away. At that time, I was at home with our three daughters. The girls were mortified and the next day we came to know they were members of the Anti-Naxal Squad. After this, I went to Hyderabad. That was the first time I met Narasimha Reddy, the legislator. He too had been with VV in jail during the Emergency. He took me to the Home Minister, to whom I submitted my petition about the police barging into our house at midnight. After that, such incidents stopped.

NK: You mentioned that the edition of *Srujana* on the Railway strike was banned. Were you arrested and how did you cope with three young daughters?

PH: Now, after the trial was over and the judge was dictating the order, before pronouncing the order, he turned towards me and asked me how many children did I have? I replied, 'Three daughters.' He then asked me if I was repentant. I just smiled and did not reply (*smiles*). The judge wrote in the order that despite having three daughters, he didn't see repentance on my face and that is why he was giving me two years of rigorous imprisonment.[92] VV wrote the poem 'Undertaking' about this in *Srujana*, as I told you before.[93] I hadn't made any mistake, so why should I have felt bad? I was willing to go to jail and I was put in prison for 10 days. The women's jail was separate and the conditions within were poor. The good part was I was kept in Warangal. The constables knew us and they treated me with immense respect. My older children were with my parents and I had taken the youngest with me to prison. She was three years old. She would stay with me for a day or two and then would go to my parents and would return to me at the prison. Today, she has vague memories of those days in jail. At that time, VV was out on bail. My arrest was a big shock to people, because the Emergency had been lifted and they didn't know why I had been arrested.

NK: Prisons are scary and have pathetic conditions. How bad was it back then and how did you cope?

PH: I was treated well and was given food. In fact, adjacent to our women's jail was the general prison, where a lot of friends we knew were imprisoned. They would regularly send me food from there. I was treated with respect, though overall, the conditions in that prison were poor. However, the people and jail staff were aware of my background and behaved well with me. Finally, the High Court acquitted me on technical grounds. I had my third daughter's birth certificate. The HC noted that the date of publishing was on the same day my daughter was born, which meant I was in the hospital. That is how the case was struck down. Now, it so happened, when I was in jail, the union leader who had called the railway strike (in May 1974), George Fernandes, was made the Minister for Industries at that time. At a press conference, a few journalists had asked him, how come after the railway strike, he was promoted and had become a central government minister, while a woman editor and publisher who had supported that strike through the edition was jailed? Fernandes had replied, 'It was a drama of absurd.' Later, he took an interest in my case and many years later, came to visit us. Through all these cases and experiences, K G Kannabiran, a senior advocate helped us in most of our cases. He is a father figure to me and I would consult him always.

NK: Why were you arrested in a second case?

PH: In 1984, the police raided our printing press in Warangal and ransacked it for publishing the issue of *Srujana*. Meanwhile, they also surrounded our house and took me into custody yet again. This happened at around 7pm. They claimed that the May 1984 edition of *Srujana* was banned. VV was not around and when he returned, he learnt I had been taken into custody. My father was at home when the police took me away and he had protested. He had insisted on accompanying me to the police station. No policewomen had come at that time. He insisted on spending the night at the police station when they put me in the lock-up. My father had gone to the SP and pleaded to stay outside the lock-up the whole night, to ensure I was safe. The next day they produced me in court and I got bail. However, the police did not pursue this case. This was done only to harass me and my children.

NK: I heard VV was one of the representatives in the peace talks between the CPI (Maoist) Party and the Government. What happened?

PH: Yes, VV was asked to mediate in October 2004; however, the talks failed. After this, the police encounters and retaliation started. For the first time in Telugu literary history, on August 17, 2005, Virasam was banned along with CPI (Maoist) and its alleged frontal mass organisations. We had noticed a pattern emerging from 2000, when the government had begun killing Maoist sympathisers and there were attempts even on VV's life. On August 19, 2005, at 3am, some people in civil clothes came to our apartment, along with the watchman of our society. Our watchman knocked on the door. We wondered who could have come this early. I saw from the kitchen window that 10-15 hefty men and some wearing masks were holding the watchman by his collar. I reported this to my youngest daughter who was staying with us and asked her not to open the door. I told her to call the journalists. Those men continued to stand at the door. My daughter and I told them from inside that unless they come with a warrant and in uniform, we won't open the door. Meanwhile, we informed our contacts in the media. This went on till 5.30-6am, after which these people disappeared. Then just after 6am, a police inspector came with a warrant and some other policemen to take VV. I insisted on accompanying him to the police station to ensure that he was safe. Though it was under the Andhra Pradesh Security Act, while he was in jail, eight more warrants were issued from different police stations. He got bail after seven months.

NK: You have witnessed all the cases in which VV has been arrested since the seventies. How different is the Bhima Koregaon case?

PH: Oh! There is a lot of difference. The first time, on August 28, 2018, the Maharashtra police conducted day-long searches.

Our whole house was ransacked. Everything was taken away. They confiscated our mobile phones, our computer, and books.[94] Later, I learnt, the Maharashtra police had also been to the homes of our two daughters and raided their residences too. One lives a bit farther away while the second one has an apartment next to ours. The officials took away their mobiles as well as those of our sons-in-law. They also took the mobile of a Virasam member, whom the police alleged to be VV's student. They didn't stop there. The police even took away the Kindles and tablets of my grandchildren. Our third son-in-law teaches in the English and Foreign Languages University in Hyderabad. The police went there too and raided their premises on the university campus. They took away their cellphones too. Our second son-in-law is a journalist and even his phone was taken. They took everything and went to Pune. Then on August 29, 2018, through the SC's intervention, VV was sent back to be under house arrest and there was no problem then.[95] The second time, on November 17, 2018, they came again and took him to Pune. The following day, I was in Pune with my granddaughter. We didn't know that city, we don't understand the language or know any people there. From November 2018 to January 2020, I slowly got accustomed to travelling between Hyderabad and Pune in overnight trains to visit VV in jail and court. I would leave the previous night to go to meet him in jail and court and leave that night for Hyderabad. Suddenly, I was faced with new problems after the NIA took over the case and shifted him to Mumbai.

NK: Venugopal, this seems to have been just the beginning of VV's problems. How challenging was it to get timely medical intervention for him?

NVR: After his arrest in November 2018 till January 2020, VV was in Yerawada. Later, he was moved to Taloja and we faced the pandemic. After that, in March 2020, the national lockdown was declared. At that time, we were only allowed phone calls; initially, it was every fortnight and later, it became once a month and finally even those completely stopped. Around June, VV had begun talking differently; it wasn't normal. Initially, we felt he must be in a different mood due to the strict prison rules in Maharashtra. In the first week of July, the same kind of conversation continued and he sounded delirious. He would say something about his childhood and there was absolutely no connection. At that time, Vernon was around VV and he took the cellphone. He then told us that for nearly a fortnight, VV was facing memory loss and he wasn't able to comprehend things. We held a press conference and demanded he be shifted to a private hospital. Then around July 12–13, 2020, the local police called and informed that VV has been shifted to JJ Hospital. They asked us to go to Taloja Jail to seek permission to visit him. My sister, her two daughters and I went to Taloja and they gave us a letter allowing us to visit the hospital. At JJ Hospital, however, the police refused to allow all of us. VV's bed was the last one in the ward and when we went to meet him, we couldn't even recognise him. He was in a pathetic condition and on top of that, he couldn't recognise his wife. Earlier, he had told Vernon that Hemalatha had died.[96] At that time, in the hospital, he recognised me and then looked at his wife. He asked her, 'How come you are here?' His bed sheet was urine-soaked and his pyjamas were wet. I quickly changed his clothes and the bed sheet, as no hospital staff was around. Then the police ordered us out within 15 minutes. We went to meet our advocate, Susan Abraham. She asked us to write down the exact sequence of events and what we had witnessed. We did so and said if he were kept in this condition, he would definitely die.[97] We wrote an open letter to the administration. Later, we learnt that VV had caught the Coronavirus and had been shifted to St George's Hospital. Obviously, we couldn't meet him there. We returned to Hyderabad and Hemalatha held an online press conference. After this, many people and politicians intervened and we approached the National Human Rights Commission (NHRC).[98] The NHRC instructed the Maharashtra government to shift VV to a private hospital. He was shifted to Nanavati hospital on July 18, 2020.[99] He was there till August 28, 2020. At that time, we were informed by the hospital doctors that VV was in delirium and was in an unconscious condition for one-and-a-half months. VV has survived only because they shifted him to Nanavati Hospital.

NK: Do you specifically remember when all his problems began?

PH: Yes, our lawyer informed me, it started on the day of Ramzan when he was in Taloja jail. It was in May and he was admitted to JJ Hospital in the last week of May. Our lawyers met him in the hospital and they informed us that he was to be kept there till the first week of June. I came to Mumbai on June 1, to attend his hearing in court and when I went to JJ Hospital to meet him, the staff informed me that he was shifted back to the jail. I hadn't been informed of it till then. Worse, I realised they had sent him back to the prison despite his ill health. VV was suffering from dysentery and was vomiting. He suffered from a urinary tract infection. We were told VV was kept in the cell, in the prison with 30 other people. There were only three toilets and no bathrooms. He told us later, he would have baths in front of the toilets, such were the pathetic conditions. There was all likelihood of him falling down. In fact, the police rushed him back to the prison from the hospital without removing the catheter tube. It had to be changed after every fortnight which they didn't. It was removed only after VV was shifted to Nanavati hospital.

That was possible only after the Bombay High Court gave the order of shifting him to a private hospital. As VV had stated in his affidavit, all three doctors at JJ were Ayurvedic doctors, not medical professionals.

NK: The conditions inside the prison seem rather pathetic. There seem to be huge space constraints, wasn't there any regard for VV's age and health?

PH: It was really bad in Taloja. Vernon was there with him, but the fact is the prisons are overcrowded. He was put in with 30 other inmates. He couldn't stretch his hands and legs and he literally slept stiff, like a dead person. If VV had to turn, his face would be close to another person's. He once shared that as he breathed, he felt as if he was breathing the other person's breath. In fact, because of his ill health, he had to often go to the toilet (due to dysentery) and would end up standing in a queue. He brought this to the notice of the Superintendent and asked to be shifted to another cell because he said he could have fallen. The Superintendent told him, 'Let us see when you fall down.' Then the jailer added, 'There are at least people here, if you fall down, they will lift you. If you are shifted to another place there will be nobody.' Such is the treatment VV was given inside the prison.

NK: This arrest seems like the worst nightmare of your life. He is an octogenarian and you are 74 years, living in a completely new city. How has imprisonment in Maharashtra been?

PH: This has been an extremely bad experience. After over one-and-a-half years, the National Investigation Agency took over the investigations and VV was shifted to Mumbai. That too he was shifted to Taloja. Now to go there, I had to take the help of a friend to visit Mumbai, stay here, and meet him in court on February 28, 2020, when he was produced. The next day I went with my friend to Taloja jail, but they refused to let me see him because my credentials were not approved by the court. This was troublesome. Since my friend was a lawyer, she could see VV, but I couldn't see him. Mumbai has been the toughest. After that there was the pandemic and the lockdown. So imagine since that day till he was hospitalised in JJ, I couldn't see him. Then too I could barely see him for 10 minutes and he couldn't recognise me. Then we met and spoke only after he was shifted to Nanavati Hospital. This has been the longest period in our lives of not meeting in person when he has been in prison.

VV has great respect for women. His poem 'Stree' reflects his views about women. Even at home, he doesn't cause inconvenience to anybody. VV can't spend time alone. He goes to our daughter's house who lives nearby or to friends' residence. He has abundant love for children. VV always wants to live near people. His commitment to the cause of the poor and oppressed is exceptional. We both share and discuss everything together. I am happy that I have lived a purposeful life and an ideal life. Thousands of people call me 'Akka' or 'Amma' affectionately! Tell me. What more is required to be happy and satisfied?

NK: How has the forced shift to Mumbai been? All of a sudden, you are in a strange city amongst strangers and trying to remain anonymous. What about the travel? Can you go anywhere?

PH: That is the worst. It has been over two-and-a-half years since we have begun living here, 'abhi tak man achcha nahi lagta' (We still don't feel fine). This city is confusing for me. I can't go anywhere alone; I can't speak or even understand the local language. It is really difficult for us. We walk inside the compound but I feel scared for us to step out. His bail has become jail for me. We can't even take the bus, train or use the metro. We are forced to engage a taxi to take us to the court and this takes two hours. On top of that, we incur more expense. There is so much traffic and noise in this city. It will be much easier to shift him to Hyderabad. We feel like fish out of water though this city has so much water. If something happens to either of us, who do we call? Where can we go and who do we ask to help? Every minute is stressful in this city—city is a problem, health is a problem, language is a problem. In the last two years, we have shifted four times. Now where we are living is the fifth place. This city is rather expensive. Yes, and some neighbours are rather inquisitive and ask isn't there a good hospital in Hyderabad?

NK: Speaking of jails, Venugopal, there seems to be resistance to implementing prison reforms in many states. How different are mulaqats and prison conditions in Andhra Pradesh and Telangana jails as compared to Maharashtra?

NVR: Andhra Pradesh and Telangana jails are much better than prisons in Maharashtra, the main reason being the social movements in our states. Many non-criminals, activists, writers and poets go to jail. Most importantly, the prison staff too know these are not criminals and treat them with respect. Inside the prisons, people have gone on hunger strikes and protested for prison reform. At the same time, outside the prisons, in 1994–1995, there was a movement for prison reform, and 200 organisations joined a forum for a sit-in before the secretariat, demanding better prison conditions. There were dharnas for three months continuously. Even VV sat in on this dharna. Finally, the government agreed and formed a tri-partite agreement with civil society groups. Varavara Rao, M. T. Khan, Kannabiram and prisoners drafted reforms and we got far better conditions in jails.

Whereas in Maharashtra, there haven't been so many social movements for such changes, such as in prisons. Another important reason is that prisons in Maharashtra are somehow or the other, linked to crime. Prisoners are looked down upon here and the prison staff treats all prisoners as criminals. Here, the jails don't differentiate between activists, intellectuals, writers and poets. These are prisoners of conscience and not criminals, but they don't have any idea about the concept of prisoners of conscience.

VV is a gregarious person and during his jail terms he missed meeting and speaking with people. He has written many poems about this. VV is known in Andhra and Telangana for his public speaking skills. He has an elephantine memory and knew each person by name. Now such a personality is jailed and is forced not to meet people, that is the most difficult part of being jailed.

NK: As you look back on your life Hemalatha, how do you think it has been? What would you like to say?

PH: I wrote a small piece on our relationship in Telugu, *Sahas Gatha* (Courageous journey). My whole life is Sahas Gatha. Today we have our grandchildren and three daughters. It all started with my involvement and attachment with *Srujana* leading to Virasam and the political beliefs. All the repression, bans, even physical attacks, and attempts on life; this intermittent exile and prison life and this restricted stay in Mumbai, all of this has been a part of 58 years of our married life. We have experienced the days and nights of love and war. These come along with all its tragedies and joy. In a way, from approximately 1973 onwards our journey has been that of living on the edge of a sword. There always has been a threat to his life. It fell on us to be vigilant all the time and to suffer along with our children. Of course, there are so many intimate friends, relatives, and well-wishers. I want to mention particularly, the people in Kumarpalli and the youth in GTB Enclave Delhi. This is the life I will cherish always.

NK: There have been years spent behind bars and many years of struggle. Did you get time together?

PH: We have been everywhere together …

We both (VV and I) faced severe repression. Despite encountering several hardships for over 40 years, VV never stepped back. I am very proud of this. Sometimes I feel that I could not provide my children with all the facilities required to lead a comfortable life while bringing them up. But VV always used to say, 'Our children will also live as every other child lives.' It's true. How many people laid down their lives to realise the objectives of the 'movement'… countless missing cases … many encounters …! I also toured many places along with him. I have witnessed the blood of turbulent times … tears too … experienced the darkness of Emergency … we did everything together. Together we demanded justice. As VV says, 'The strength in our love brings unity in our faiths. It formulated our value system.'

I end this chapter with a poem VV wrote for Hemalatha:

There is no path we walked without your company. There are no dangers we encountered without your love. No love we have got. By becoming 'Srujana' not only you waited for long but underwent rigorous imprisonment too… you went through night lock-ups … heartful of aspirations … your two eyes became wet in prolonged waiting … in our village in our marriage in the palanquin we have our own amorous experience of seeing 'aadhi hai chandrama'. We have the wretched experience of hiding the children in your lap when the axes wearing mufti dress broke the doors in the utter darkness of new moon night. From Kumarapalli to New Delhi not only our own daughters but how many children encircle you calling 'amma' amma' … so many brothers, sisters and fearless fighters shared their love and affection addressing you 'akka' 'akka'… we wiped of how many mothers', life-companions' of martyrs tears.

We checked up on how many missing cases … We walked seven steps together, Star Arundhathi being the witness whatever oath we took… We heard what the river of seven streams had uttered … We heard the rhythmic sounds from the voices of Ganga, Sindhu, Godavari, Kaveri, Krushna … we witnessed the tears and blood dripping from turbulent times. We enjoyed the moon-lit nights … we also went through the emergency darkness … the days when you came to the far off 'mulaqat' leaving a newborn 20 days kid just like a woman just after giving birth to a baby coming to the field to work … when in a jail commune or in the company of a comrade… or while in solitary confinement or amidst high security … in Emergency, in the hard times when song, performance, public talk were banished, helpless you and the girl children subdued much grief but also were fearless. Without your friendship I would not have got any other companion, without your support I would not have got affection from others. All the people who were ready to face any consequences for me thought that you were very much there within me. Without your involvement and backing this adventurous episode would not have been written. The strength in our love brought unity of our faiths. The strength of our love formulated our value system. We are projected as ideal only because of your magnanimity and also because you kept the dark side in me and my weaknesses out of sight. Without your active involvement, this adventurous episode would not have been written.

Notes

1. According to the party's official website, the CPI(M) was formed at the Seventh Congress of the Communist Party of India held in Calcutta from October 31 to November 7, 1964. Since its formation the party has grown to be a national party. The party has a strong presence in Kerala, Tripura Bihar, Rajasthan, Himachal Pradesh, Odisha, Tamil Nadu, Maharashtra and Assam. The All-India Party Congress is the supreme authority of the Communist Party of India (Marxist). They are often termed as the Maoist party. This party is said to be founded in September 2004, after Communist Party of India (Marxist-Leninist), Peoples War Group and the Maoist Communist Centre of India merged. See: "Communist Party of India (Marxist): About Us," Communist Party of India (Marxist), https://cpim.org/page-about-us/.
2. This report gives timeline of Tushar Damgude's complaint followed by the arrest of Sudha Bharadwaj and five more: "Tushar Damgude, Whose Complaint Sparked Nationwide Raids, Is a Bhide Disciple," *India Today*, August 29, 2018, https://www.indiatoday.in/india/story/tushar-damgude-sambhaji-bhide-bhima-koregaon-1326777-2018-08-29.
3. For more details on zero tolerance policy, read: Sheikh Saaliq, "Critics of India's Modi Government Face Sedition Charges," *AP News*, April 20, 2021, https://apnews.com/article/india-international-news-asia-pacific-religion-weekend-reads-8c675cc2b23c5c83b0df523b09fa23f8.

4 Read more on the order by a bench of Supreme Court Justices M M Sundresh and Aravind Kumar: Utkarsh Anand, "'Bail Is Rule, Jail an Exception' Does Not Apply in Terror Cases: Supreme Court," *Hindustan Times*, February 8, 2024, https://www.hindustantimes.com/india-news/bail-is-rule-jail-an-exception-does-not-apply-in-terror-cases-sc-101707416805240.html.

5 Because of his health, he required a straw to drink and swallow. (See: The Wire Staff, "Stan Swamy Files Plea for Straw, Sipper in Jail; NIA Seeks 20 Days to Reply," *The Wire*, November 7, 2020, https://thewire.in/rights/stan-swamy-jail-nai-straw-sipper-parkinsons.) (See: "Stan Swamy," USCIRF, https://www.uscirf.gov/religious-prisoners-conscience/forb-victims-database/stan-swamy.)

6 Read the report by the Comptroller and Auditor General of India on 'Management of Prisons in Telangana'. It was reported that the Telangana prisons department, since the formation of the state in June 2014, has taken several measures such as providing hygienic living conditions, recreation and sports facilities, increased interaction with families, better diet and clothing, 'Which are compatible with human dignity in all respects.' The CAG further noted, 'Measures initiated by the government for reform and rehabilitation of prisoners were in conformity with the objectives of the extant Act and the Rules, and have achieved the desired objectives.' Government of Telangana, Report of the Comptroller and Auditor General of India on General, Social &; Economic Sectors for the year ended March 2019, https://cag.gov.in/webroot/uploads/download_audit_report/2020/GSSA%20English%2019-0605c3c822ad8d3.00058868.pdf. Read more on the report on how Telangana jails have brought down deaths: Murali Karnam, "The Successful Reformation of Prisons in Telangana," *The Wire*, December 25, 2018, https://thewire.in/rights/the-successful-reformation-of-prisons-in-telangana

7 Read here for more on 'outlawing the opposition': "Outlawing The Opposition," Facing History &; Ourselves, August 2, 2016, https://www.facinghistory.org/resource-library/outlawing-opposition?__cf_chl_rt_tk=Os29PZR.JFh0.wj02KQF.eB3O3X5tyhQDRpYDHOi9pA-1704951023-0-gaNycGzND9A.

8 For more on Ex-PM Dr Singh's speech on Naxalism, see: "PM's Speech at the Chief Minister's Meet on Naxalism," Former Prime Minister of India: Dr. Manmohan Singh, accessed October 4, 2024, https://archivepmo.nic.in/drmanmohansingh/speech-details.php?nodeid=302.

9 For more on P Chidambaram's statement of use of air strikes against Naxals. See: NDTV Correspondent, "May Consider Air Power against Naxals: Chidambaram," NDTV.com, April 7, 2010, https://www.ndtv.com/india-news/may-consider-air-power-against-naxals-chidambaram-414729

10 For more details on Dr Sen's case, see: "Indian Activist Binayak Sen Released from Prison," BBC News, April 19, 2011, https://www.bbc.com/news/world-south-asia-13125572.

11 Read more on the protests by Muslim women: Yash Sharma and Shatakshi Singh, "Shaheen Bagh and the Politics of Protest in the Anti-CAA Movement in India," *Feminist Encounters: A Journal of Critical Studies in Culture and Politics*, March 1, 2023, https://www.lectitopublishing.nl/Article/Detail/shaheen-bagh-and-the-politics-of-protest-in-the-anti-caa-movement-in-india-12888.

12 For more on the media campaign against Shaheen Bagh protests. See: Omer Fayaz and Rayees Amin, "How Rightwing Media Outlets' Obsession with Shaheen Bagh Led to False Reporting," *The Wire*, March 11, 2020, https://thewire.in/media/rightwing-media-channels-shaheen-bagh.

13 For more on allegations made against the farmers. See: DHNS, "From 'Khalistanis' to Defeat of 'Anti-National' Forces: Rhetoric around Farmers Protest Comes a Full Circle," *Deccan Herald*, November 20, 2021, https://www.deccanherald.com/

india/from-khalistanis-to-defeat-of-anti-national-forces-rhetoric-around-farmers-protest-comes-a-full-circle-1052696.html.

14 Read for more details: "Why Are Farmers Protesting in India?," *Reuters*, March 14, 2024, https://www.reuters.com/world/india/why-farmers-are-protesting-new-delhi-2024-03-14/.

15 For more on this, see: Neel Kamal, "NIA Raids Woman Farmer Leader's Residence in Bathinda," *The Times of India*, August 30, 2024, https://timesofindia.indiatimes.com/city/chandigarh/nia-raids-woman-farmer-leaders-residence-in-bathinda/articleshow/112922031.cms.

16 Read more on the anti-national list here: The Wire Staff, "The Updated List of India's 'Anti-Nationals' (According to the Modi Government)," *The Wire*, February 19, 2021, https://thewire.in/rights/india-modi-anti-national-protest-arrest-sedition-authoritarianism.

17 For details on Indian journalists arrested, see: Geeta Seshu, "Behind Bars: Arrests and Detentions of Journalists in India 2010-2020," *Free Speech Collective*, December 24, 2020, https://freespeechcollective.in/behind-bars-arrests-and-detentions-of-journalists-in-india-2010-2020/.

18 For more on the rise in sedition cases, see here: Kunal Purohit, "Our New Database Reveals Rise In Sedition Cases in the Modi Era," *Article 14*, February 2, 2021, https://www.article-14.com/post/our-new-database-reveals-rise-in-sedition-cases-in-the-modi-era.

19 Gautam Doshi, "Data Dive: In Last 7 Years, 10,552 People Arrested Under UAPA, 253 Convicted," Factchecker, November 12, 2021, https://www.factchecker.in/data-dive/seven-years-uapa-cases-arrests-786935.

20 For more on politicians arrested. See: Rajashree Seal, ed., "95% of Politicians Booked by ED Since 2014 from Opposition: Report," India.com, September 21, 2022, https://www.india.com/news/india/enforcement-directorate-casebook-95percent-of-politicians-booked-by-ed-since-2014-from-opposition-report-5643576/.

21 For more on politicians from Congress, NCP and Shiv Sena who got reprieve after joining the BJP, see: Livemint, "23 of 25 Opposition Leaders Accused of Corruption Got Reprieve after Joining BJP since 2014: Report," Livemint.com, April 3, 2024, https://www.livemint.com/politics/news/23-of-25-opposition-leaders-accused-of-corruption-who-joined-bjp-since-2014-got-reprieve-report-11712116448479.html.

22 For details on how the UPA Govt used section 124A (sedition) against 9000 citizens, see: Maneesh Chhibber, "Why BJP and Congress Love to Hate Sedition (till They Come to Power)," ThePrint, January 21, 2019, https://theprint.in/opinion/why-bjp-and-congress-love-to-hate-sedition-till-they-come-to-power/180648/.

23 For details on the seven journalists arrested, see: The Wire Staff, "Number of Jailed Journalists at New Global Record, Seven Behind Bars in India," *The Wire*, December 14, 2022, https://thewire.in/media/cpj-jailed-journalists-india-seven.

24 For more on this issue, see: Harpreet Singh Dhillon and Shibu Sasidharan, "Prison Mental Health—an Indian Perspective," Annals of Indian Psychiatry 8, no. 1 (January 2024): 80–82, https://doi.org/10.4103/aip.aip_105_21.

25 For details on the Bhima Koregaon case and Sudha's arrest, see: "Woman Human Rights Defender Sudha Bharadwaj Released on Bail," Front Line Defenders, December 9, 2022, https://www.frontlinedefenders.org/en/case/woman-human-rights-defender-sudha-bharadwaj-released-bail.

26 Sen is a women's rights activist and she was assistant professor and head of the English Literature department at Nagpur University. On June 8, 2018, she was arrested by the Pune Police for her alleged involvement in the Elgar Parishad and Bhima-Koregaon riots cases. After six years of incarceration, Sen was granted bail on April 5, 2024, by an Apex Court bench of Justices Aniruddha Bose and Augustine George Masih. In the bail order they stated, the restriction for grant of bail

as per Section 43D(5) of the UAPA would not apply in case of Sen. See: The Wire Staff, "Supreme Court Grants Bail to Shoma Sen, in Jail for 6 Years," *The Wire*, April 5, 2024, https://thewire.in/law/supreme-court-bail-to-shoma-sen-elgar-parishad-case.

27 Sudha Bharadwaj, *From Phansi Yard : My Year With The Women Of Yerawada* (New Delhi: Juggernaut Books, 2023).

28 For details on the textile mills, see: "Tale of the Iconic Textile Mills of Bombay," Needle & Quest, https://www.needleandquest.com/diaries/tale-of-the-iconic-textile-mills-of-bombay.html.

29 For details on Malik's interim bail on medical grounds, see: Express News Service, "SC Grants 2 Months' Interim Bail to Nawab Malik, Sharad Pawar-Led NCP Welcomes Party's 'Strong, Loud Voice,'" *The Indian Express*, August 13, 2023, https://indianexpress.com/article/cities/mumbai/sc-2-months-interim-bail-nawab-malik-sharad-pawar-ncp-welcomes-partys-strong-loud-voice-8888025/.

30 For details on Sameer Khan's bail, see: Vidya, "Maharashtra Minister Nawab Malik's Son-in-Law Granted Bail in Drugs Case," *India Today*, September 27, 2021, https://www.indiatoday.in/india/story/maharashtra-nawab-malik-son-in-law-granted-bail-drugs-case-1857879-2021-09-27.

31 Read here for details on Malik's arrest: "Nawab Malik, Arrested in Money Laundering Case, Sent to ED Custody till March 7," *Hindustan Times*, March 3, 2022, https://www.hindustantimes.com/india-news/nawab-malik-arrested-in-money-laundering-case-sent-to-ed-custody-till-march-7-101646301438465.html.

32 J Dey, a senior crime reporter in leading publications in Mumbai, was murdered on June 11, 2011 by members of Mumbai's underworld gang. J Dey authored two books on underworld activities, *Zero Dial: The Dangerous World of Informers* and *Khallas: An A to Z Guide to the Underworld*, Express Web Desk, "J Dey Murder: A Complete Guide to the Case That

Inspired Netflix Series 'Scoop,'" *The Indian Express*, June 8, 2023, https://indianexpress.com/article/india/j-dey-murder-case-netflix-scoop-8652418/.

33 *Damini* is a film in which the lead female actor tries to get justice for her deceased domestic help who was sexually assaulted by the lead's own brother-in-law. She moves the court but faces many legal hurdles, mainly several adjournments which add to the severe delay in getting justice.

34 Sameer Khan is the son-in-law of ex-Minister, Nawab Malik. Nawab Malik has been a politician and minister from the Nationalist Congress Party since 2004. He had been critical of the Hindu right-wing Bharatiya Janata Party and also the Narcotics Control Bureau's handling of various cases. Sameer Khan had made a Google transaction with a British national Karan Sajnani who was accused in another case. The authorities suspected Sameer Khan of having purchased drugs. Nawab Malik was a Minister at the time Sameer was arrested. Also, the party for which Malik was the minister had the state Home Ministry portfolio. The NCB claimed that the accused had conspired to procure, sell, purchase, and transport 194.6 kilograms of ganja, and charged Khan and five others for dealing with commercial quantities of the drug, a crime that carries a maximum punishment of 20 years. The court said there was no evidence of drugs and the NCB had not brought anything on record to prove a conspiracy.

35 For more on this, see: Sarah Thanawala, "Bhima Koregaon Case: Shoma Sen's Discharge Application at NIA Asserts Discrepancies in Evidence against Her," *The Leaflet*, June 5, 2023, https://theleaflet.in/bhima-koregaon-case-shoma-sens-discharge-application-at-nia-asserts-discrepancies-in-evidence-against-her/. For more on the BK case and the accused arrested, see: Sayantani Biswas, "Bhima Koregaon Case: 16 Arrested, 1 Died in Custody, Some Got Bail- a 2023 Update," mint, July 28, 2023, https://www.livemint.com/news/india/

bhima-koregaon-elgaar-parishad-case-16-arrested-1-died-in-custody-some-got-bail-a-2023-update-11690537456618.html.

36 For more details on Shoma Sen's bail rejection, see: Sharmeen Hakim, "Special Nia Court Rejects Professor Shoma Sen's Interim Medical Bail Plea in Bhima Koregaon—Elgar Parishad Case," *Live Law*, September 22, 2021, https://www.livelaw.in/news-updates/shoma-sens-interim-medical-bail-rejected-bhima-koregaon-violence-nia-court-182140.

37 For more details on Shoma Sen's SC bail order, see: The Wire Staff, "Supreme Court Grants Bail to Shoma Sen, in Jail for 6 Years," *The Wire*, April 5, 2024, https://thewire.in/law/supreme-court-bail-to-shoma-sen-elgar-parishad-case.

38 For more details on Sen's case and bail terms, read: "Explained: The Shoma Sen Bail Judgment," *The Leaflet*, April 8, 2024, https://theleaflet.in/explained-the-shoma-sen-bail-judgment/.

39 For more details on the conditions placed by the Supreme Court on Sen, see: Akriti Anand, "Activist Shoma Kanti Sen Gets Bail in Bhima Koregaon Case, but SC Sets Conditions," *Mint*, April 5, 2024, https://www.livemint.com/news/india/activist-shoma-kanti-sen-gets-supreme-court-bail-in-elgar-parishad-maoist-links-case-bhima-koregaon-case-11712306316133.html.

40 For more details on acquittal of Rahi and others, see: Jyoti Punwani, "Police Case Collapses. Journalist Acquitted after 14 Years," justicenews, October 15, 2022, https://www.justicenews.co.in/police-case-collapses-journalist-acquitted-after-14-years-2/.

41 Refer for more information on this case, here: The Hindu Bureau, "Bombay High Court Acquits DU Ex-Professor G.N. Saibaba, Five Others in Maoist Link Case," *The Hindu*, March 6, 2024, https://www.thehindu.com/news/national/ex-du-professor-gn-saibaba-acquitted-hc-sets-aside-his-life-sentence/article67915870.ece

42 For more details on Pandu's case, see: Susan Abraham, "Misuse of the Unlawful Activities (Prevention) Act," *Economic and Political Weekly*, January 20, 2024, https://www.epw.in/

journal/2017/12/web-exclusives/misuse-unlawful-activities-prevention-act.html-0. Refer to the legal details regarding bail rejection of Prashant Rahi and others here: Vaibhav Ganjapure, "Major Jolt to Naxals, HC Rejects Bail Pleas of Rahi, Tirki," *The Times of India*, January 26, 2018, https://timesofindia.indiatimes.com/city/nagpur/major-jolt-to-naxals-hc-rejects-bail-pleas-of-rahi-tirki/articleshow/62654170.cms.

43 For more details on the political turmoil in Maharashtra, see: R. Sai Spandana and Joyston D'Souza, "Understanding the Shiv Sena Conflict," *Supreme Court Observer*, March 31, 2023, https://www.scobserver.in/journal/understanding-the-shiv-sena-conflict/.

44 For details on Sanjay Raut's case, see: India News Desk, "What Is the Patra Chawl Redevelopment Case and Why Is Sanjay Raut under ED Scanner?," *The Financial Express*, June 28, 2022, https://www.financialexpress.com/india-news/what-is-the-patra-chawl-redevelopment-case-and-why-is-sanjay-raut-under-ed-scanner/2574951/.

45 For more details on Patra chawl redevelopment controversy, see: "Sanjay Raut Was Directly Involved in Patra Chawl Project Right from Start: ED," *Hindustan Times*, September 20, 2022, https://www.hindustantimes.com/cities/mumbai-news/sanjay-raut-was-directly-involved-in-patra-chawl-project-right-from-conception-ed-101663614323601.html.

46 Sanjay Raut, a Member of Parliament in the Rajya Sabha has been a loyalist of first Balasaheb Thackeray and later his son Uddhav Thackeray who took over the party reins in 2004. Since the nineties, Shiv Sena, a Hindutva ideology party had always been integral to the saffron alliance with the Bharatiya Janata Party. However, in the 2019 Maharashtra state assembly elections, the two parties fell out over power sharing and Uddhav joined the post-poll tripartite alliance with the Nationalist Congress Party and the Congress and became the Chief Minister of Maharashtra. However, within two years, the BJP led a faction within the Sena, with Eknath

Shinde leading the rebellion. A majority of the elected legislators went with Shinde and the Shiv Sena party was divided into two factions. This was challenged by Uddhav in Supreme Court, after he resigned from the post of CM. In June 2023, the Election Commission ruled in favour of the Shinde faction to use the original Shiv Sena party name and its symbol of a Bow and Arrow. Since then, Uddhav and Raut have been critical of the BJP, the new CM Shinde and his faction. Raut has alleged he was arrested for his strong criticism against the BJP and the PM. For more details on Maharashtra politics, see: "Maharashtra Political Crisis: Current Affairs," Shankar IAS Parliament, May 15, 2023, https://www.shankariasparliament.com/current-affairs/maharashtra-political-crisis.

47 For more details on the arrest of Sanjay Raut, see: TN National Desk, "Ed Finds Rs 11.50 Lakh Unaccounted Cash at Sanjay Raut's Residence, His Lawyers Say Rs 10 Lakh Belongs to Shiv Sena," Times Now, July 31, 2022, https://www.timesnownews.com/india/ed-detains-shiv-sena-mp-sanjay-raut-in-land-scam-case-after-raids-at-his-mumbai-residence-article-93252152.

48 Vijay V. Singh, "Ed Arrests Raut after Day-Long Raid in Money Laundering Case," *The Times of India*, August 1, 2022, https://timesofindia.indiatimes.com/city/mumbai/ed-arrests-raut-after-day-long-raid-in-money-laundering-case/articleshow/93262357.cms.

49 As per the Principle of Justice one is innocent until proven guilty, thereby the mandate is to be granted bail. Refer to: General Principles of Trial, https://districts.ecourts.gov.in/sites/default/files/GENERAL PRINCIPLES OF TRIAL—Mayakuntla Manasa.pdf.

50 "'PMLA Most Draconian Statute Ever in the Country': Kapil Sibal Urges Supreme Court to Reconsider 'Vijay Madanlal Choudhary' Judgment," *Live Law*, April 10, 2023, https://www.livelaw.in/top-stories/prevention-of-money-laundering-act-draconian-kapil-sibal-pvijay-madanlal-choudhary-

judgmentenforcement-directorate-supreme-court-225950; Ananthakrishnan G, "Supreme Court Upholds PMLA, Says Presuming Innocence Can Be Reversed by Law," *The Indian Express*, July 28, 2022, https://indianexpress.com/article/india/supreme-court-pmla-validity-enforcement-directorate-8054053/.

51 For details on Raut's bail, see: The Wire Staff, "Sanjay Raut's Arrest by ED 'Illegal', a 'Witch Hunt' Says Court While Granting Bail," *The Wire*, November 9, 2022, https://thewire.in/law/sanjay-raut-uddhav-thackerays-close-aide-gets-bail-in-pmla-case.

52 For details on the cases against Shiv Sena leaders, see: Sadaf Modak, "Status of Cases against Sena Leaders—Both in Shinde Camp & Those with Uddhav," *The Indian Express*, July 11, 2023, https://indianexpress.com/article/cities/mumbai/status-of-cases-against-sena-leaders-both-in-shinde-camp-those-with-uddhav-8695033/; The Hindu Bureau, "Bookie Claimed Amruta Fadnavis Had Discussed Bringing down MVA Government and Trapping Eknath Shinde, According to Chargesheet," *The Hindu*, June 9, 2023, https://www.thehindu.com/news/cities/mumbai/bookie-claimed-amruta-fadnavis-had-discussed-bringing-down-mva-government-and-trapping-eknath-shinde-according-to-chargesheet/article66938636.ece.

53 For information on the case against Eknath Khadse's son-in-law, see: Express News Service, "Land Grab Case: Two Years Later, SC Grants Bail to Eknath Khadse's Son-in-Law," *The Indian Express*, July 21, 2023, https://indianexpress.com/article/cities/mumbai/land-grab-case-two-years-later-sc-bail-eknath-khadses-son-in-law-8853217/.

54 For more details on Anand Teltumbde's bail case: Sayantani Biswas, "Bhima Koregaon Case: Sc Rejects Nia's Plea to Cancel Anand Teltumbde's Bail: Today News," *Mint*, November 25, 2022, https://www.livemint.com/news/india/bhima-koregaon-case-sc-rejects-nia-s-plea-to-cancel-anand-teltumbde-s-bail-11669376265435.html.

55 NDTV, "Prime Time With Ravish | 'Sanjay Raut Arrested Illegally': Court Shreds Probe Agency, Grants Bail," YouTube, November 9, 2022, https://www.youtube.com/watch?v=R9kbMZxUG4k.

56 Nandita Haksar, "Stop Identity Politics," *Force*, June 5, 2023, https://forceindia.net/guest-column/stop-identity-politics/.

57 Read for more details: Ajmal Abbas, "Rahul Gandhi Kicks off over 6,000 Km Long Bharat Jodo Nyay Yatra from Manipur," *India Today*, January 14, 2024, https://www.indiatoday.in/india/story/rahul-gandhi-bharat-jodo-nyay-yatra-manipur-congress-prime-minister-narendra-modi-manipur-violence-2488559-2024-01-14.

58 For details on the Rani Laksmi controversy, see—https://m.facebook.com/ilmmanipur/posts/why-rani-lakshmibai-in-manipurwhat-had-she-done-for-our-statethis-is-too-much-of/1980744121974263/?_rdr

59 Section 504—India Code on criminal intimidation, states—'Whoever intentionally insults and thereby gives provocation to any person, intending or knowing it to be likely that such provocation will cause him to break the public peace or to commit any other offense, shall be punished with imprisonment of either description for a term which may extend to two years, or with a fine, or with both.'

60 For details on Erendro's case, see: Utkarsh Anand, "SC Orders the Release of Activist Held under NSA," *Hindustan Times*, July 20, 2021, https://www.hindustantimes.com/india-news/sc-orders-the-release-of-activist-held-under-nsa-101626717268994.html.

61 For details on Kishorechandra's release, see: Shrutika Pandey, "Manipur High Court Orders Release of Journalist Detained under NSA over Facebook Post on Cow Dung Cure for Covid," *Live Law*, July 23, 2021, https://www.livelaw.in/news-updates/manipur-high-court-orders-interim-release-of-journalist-kishorchandra-wangkhemcha-178003.

62 For details on Milind Teltumbde's life, see: Soumitra Bose, "Gadchiroli Encounter: 'Milind Teltumbde Died for the Cause of Displaced and Jal-Jungle-Jameen'," *The Times of India*, November 16, 2021, https://timesofindia.indiatimes.com/city/nagpur/milind-died-for-the-cause-of-displaced-and-jal-jungle-jameen/articleshow/87723112.cms.

63 For details on need for mosquito nets in jail, see: Scroll Staff, "Bhima Koregaon Accused Gautam Navlakha, Sagar Gorkhe Denied Permission to Use Mosquito Nets in Jail," *Scroll.in*, July 8, 2022, https://scroll.in/latest/1027913/bhima-koregaon-accused-gautam-navlakha-sagar-gorkhe-denied-permission-to-use-mosquito-nets-in-jail.

64 Read the letter written by Dr Sen's mother: Anasuya Sen, "An Appeal from Dr. Binayak Sen's Mother," *Counter Currents*, January 5, 2008, https://countercurrents.org/sen261210.htm.

65 Read here for the campaign to free Binayak Sen: Mari Marcel Thekaekara, "Free Binayak Sen!" *New Internationalist*, September 3, 2007, https://newint.org/features/special/2007/09/03/freebinayaksen.

66 For more details on the SC bail to Binayak Sen, see: "SC Grants Bail to Dr Binayak Sen," *Rediff*, May 25, 2009, https://news.rediff.com/report/2009/may/25/supreme-court-grants-bail-to-binayak-sen.htm.

67 For details on the Raipur court verdict, see: Headlines Today Bureau, "Raipur Court Holds Binayak Sen Guilty of Treason," *India Today*, December 24, 2010, https://www.indiatoday.in/india/story/raipur-court-holds-binayak-sen-guilty-of-treason-87674-2010-12-23.

68 For more details on Binayak Sen case, see: B. Raman, "Dr Binayak Sen & Two Others vs the State," *Outlook India*, December 28, 2010, https://www.outlookindia.com/website/story/dr-binayak-sen-two-others-vs-the-state/269805.

69 For more information on the SC order, see: ITGD Bureau, "Binayak Sen Gets Bail, SC Trashes Sedition Charge," *India Today*, April 18, 2011, https://www.indiatoday.in/india/

north/story/sc-grants-bail-to-binayak-sen-drops-sedition-charge-132224-2011-04-14.

70 See here for information on the new law replacing sedition: Bharti Jain, "Explanation to Section on New Law Replacing Sedition Appears Incomplete," *The Times of India*, August 12, 2023, https://timesofindia.indiatimes.com/india/explanation-to-section-on-new-law-replacing-sedition-appears-incomplete/articleshow/102663906.cms?from=mdr.

71 For more information on the new law, see: Ashish K James and Dyuti Anand, "A Thorn by Another Name Pricks Just as Sharply: India's New Laws Intensifying the Sting of Sedition," *Law and Other Things*, September 8, 2023, https://lawandotherthings.com/a-thorn-by-another-name-pricks-just-as-sharply-indias-new-laws-intensifying-the-sting-of-sedition/.

72 Read for more information on Ilina Sen: Gabriele Dietrich, "A Passionate Teacher and Activist," *Economic and Political Weekly*, September 3, 2020, https://www.epw.in/journal/2020/35/commentary/passionate-teacher-and-activist.html.

73 Express News Service, "Help Free Binayak Sen: Citizens Write to Advani," *The Indian Express*, April 27, 2009, https://indianexpress.com/article/cities/pune/help-free-binayak-sen-citizens-write-to-advani/.

74 "Life Sentence for Activist Indian Doctor Stokes Outrage," *Voice of America*, December 29, 2010, https://www.voanews.com/a/life-sentence-for-activist-indian-doctor-stokes-outrage-112600044/132888.html.

75 For more details: T.K. Rajalakshmi, "India at 75: Timeline: Labour," *Frontline*, August 15, 2022, https://frontline.thehindu.com/social-issues/india-at-75-timeline-labour-75-years-of-independence/article65726761.ece.

76 For more details on Niyogi's death, see: "Remembering com. Shankar Guha Niyogi: A martyr of class struggle", accessed October 4, 2024, https://gaurilankeshnews.com/remembering-com-shankar-guha-niyogi-a-martyr-of-class-struggle/.

77 For more details on Salwa Judum, see: "Fact Finding Reports on Salwa Judum," Campaign for Peace and Justice in Chhattisgarh, August 11, 2008, https://cpjc.wordpress.com/reports-by-fact-finding-teams-on-salwa-judum/.

78 The WHO report: Covid-19 and the Social Determinants of Health and Health Equity: Evidence Brief, World Health Organisation (Geneva: World Health Organization, 2021), https://www.who.int/publications/i/item/9789240038387.

79 For details on the life sentence to Dr Sen, see: NDTV Correspondent, "Dr Binayak Sen Found Guilty of Treason, Sentenced to Life Term," NDTV.com, December 24, 2010, https://www.ndtv.com/india-news/dr-binayak-sen-found-guilty-of-treason-sentenced-to-life-term-442896.

80 For information on Bhilai workers movement, see: Dr Punyabrata Gun, "'Struggle and Create: My Days with Com. Shankar Guha Niyogi'—Chapter 7: Bhilai Workers Movement," *Countercurrents*, February 15, 2018, https://countercurrents.org/2018/02/struggle-create-days-com-shankar-guha-niyogi-chapter-7-bhilai-workers-movement/.

81 Mitanin Programme in Chhattisgarh, India: India's Largest Community Health Volunteer Programme, accessed October 4, 2024, https://cghealth.nic.in/cghealth17/Information/content/MediaPublication/MitaninProgrammedraft.pdf.

82 For more on this topic, read: Alya Mishra, "India: Maoist Sympathisers Targeted," *University World News*, June 27, 2010, https://www.universityworldnews.com/post.php?story=20100625183627800.

83 Satish Jha, "73 Yr Old Maoist Ideologue Kobad Ghandy Gets Bail," *Deccan Herald*, October 14, 2019, https://www.deccanherald.com/national/west/73-yr-old-maoist-ideologue-kobad-ghandy-gets-bail-768352.html.

84 *Fractured Freedom: A Prison Memoir*, Roli Books.

85 For more details on the controversy surrounding the award for the Marathi translation of *Fractured Freedom*, see: Chaitanya

Marpakwar, "Maharashtra Government Scraps Award, and Jury, for Kobad Ghandy's Book," *The Times of India*, December 13, 2022, https://timesofindia.indiatimes.com/city/mumbai/maharashtra-government-scraps-award-and-jury-for-kobad-ghandys-book-translation/articleshow/96184157.cms.

86 Prime Minister Indira Gandhi had declared a state of emergency in India between 1975 to 1977. Members of the Communist Party of India (Marxist) were arrested in Kerala at this time.

87 For details on arrest of Muralidharan, see: Atikh Rashid and Chandan Shantaram Haygunde, "Top Maoist Leader from Kerala, Aide Held near City," *The Indian Express*, May 10, 2015, https://indianexpress.com/article/india/maharashtra/maharashtra-ats-claims-to-have-arrested-senior-maoist-leader/.

88 Read more on Kanchan Nanaware's death: Sukanya Shantha, "Awaiting Trial for Six Years, UAPA Prisoner Dies While in Custody," *The Wire*, January 25, 2021, https://thewire.in/rights/uapa-undertrial-prisoner-death-custody.

89 Chaphekar brothers—Damodar Hari Chapekar (25 June 1869—18 April 1898), Balkrishna Hari Chapekar (1873—12 May 1899, also called Bapurao) and Vasudeo Hari Chapekar (1880–8 May 1899), also spelt Wasudeva or Wasudev, were Indian revolutionaries involved in assassinating W. C. Rand, the British Plague Commissioner of Pune, after the public of Pune got frustrated with the vandalism from the officers and soldiers appointed by him, in the late 19th century. Mahadev Vinayak Ranade was also an accomplice in the assassination.

90 Madhukar Dattatraya Deoras, Sarsanghchalak, born on December 11, 1915–June 17, 1996.

91 Read here on Bapu Nayar: TNN, "Criminal on the Run Held in Noida," *The Times of India*, May 10, 2016, https://timesofindia.indiatimes.com/city/pune/criminal-on-the-run-held-in-noida/articleshow/52196830.cms.

92 "P. Hemalatha vs the Govt. of Andhra Pradesh on 23 April, 1976," *Indian Kanoon*, https://indiankanoon.org/doc/40528/.

93 'Undertaking' by VV:
You have given a judgement against the change and against the rising sun
And demanding me to confess
If jails can run the rails
If jails can barricade the mind
If jails can scuttle the voices of struggle
If sun rises on the west
Then I will give my undertaking for repentance, My Lord!

94 Sanjay Sharma, "House Arrest for Varavara Rao, Other Activists: Supreme Court Provides Interim Relief," *India Today*, August 29, 2018, https://www.indiatoday.in/india/story/supreme-court-gives-varavara-rao-other-activists-interim-relief-orders-house-arrest-1326553-2018-08-29.

95 "Pune Police Takes Activist Varavara Rao into Custody from Hyderabad," *India Today*, November 17, 2018, https://www.indiatoday.in/india/story/varavara-rao-custody-pune-police-hyderabad-elgar-parishad-1390835-2018-11-17.

96 "Varavara Rao Unwell & Hallucinating; Family Alleges Negligence," *The Quint*, July 12, 2020, https://www.thequint.com/news/india/varavara-rao-unwell-and-hallucinating-family-alleges-negligence.

97 "As Varavara Rao's Health Worsens in Jail, Family Alleges Severe Negligence by Authorities," *The Wire*, July 12, 2020, https://thewire.in/rights/as-varavara-raos-health-worsens-in-jail-family-alleges-severe-negligence-by-authorities.

98 "Unable to Get Information About His Health, Varavara Rao's Family Asks NHRC to Intervene," *The Wire*, July 24, 2020, https://thewire.in/rights/varavara-rao-health-nhrc.

99 "Varavara Shifted from Taloja Jail to Nanavati Hospital," *The Times of India*, November 20, 2020, https://timesofindia.indiatimes.com/city/mumbai/varavara-shifted-from-taloja-jail-to-nanavati-hospital/articleshow/79314775.cms.

About the Author

Neeta Kolhatkar is a senior journalist from Mumbai, with over 35 years of experience in broadcast, print and digital media. In 2008, she won the Mumbai Mayor's award for excellence in journalism. Powered by a Master's in Social Work, she has focussed on marginalised communities and human rights issues. Moreover, she equipped herself with the Rotary certificate course in Peace and Conflict Resolution Studies from Chulalongkorn University, Bangkok in 2009.